MW00986935

Humana Festival 2014
The Complete Plays

About the Humana Foundation

The Humana Foundation was established in 1981 as the philanthropic arm of Humana Inc., one of the nation's leading health care companies. Located in Louisville, Ky., the site of Humana's corporate headquarters, the Foundation focuses on supportive relationships and healthy behaviors. We believe that people who are engaged in caring relationships are receptive and more likely to exhibit healthy behaviors; and healthy behaviors result in healthier communities. For more information, visit www.HumanaFoundation.org.

Humana and the Humana Foundation are dedicated to Corporate Social Responsibility. Our goal is to ensure that every business decision we make reflects our commitment to improving the health and well-being of our members, our associates, the communities we serve, and our planet.

Humana Festival 2014
The Complete Plays

Edited by
Amy Wegener and Kimberly Colburn

Playscripts
Inc.

New York, NY

Published by Playscripts, Inc.
7 Penn Plaza, Suite 904
New York, New York, 10001
www.playscripts.com

Cover Design by Mary Kate Zihar
Cover Image by Ellen Weinstein
Text Design and Layout by Erin Salvi

First Edition: April 2015
10 9 8 7 6 5 4 3 2 1

LCCN: 95650734
ISSN: 1935-4452

ISBN-13: 978-1-62384-004-4

Contents

Acknowledgments

The editors wish to thank the following persons for their invaluable assistance in compiling this volume:

Jennifer Bielstein
Robyn Carroll
Sara Durham
Kirsty Gaukel
Justin Kleiner
Steve Knight
Sarah Lunnie
Danielle Manley
Meredith McDonough
Hannah Rae Montgomery
Steve Moulds
Andy Perez
Jessica Reese
Jeffrey S. Rodgers
Erin Salvi
Zan Sawyer-Dailey
Ariel Sibert
Stephanie Spalding
Les Waters
Sam Weiner
Eric Werner
Mary Kate Zihar

Scott Chaloff
Val Day
Di Glazer
Seth Glewen
Leah Hamos
Jonathan Lomma
Kate Navin
Antje Oegel
Michelle Preston
Mark Subias
Rachel Viola
Alana Zalas

Actors Theatre of Louisville Staff
Humana Festival 2014

ARTISTIC DIRECTOR, Les Waters

MANAGING DIRECTOR, Jennifer Bielstein

ARTISTIC

Associate Artistic Director . . . . Meredith McDonough
Associate Director . . . . Zan Sawyer-Dailey
Artistic Manager . . . . Meg Fister
Company Manager . . . . Dot King
Arts Administration Intern . . . . Sterling Franklin
Directing Interns . . . . Cara Phipps, Jacob Sexton

Literary

Literary Director . . . . Amy Wegener
Interim Literary Manager . . . . Steve Moulds
Literary Associate . . . . Hannah Rae Montgomery
Humana Festival Literary Assistant . . . . Jessica Reese
Dramaturgy/Literary Management Interns . . . . Sam Weiner, Eric Werner

Education

Director . . . . Steven Rahe
Education Manager . . . . Jane B. Jones
Education Coordinator . . . . Betsy Anne Huggins
Education/Teaching Artist Interns . . . . Rebecca Goldstein, Jeff Sachs
Teaching Artists . . . . Justin Dobring, Liz Fentress,
Keith McGill, Amanda Simmons

Apprentice/Intern Company

Director . . . . Michael Legg
Assistant Director . . . . John Rooney
A/I Administration Intern . . . . Zachary Meicher-Buzzi
Directing Interns . . . . Kate Eminger, Rachel Karp
Apprentices . . . . Jamal Abdunnasir, Rachael Balcanoff, Julia Bynum,
Derek Grabner, Peregrine Heard, Jason Huff,
David Jackson, Cyndii Johnson, Lindsey Kite,
Lauren LaRocca, Madison Niederhauser,
Devon Nimerfroh, Daniel Rodriguez, Conrad Schott,
Alex Seeley, Mirirai Sithole, Emily Stout,
Casey Worthington, Zach Wymore

ADMINISTRATION

General Manager . . . . Jeffrey S. Rodgers
Human Resources Manager . . . . Cora Brown
Systems Manager . . . . Dottie Krebs

Executive Assistant . . . . Janelle Baker
Administrative Services Coordinator . . . . Alan Meyer

AUDIENCE SERVICES AND SALES

Ticket Sales Director. . . . . Kim McKercher
Senior Box Office Manager . . . . Saundra Blakeney
Training Manager . . . . .Steve Clark
Season Tickets Manager . . . . Julie Gallegos
Customer Service & Special Projects Manager. . . . . Kristy Kannapell
Customer Service Representatives . . . . Cheryl Anderson,
Matthew Brown, Samantha Dzirko,
Tony Hammons, Marty Huelsmann,
Jessica Hughes

Volunteer and Audience Relations
Director . . . . .Allison Hammons
House Managers . . . . Chadwick Ballard, Elizabeth Cooley,
Will Farrell, Sterling Franklin
Lobby Manager . . . . Tiffany Walton
Coat Check Supervisor . . . . Patrick Vaughn
Coat Check Attendants . . . . Tanisha Johnson, Jordan Lingreen

DEVELOPMENT

Director . . . . Julie Roberts
Associate Director, Individual Giving. . . . . .Kate Chandler
Associate Director, Institutional Partnerships . . . . Danielle Manley
Development Planning Manager . . . . .Gretchen James
Manager, Institutional Partnerships . . . . .Katie McCandless
Development Coordinator . . . . Liz Magee
Development Intern . . . . .Holly Fisher

FINANCE

Finance Director . . . . .Peggy Shake
Accounting Coordinator. . . . . Jason Acree
Accounting Assistant. . . . . .Dara Tiller

MARKETING AND COMMUNICATIONS

Director . . . . .Kory P. Kelly
Public Relations Manager. . . . . Kirsty Gaukel
Marketing and Sales Manager. . . . . .Olivia Pedolzky
Audience Development and Special Events Manager . . . . Stephanie Spalding
Communications Coordinator . . . . Sara E. Durham
50th Anniversary Projects Coordinator . . . . Evan McMahon
Graphic Designer . . . . Andy Perez
Group Sales Manager . . . . .Sarah Peters
Group Sales Associate. . . . . Chris O'Leary

Marketing and Public Relations Intern . . . . .Jessica Hughes
Audience Development/Festival Management Intern . . . . Jordan Lingreen
Graphic Design Intern . . . . Joshua Nicholson

OPERATIONS

Director . . . . Mike Schüssler-Williams
Operations Manager . . . . Barry Witt
Maintenance. . . . . .Ricky Baldon, John Voyles
Building Services. . . . . LaTroy Booth, Patricia Duncan,
Joe Spencer, Cindy Woodward
Receptionist . . . . Griffin Falvey

PRODUCTION

Production Manager . . . . .Paul Werner
Assistant Production Manager . . . . .Michael Whatley
Production Management Intern. . . . . Samantha Dzirko
Production Stage Manager . . . . .Paul Mills Holmes
Resident Stage Managers. . . . . Stephen Horton, Katie Shade
Production Assistants . . . . Jessica Potter, Suzanne Spicer
Stage Management Interns . . . . Joshua Mark Gustafson, Rachel Nin,
Jason Pacella, Leah Pye

Scenic
Technical Director. . . . . Justin Hagovsky
Assistant Technical Director . . . . Braden Blauser
Shop Foreman . . . . Javan Roy-Bachman
Master Carpenter. . . . . .Ashley Crockett*
Carpenters .Alexia Hall, Brandon Hickman, Eric Kneller,
Winslow Lindsay, Jason Pacella,
Joen Pallesen, Pierre Vendette
Pamela Brown Deck Carpenter . . . . .Peter Regalbuto
Bingham Theatre Deck Carpenter. . . . . .Matthew Krell
Scenic Charge. . . . . Kieran Wathen
Scenic Painter. . . . . .Sabra Crockett
Scenic Journeyman . . . . G.E. Simmons Falk*
Costumes
Costume Director . . . . Kristopher Castle
Costume Coordinators . . . . .Rhianna Reardon, Beatrice Vena
Crafts Master . . . . Shari Cochran
Wig and Makeup Supervisor. . . . . Jehann Gilman
Draper/Tailor . . . . Jeffery Park
First Hand . . . . Natalie Maynard
Stitcher Captain . . . . .Elizabeth Hahn
Stitcher . . . . Andrea Washington
Wardrobe Manager . . . . .Jacob Freund
Bingham Wardrobe Supervisor . . . . .Megan Shuey

Stitcher Journeymen ....Faith Brown*, Christine Leidner*
Wig Journeyman ....Hannah Blosser
Costume Intern ....Caitlyn deAraujo

Lighting

Supervisor .... Nick Dent
Assistant Lighting Supervisor............................. Christine Ferriter
First Electrician ....John Newman
Lighting Technicians............................. Jesse AlFord, Jon Harden,
Melanie Medeiros, Peter Martino
Lighting Intern ....Victoria Bain

Sound

Supervisor ....Paul Doyle
Assistant Sound Supervisor ....Jessica Collins
Sound Technicians................ Amanda Neild, Rachel Spear, Amanda Werre

Properties

Director .... Mark Walston
Properties Master...Joe Cunningham
Assistant Properties Master .... Jay Tollefsen
Carpenter Artisan .... Karl Anderson
Soft Goods Artisan.. Heather Lindert
Artisan/Shopper ....Jessie Combest
Props Artisans............................... Aaron O'Neill, Aimee Plant

VIDEO

Media Technologist...Philip Allgeier

USHER CAPTAINS

Dolly Adams, Marie Allen, Katherine Austin, June Blair, Libba & Chuck Bonifer,
Tanya Briley, Maleva Chamberlain, Donna Conlon, Terry Conway, Laurie Eiden,
Doris Elder, Reese Fisher, Joyce French, Carol Halbleib, Sandy Kissling, Nickie
Langdon, Barbara Nichols, Cathy Nooning, Teresa Nusz, Judy Pearson, Nancy
Rankin, Bob Rosedale, Bernadette Stone, Tim Unruh, David Wallace, Megg Ward

Denotes Paul Owen Fellow

Foreword

Scientific studies have attempted to quantify the human need for storytelling. Jonathan Gottschall's book, *The Storytelling Animal*, posits that "the constant firing of our neurons in response to fictional stimuli strengthens and refines the neural pathways that lead to skillful navigation of life's problems." We must tell stories—our very survival depends on it. Plays communicate stories in a way no other medium can. Plays are a blueprint for a theatrical event, and their creation involves hundreds of people before an audience even enters the building. By the closing of the Humana Festival, thousands of people have shared in many tales, both onstage and off.

The plays in this year's anthology cover all manner of human experience, from the exploration of an American folk hero to a crisis of faith, from celebrating a young man lost too soon to the heartbreaking realization that even a long life can pass by in the blink of an eye. The variety of these stories is inspiring, and they compel us to exercise the most important muscle we have—imagination. The storytellers in this volume are an impressive group. They include my longtime friends and collaborators such as Jordan Harrison and the SITI Company, along with exciting writers I've met only recently, like Dorothy Fortenberry and Kimber Lee.

It's a great credit to these playwrights that they can harness so much storytelling skill. *The Grown-Up* jumps time and space as its protagonist hurtles through life, and his madcap adventure leads us toward serious meditations. You may not have witnessed their intense physicality during the production's run, but you can almost hear *Steel Hammer*'s pounding rhythms bouncing off the page while reading the words of Kia Corthron, Will Power, Carl Hancock Rux, and Regina Taylor. I had the great pleasure of directing Lucas Hnath's *The Christians*, and was gratified by the many exciting discoveries we made in finding how that story should be told (listen to Lucas's instructions; you really need the microphones to do the story justice). Lena tells the audience her grandson is dead in the first moments of *brownsville song (b-side for tray)*, but the depth and emotional resonance in Kimber's contemporary urban poetry still surprises me. And *brownsville song* stands in sharp relief to the rapid comedic banter of *Partners*. *Partners* tells a modern story about the things we don't talk about in polite society and the ways that can destroy our relationships. Even though the Ten-Minute Plays are brief in duration, they are vast in storytelling ambition and humor, and can even manage to tell the tale of an entire life in less time than you'd stand in line at Starbucks.

Reflecting on last year's festival, I realize that the Humana Festival is a large part of the story of Actors Theatre. The 38th Humana Festival was the capstone on a landmark year celebrating Actors Theatre's 50th Anniversary, and the many different stories found in this volume continue that richly diverse legacy—wildly different but all pulsing with the same high potency. This enduring link to the past while moving ever forward was what inspired the writers of *Remix 38*, and while they may have started with famous plays from our festivals past as their inspiration, they pushed the scope of theatricality in ways that were all their own.

The Humana Festival is one of my favorite times of the year. It both requires and brings an overwhelming amount of energy, with throngs of supporters filling the lobbies and theatres to capacity. I'm writing this just before we're heading into rehearsals for the 2015 Humana Festival, and already there is an electricity around the building as our staff prepares to help launch new stories into the world. I can't speak to the alchemy of storytelling and how it might strengthen our neural pathways, but I can attest to the power of sharing stories through the Humana Festival.

—*Les Waters*
Artistic Director
Actors Theatre of Louisville

Editors' Note

Vividly present and then gone, unfolding right before our eyes for a limited duration (and without a rewind button), theatre might be said to be one of the most time-conscious and time-bound of art forms. The experience of a good play envelops and maybe even changes us, and then just as quickly becomes a memory. But in its formal magic, a theatrical event can reorder, jump, and defy time, traversing great temporal and emotional distances or even raising the dead.

As of this writing, almost a year has passed since the plays of the 2014 Humana Festival first premiered on Actors Theatre of Louisville's stages, and perhaps that's why we're feeling philosophical about time. However, we think there's a bit more to it than that. While festival selections are never intended to cohere thematically, the wildly different plays in this collection seem (in retrospect) to capture the way that time transforms us and shakes up our assumptions about who we're supposed to be, or brings about losses we can't reverse alongside moments we can't forget. In myriad elegant ways, these theatrical texts also bend and contemplate time through style and form—by moving between then and now, by telescoping time to show how a new idea that takes hold can upend everything, or by simulating the speed at which we perceive life accelerating as we grow older.

Put another way, the brilliant writers of the 2014 Humana Festival have us thinking a lot about theatre as a medium that's uniquely equipped to distill the sometimes enlightening, sometimes disorienting process of change as time slips onward. In *The Grown-Up*, playwright Jordan Harrison sends his protagonist, Kai, hurtling through his own life at a bewildering pace, arriving at destinations that he (like all of us) might never have imagined. A charmed crystal doorknob supplies the magic that makes Kai's quantum leaping possible, and with thrilling transformative agility, Harrison's funny and sad fable captures the fleeting nature of experience. Employing the more compact ten-minute play form, Jason Gray Platt's *Some Prepared Remarks (A History in Speech)* also pulls off the feat of encapsulating one human's trajectory through a life. Via a series of gracefully rendered speeches—at a graduation, a wedding, a funeral—we witness a consciousness struggling toward understanding as time moves inexorably forward. "It seems the only things you remember in life," Platt's Speaker muses, "are the ones you never imagined until the moment they become real."

In a different context, memory and the skillful manipulation of time are also keys to the texture of Kimber Lee's beautiful *brownsville song (b-side for tray)*, which moves fluidly between past and present to drive home the impact of a tremendous loss. Tray, a bright eighteen-year-old boxer, aspiring college student, loving grandson and big brother, has been killed in a senseless act of violence in his inner city neighborhood that pulses with life even as it witnesses too much death. Lee's remarkable elegy travels seamlessly between the before and after as Tray's family grieves and remembers, evoking the vitality of his presence in a way that makes his absence all the more heartbreaking. The dexterity with which the play glides through time is integral to its powerful and personal depiction of loss, affirming that this particular young man is not defined by his death—but rather, lives on in the memories of those who love him.

Collective memory and layered narratives of history—in this case, on the level of a national legend—also inform the construction of *Steel Hammer*, the latest work from festival veteran Anne Bogart and the SITI Company to receive its world premiere in the Humana Festival. Conceived as a collaboration with composer Julia Wolfe, whose intricate score of the same title was inspired by hundreds of variations on the folk ballad "John Henry," this partnership led to a piece of music-theatre with rich choreography. The event is anchored textually by pieces written by four playwrights who tell their own versions of the John Henry story—Kia Corthron, Will Power, Carl Hancock Rux and Regina Taylor. Together, these diverse representations span time and space to powerfully connect the African-American folk hero's triumph and tragic end in his race against the machine to the contemporary moment. By considering the many incarnations of this steel-drivin' railroad laborer throughout history, tall tales and song, *Steel Hammer* eloquently articulates John Henry's multiple meanings in American culture.

While *Steel Hammer* interrogates inherited myths spun from the past, other plays from this festival feature characters wrestling with new ideas about the future—even eternity—that will scramble the timeline they once thought they were supposed to follow. In Lucas Hnath's extraordinary drama, *The Christians*, a pastor changes his mind about a central article of faith, embracing a new belief whose consequences threaten to shake his ties to the church he's helped to build. Taking the form of a church service, the play compresses a span of time into an urgent series of gripping dialectical arguments between the pastor and all who question how he can be so certain of what he claims to know. In *Partners*, an event from the past sets a timeline in motion that leads to a sudden windfall of wealth for one of its characters that, like a bomb, changes the dynamics of the play's relationships. Dorothy Fortenberry's witty comic drama about two couples at a crossroads (and a pair of best friends) contemplates the seismic shift caused by money—which might change everything, including marriage. Events long since relegated to personal historical narrative can have an unforeseen impact on the present and the newly uncertain future, unsettling assumed bonds as time marches forward.

On the shorter and sillier side of unsettled expectations, Gregory Hischak's delightfully absurd office satire, *Poor Shem*, imagines three co-workers' encounter with a malfunctioning photocopier—and what, or rather whom, they find jammed in the bypass tray. Here, stage time unfolds with heightened rhythmic precision through the poetry and repetition of the dialogue, as the bizarre demise of a colleague is eventually eclipsed by other concerns. The other ten-minute play in this volume, Rachel Bonds' award-winning *Winter Games*, is a conversation between co-workers as well, but in a very different register. On a break before opening up a small-town bakery one morning, we find Jamie and Mary—who've known each other since their school days—in a moment of contemplation about where life has landed them. As ever, it is thrilling to see how much distance can be traveled in such a short time, whether via subtle character development or crazier comical leaps.

The potential for variety and experimentation in the short play form was also a key ingredient in the recipe for *Remix 38*, a project that had an awareness of time past built into its very premise. Commissioned to be performed by the 19 young actors in our 2013-2014 Apprentice Company, this collection of short pieces was written by five enormously talented playwrights—Jackie Sibblies Drury, Idris Goodwin, Basil Kreimendahl, Justin Kuritzkes, and Amelia Roper. Their writing prompt was inspired by Actors Theatre's 50th Anniversary Season: the five were asked to consider Humana Festival history in order to make something new, using memorable plays selected from nearly four decades of work as jumping-off points for their own scenes. From an invitation to recall every play the audience has ever seen to a wedding reception where a bridesmaid-turned-bride finally arrives at her own party, the pieces that comprise *Remix 38* play with theatrical time in a multitude of imaginative ways, and their authors boldly took up the challenge to mine festivals past for creative fuel.

The 2014 Humana Festival of New American Plays has now become part of Actors Theatre's history—a warm, shared memory of several months last spring when a cadre of collaborating artists came together to fully realize all of these marvelous visions, and nine productions filled the theatre complex's three performance spaces. Editing this book has been a form of time travel; we've revisited each piece, feeling every bit as moved and delighted as when we first encountered these scripts. Luckily, though, this time travel works in both directions. While the plays might hold fond memories for us, the publication of this book means that they'll become future adventures for readers and audiences everywhere. Sure, theatre may be a time-bound and often time-obsessed art form, but all it takes to experience a play is a few hours (or even ten minutes) and your fired-up imagination.

—Amy Wegener and Kimberly Colburn

WINTER GAMES
by Rachel Bonds

BIOGRAPHY

Rachel Bonds' plays have been developed or produced by South Coast Repertory, Manhattan Theatre Club, McCarter Theatre, Roundabout Underground, Atlantic Theater Company, New Georges, Ars Nova, Ensemble Studio Theatre, SPACE on Ryder Farm, Williamstown Theatre Festival, Actors Theatre of Louisville, Studio Theatre, Arden Theatre Company, and New York Stage and Film, among others.

Her plays include: *Five Mile Lake*, winner of the 2013 L. Arnold Weissberger Award, which received its world premiere at South Coast Repertory, directed by Daniella Topol, and will receive its East Coast premiere at the McCarter Theatre in May 2015, directed by Emily Mann; *The Wolfe Twins*, her commissioned play for Studio Theatre in Washington, D.C., which received its world premiere in October 2014, directed by Mike Donahue; *At the Old Place*, developed during her 2013 Writers' Room Residency at the Arden; *Swimmers*, featured in New York Stage and Film's 2013 Powerhouse Reading Series and Roundabout Underground's Reading Series, receiving top ranking on The Kilroys' List; *Michael & Edie*, named a *New York Times* Critics' Pick in 2010, directed by Robert Saenz de Viteri; *Winter Games*, winner of the 2014 Heideman Award and part of The Ten-Minute Plays at the 2014 Humana Festival; *The Noise*, developed at New Georges and Ars Nova; and *Anniversary*, winner of the 2012 Samuel French Festival and featured on Public Radio's *Playing on Air.*

Bonds is an alumna of EST's Youngblood, Ars Nova's Play Group and New Georges' The Jam, and was the Father William Ralston Fellow at the 2011 Sewanee Writers' Conference. She was a member of SPACE on Ryder Farm's 2014 Working Farm Writers' Group, and is currently working on commissions for Ars Nova/Manhattan Theatre Club's The Writer's Room, South Coast Repertory, and Atlantic Theater Company. She is a graduate of Brown University.

ACKNOWLEDGMENTS

Winter Games was produced at the Humana Festival of New American Plays in April 2014. It was directed by Pirronne Yousefzadeh with the following cast:

MARY...Julia Bynum
JAMIE .... Jason Huff

and the following production staff:

Scenic Designer......................................Dane Laffrey
Costume Designer .... Kristopher Castle
Lighting Designer.....................................Seth Reiser
Sound Designer....................................Christian Frederickson
Stage Manager .... Stephen Horton
Dramaturg...Jessica Reese
Directing Assistants........................Cara Phipps, Jacob Sexton
Production Assistant ....Suzanne Spicer

The play was originally developed at Ars Nova as part of Play Group's "The Urban Dictionary Plays." It premiered on February 1, 2012, directed by Wes Grantom, with Susan Kelechi Watson as Mary and Zach Shaffer as Jamie.

CHARACTERS

MARY (28-30ish). Defensive, frank, very smart. Her humor/brashness covering up her vulnerability. Claustrophobic in her life, she always has the feeling that the world is going on in some fantastic way—far away and without her.

JAMIE (29-30ish). Playful and warm. He's resilient and practical; it is not in his nature to brood or worry.

PLACE

Behind a bakery in a small, somewhat desolate town near Scranton, PA. Winter.

NOTES

A / indicates where the next line should begin:

JAMIE. It's freezing /out here.

MARY. I know.

JAMIE. You don't wear coats /anymore?

MARY. Jamie I'm on my break.

Julia Bynum and Jason Huff
in *Winter Games*

38th Humana Festival of New American Plays
Actors Theatre of Louisville, 2014
Photo by Bill Brymer

WINTER GAMES

Early, early morning. MARY *stands behind the bakery, smoking, her eyes closed. It's quiet and cold out, grey, a little bleak. She doesn't wear a coat.*
JAMIE *opens the back door and peers at her.*

JAMIE. You're smoking already?

MARY. I'm tired.

JAMIE. So you're smoking.

MARY. It helps me wake up.

(He steps outside.)

JAMIE. It's freezing /out here.

MARY. I know.

JAMIE. You don't wear coats /anymore?

MARY. Jamie I'm on my break.

JAMIE. We open in like /ten minutes.

MARY. I know I'm taking my break before everyone starts screaming at me about what kind of bran muffin they want.

JAMIE. There's pretty much just the /one kind.

MARY. Jamie I'm on my break.

JAMIE. Okay, sorry.

(He stares at his breath.)

Why're you so tired?

MARY. I was up late.

JAMIE. Ahhhhh okay.

MARY. *(Opening her eyes.)* Shut up, not like that.

JAMIE. Okay.

MARY. I was watching the Olympics.

JAMIE. Figure skating?

MARY. Yes.

(He cringes.)

It's a sport, /Jamie.

JAMIE. Yeahhh, not really /a sport.

MARY. It's a /sport.

JAMIE. Not really a sport, /Mary.

MARY. Have you seen the legs on those people? Their muscles are like bulging out all over the—they are super-athletes, Jamie.

JAMIE. I don't know if they're *super* /athletes…

MARY. Jamie I'M ON MY BREAK.

JAMIE. Okay okay okay okay.

(*Quiet, almost to himself.*)

I mean they wear glittery costumes.

MARY. Fuck off.

JAMIE. Whoa!

MARY. Well I'm tired and you're pissing me off!

JAMIE. I'm sorry.

(*They both stare at their breath.*)

Haven't seen Mr. Belvedere around lately.

MARY. I know. I brought some food out for him and the little grey guy yesterday and usually they greet me at the door, but I didn't see them anywhere. The orange one /wasn't around either.

JAMIE. John Adams.

MARY. Yeah, John Adams.

Auugghh I'm worried about them in the cold. That little grey guy is so little.

JAMIE. Yeah.

You shouldn't worry, though. They're like little ninjas. Did you see Mr. Belvedere scale the fence /that time?

MARY. I'm just worried…

JAMIE. You worry about too much stuff.

MARY. Not really.

JAMIE. Yeah, you always have this face like aughhhh I'm really tense and worried about stuff.

MARY. I do /not.

JAMIE. (*Twisting his face.*) Yeah, since like tenth grade you've had this look, like auuughhhhh /my brain is having a heartattack.

MARY. I don't—.

I hope I don't look like that.

JAMIE. No, you—I'm kidding. You look…nice.

MARY. (*Amused.*) Right.

How come you're eternally cheerful?

JAMIE. Don't know.

MARY. Like you actually enjoy getting up at 4 a.m. and baking things for people who know every embarrassing thing about you.

JAMIE. I do enjoy it.

MARY. I know. It's weird.

JAMIE. I like that people know who I am and I know who they are.

MARY. You like serving scones to your high school girlfriend and her husband.

JAMIE. I don't know. They're good people.

MARY. Yeah, Melissa's a gem.

(*JAMIE stares at his breath, quiet.*)

...Haven't you ever wanted to get out?

JAMIE. (*Shrugging.*) I don't know.

MARY. (*Peering at him.*) You don't ever want to just, like, tear your skin off and run away and be a whole different person?

JAMIE. No.

MARY. (*Peering at him.*) No...

JAMIE. I'm happy here.

MARY. Really?

JAMIE. Yeah.

MARY. (*Sighing, staring at her breath.*) ...We are very different people, Jamie Hewitt.

JAMIE. I guess.

What happened on figure skating?

MARY. Nothing.

JAMIE. I'm not fucking with you.

(*She peers at him. He stares back at her earnestly.*)

MARY. Okay. Okay, well. This was like the final final for the women's single competition, okay?

JAMIE. Yeah.

MARY. And there's this skater from Estonia, right, and she's amazing, her short program was killer, and so everyone's looking to her, you know, because she's like come up from the bottom, like Estonia's never won a medal in this category or even this sport EVER, so she'd be making big-time history.

JAMIE. Whoa.

MARY. Yeah, AND her husband has just died.

JAMIE. Oh God.

MARY. I know. So she's skating *anyway*, despite this horrible thing that's occurred like a few *weeks* before—she just has to nail her long program and she's got the gold. So the music starts, and the entire coliseum is dead quiet. Like the air in the place is so taut, you can just feel it tightening around her. And then, like, bing!, she lifts her head and starts moving. And it's lovely and it's light and just the most graceful but also the most like—full thing you've ever seen, like every single tiny movement is full of this, this like incredible energy and presence, and they keep flashing the camera into the stands where her parents are sitting, and her dad's really frail-looking and he's wearing this hat and he's kind of stoic and Eastern European but you can tell he's like beaming underneath, and she's going and she's going and it's beautiful, like even the commentators are silent, and she nails the double axel and then she nails the triple axel and then another triple axel her mom has her arms up in the air, like victory, like—(*She demonstrates.*)—and then she goes for the last triple axel, with this like incredible force—and she screws up the landing.

JAMIE. (*Quiet.*) Oh no.

MARY. She doesn't fall—she just loses her balance for one tiny moment, like she tips forward and has to catch herself with her hand. And the crowd gasps and her dad closes his eyes and time freezes for a second.........and then she rights herself and moves on to finish the program. So she throws herself into the final pose...and everyone's cheering and her parents are holding each other and her arms are in their pose but you can just—. You can see something break in her—like a little crack running down the side of a teacup, just this terrible sense of failure like running across her skin. And she's thinking, I missed it. I missed it.

JAMIE. Wow.

MARY. Yeah.

So.

I couldn't sleep at ALL after that so I had to watch *Aladdin*.

JAMIE. Like a whole new world *Aladdin*?

MARY. Yeah.

JAMIE. Really?

MARY. I always watch it when I can't sleep.

JAMIE. Why?

MARY. Because everything turns out right in the end.

JAMIE. Not for Jafar. /Or that weird little parrot.

MARY. Yeah, but for the good guys. Why, what do you watch when you can't sleep?

JAMIE. I sleep pretty well.

MARY. Of course you /do.

JAMIE. My head hits the pillow and I'm pretty much out.

(*She shakes her head, looking away. He watches her for a moment.*)

I built a hotel.

MARY. What?

JAMIE. For the cats. See—(*He points.*)—it's over there—I kind of tucked it into that little space between the dumpster and the fence.

MARY. Oh my God.

JAMIE. It's like a double-decker type thing—I lined it with straw. Which should apparently keep them pretty warm. I looked up how to build it on feral cat villa dot org.

MARY. Jamie.

JAMIE. I checked on them when I got in this morning. Mr. Belvedere was asleep on the first floor. John Adams was up top with the little grey guy.

MARY. /Oh man...Jamie...

JAMIE. They're so damn cute.

MARY. Yeah.

JAMIE. I was worried about them. It's fucking freezing out here.

MARY. I know.

JAMIE. So.
Yeahhh.

We're not all that different.

MARY. ...No.

(*They watch their breath.*)

JAMIE. Okay. So...I'm going to go open the doors for the angry mob.

MARY. Okay.

JAMIE. You still on break?

MARY. No, no. I'm coming.

(*He opens the door. After a moment she follows him inside.*)

End of Play

PARTNERS
by Dorothy Fortenberry

ABOUT *PARTNERS*

This article first ran in the January/February 2014 issue of Inside Actors, *Actors Theatre of Louisville's subscriber newsletter, and is based on conversations with the playwright before rehearsals for the Humana Festival production began.*

We all dream of growing up to have the perfect job, the perfect love life—but not everyone is so lucky. What happens when things don't work out the way we imagined, and we're left comparing ourselves to our friends or wondering why we still feel stuck at the kids' table? In *Partners,* Dorothy Fortenberry takes a refreshingly funny, poignant, and self-deprecating look at two young couples trying to perfect the recipe for successful adulthood—and finding that it can be hard to acquire the right ingredients.

Clare and Ezra, longtime best friends, are about to take their relationship to the next level: they're going into business together. As far as Ezra's concerned, Brooklyn in early 2012 is the perfect place to start a food truck. And for Clare, an aspiring chef who regularly treats her husband Paul and their friends to lavish dinners, cooking up trendy eats for the truck should be a dream come true. Money is an obstacle, but surely if Clare and Ezra can get their fundraising campaign off the ground, they'll be good to go. When an unexpected windfall lands one of them newfound wealth, however, it becomes more and more apparent that funding might not be their biggest roadblock. As tensions begin to simmer, it's not just Clare and Ezra's work relationship that shifts, but their romantic lives too. For as they and their significant others discover, money can't buy what's most important in any partnership: communication, commitment, and trust.

For Fortenberry, an early thirty-something confronting the challenge of making a living as a writer, the issues that *Partners* dramatizes are close to home. "*Partners* is a satire of myself," she remarks wryly. "It's looking at people who have been encouraged to pursue their dreams and then are faced with the financial realities of what that really looks like." In the play there's a contrast between characters like Clare and Ezra—following their passions despite financial impracticalities—and Paul and Brady (Ezra's boyfriend), who have found the security of steady jobs with retirement plans and health insurance. "I am a person who is incredibly conscious of money and wonders what other people's relationships to it are," elaborates Fortenberry. Indeed, *Partners* also invites us to examine the gap between people's perceptions of how well-off they are, and the reality. The protagonists count one another's money constantly—How does he afford fancy leather shoes? How do they afford a cleaning lady?—holding up their friends' finances as measures of their own achievements (or lack thereof).

Fortenberry is also familiar with the pitfalls of having personal and professional relationships that overlap. "In a lot of creative fields, the person you're out with at the bar is also the person you're in a meeting with the next morning," she explains. While it might seem ideal to have close friends as colleagues, this kind of collaboration isn't without risk. "In friend-professional relationships, often there aren't set expectations and it can get murky very fast," she continues. Writing about Clare and Ezra's struggle to negotiate their "friend-professional" status is Fortenberry's own attempt to wade through said murkiness.

Romantic relationships don't always conform to expectations, either. In addition to its incisive probing into issues of money and the complicated confluence of work and social life, perhaps the biggest question *Partners* tackles is the meaning of marriage in modern society. "I'm interested in whether there's something about 'marriage' that is universal, or whether it has become something that every couple decides for itself," Fortenberry muses. For her characters, it seems to be the latter. Clare ascribes vast importance to the institution of marriage, but compromises hers by concealing secrets from her husband. And although marriage equality has recently become the law in New York, Ezra isn't sure he's interested. When Clare urges him to wed Brady, he replies, "I politely reject your assumption that I need a piece of paper to tell me my relationship matters." Meanwhile, Clare has to learn that sometimes, the promise of a piece of paper isn't enough. Just like a business arrangement, a marriage is a contract that takes work—and is it worth it when you find that you aren't on the same page? As Fortenberry quips, "If we're all so individualistic, why get married at all?"

It isn't easy to reconcile our progress through life with what we think we're supposed to want, or do, or be. It isn't easy to resist the seductive impulse to self-sabotage. And most of all, it isn't easy—or even possible—to separate what we owe ourselves from what we owe to others. With heart, wit, and unflinching candor, *Partners* explores what it's like to wrestle with these essential dilemmas at a moment when, as Ezra worries, "we only have a few more mistakes to make before we've officially squandered our potential."

—Hannah Rae Montgomery

BIOGRAPHY

Dorothy Fortenberry's work has been produced and developed by Arena Stage, Center REPertory Company, Geva Theatre Center and Oregon Shakespeare Festival, as well as by Ars Nova, Chalk Repertory Theatre, LiveWire Chicago Theatre, and The Management. She lives with her family in Los Angeles, where she writes for the CW television series *The 100* and recently developed a drama series with filmmaker Ry Russo-Young at Bravo. Fortenberry is a winner of the 2011 Helen Merrill Award for Emerging Playwrights, a two-time finalist for the O'Neill National Playwrights Conference, and holds an M.F.A. from the Yale School of Drama. She is currently working on a commission for Yale Repertory Theatre about a children's book author. Having her play *Partners* be part of Actors Theatre of Louisville's Humana Festival of New American Plays was one of the best things that has happened in her life, so far.

ACKNOWLEDGMENTS

Partners premiered at the Humana Festival of New American Plays in February 2014. It was directed by Lila Neugebauer with the following cast:

CLARE...Annie Purcell
PAUL.. David Ross
EZRA ....Kasey Mahaffy
BRADY ....LeRoy McClain

and the following production staff:

Scenic Designer..Daniel Zimmerman
Costume Designer ....Janice Pytel
Lighting Designer...Paul Toben
Original Music and Sound Design...................... Lindsay Jones
Stage Manager ....Kathy Preher
Dramaturg...Kimberly Colburn
Casting ....Zan Sawyer-Dailey, Meg Fister
Fight Director..Drew Fracher
Properties Master..Mark Walston
Directing Assistant ....Jacob Sexton
Production Assistant ....Hannah Barnes
Assistant Dramaturg...Eric Werner

Partners was written at The MacDowell Colony and developed by Creative Destruction, Page 73, and LiveWire Chicago Theatre.

CHARACTERS

CLARE, an aspiring chef

PAUL, her husband

EZRA, Clare's best friend and business partner

BRADY, Ezra's boyfriend

Annie Purcell, Kasey Mahaffy, LeRoy McClain, and David Ross
in *Partners*

38th Humana Festival of New American Plays
Actors Theatre of Louisville, 2014
Photo by Bill Brymer

PARTNERS

Scene 1

The living/dining room of CLARE *and* PAUL'S *small apartment in Brooklyn, in a neighborhood that's yet to be gentrified. Nothing has been cleaned in a while.* CLARE, PAUL, EZRA, *and* BRADY *are finishing dinner.*

CLARE. You didn't see it? It was so sweet. How did you not see it?

EZRA. I don't read Weddings & Celebrations, Clare. Because I'm trying not to kill myself.

BRADY. I hate that the brides are always teachers.

EZRA. Used to be teachers. "Until recently, she was a pre-kindergarten instructor..."

BRADY. I feel like it diminishes teaching.

PAUL. You really think that pre-kindergarten teachers can be demeaned—

BRADY. Maybe.

CLARE. You guys, you're missing the point.

EZRA. All of Sunday Styles should be abolished.

PAUL. Definitely.

BRADY. I like the advice column.

EZRA. "How high is too high for denim cutoffs?" "Mandarin tutors for your basset hound." "A father's legacy, a sister's gift: my journey to microdermabrasion." These are the issues that animate our nation.

BRADY. You seem to know an awful lot—

EZRA. We're doomed. We should just start appointing horses to the Senate and head to the vomitoriums.

BRADY. That's not actually what you think it is.

PAUL. What if, instead of "Sunday Styles" they called it "Shitty Rich People"?

BRADY. Vomitoria were exits, they vomited forth crowds. We do a unit on Ancient Rome.

EZRA. I like that. "Shitty Rich People and Also, You're Fat."

CLARE. I am not defending all of Sunday Styles. Just this one article. And, Ezra, you know you read Modern Love.

EZRA. Sometimes.

PAUL. Really?

CLARE. Look, this particular Weddings & Celebrations article was so sweet. They were, like, 80.

PAUL. I thought they were 60.

CLARE. Whatever, they were old. They were these old, Black lesbians.

BRADY. In pantsuits.

CLARE. You did see it!

BRADY. This one was sweet.

EZRA. You didn't show it to me.

CLARE. It was, it was so sweet, wasn't it? There was a photo of them dancing, where they're just looking at each other with this devotion in their eyes. I think one of the women had been with men before, so she thought she was straight, but then they found each other and now that it's legal in New York—

BRADY. It was really sweet.

CLARE. And I just felt so proud, you know, and grateful. To be living where we're living, to be a part of something so meaningful. Gay marriage.

(*She raises her glass.*)

PAUL. It's a little late in the meal to—

(*She gives him a look.* PAUL *raises his glass. They all toast. Small pause.*)

EZRA. The chicken—

PAUL. It was great, really.

BRADY. Wonderful tacos.

CLARE. I marinated the chicken in lime. Then topped it with fig foam.

EZRA. It was amazing.

CLARE. Not amazing.

BRADY. It was. Foamed figs?

CLARE. Something new, I don't know. There's tons left over. You should take some home.

BRADY. No. You don't have to—

CLARE. I'll get a Tupperware.

(*She goes to the kitchen.*)

EZRA. Fig foam. (*To* PAUL.) You get this every night, don't you?

PAUL. Not exactly this. There's a lot of experiments.

EZRA. Still. You're a lucky man.

PAUL. I don't think anything makes Clare as happy as feeding people.

(CLARE *comes back in and starts packing a Tupperware.*)

BRADY. Not too much.

CLARE. It's fine. Freezes well.

EZRA. Clare, honey, did you make your video yet?

(She stops spooning food for a second, then starts again.)

CLARE. Sorry. I've been slammed. Sorry.

EZRA. It's okay.

PAUL. What video?

CLARE. For the thing, Ezra wants me to make a video of my food.

EZRA. Not just the food, but you, talking and explaining your influences and passions, what goes into creating the recipes.

BRADY. It's for their Kickstarter.

PAUL. You're funding your food truck on Kickstarter?

CLARE. I told you about it.

EZRA. I'll come over and record it. I'll interview you.

CLARE. I'll record it. Don't worry.

BRADY. You'll do great.

EZRA. I'm not worried, I'm frustrated.

CLARE. Besides, don't we need a cute name before we go public? Like a pun or a wacky expression? I saw a bagel and pickle truck in Fort Greene called "Rise and Brine." Do you think that's adorable or repulsive?

EZRA. We'll find a cute name. We need a hundred thousand dollars.

PAUL. That's a lot of money for a Kickstarter.

EZRA. *(To* CLARE, *softly.)* Are you nervous about how you'll look on camera, because I can—

CLARE. No.

(CLARE does not have good skin.)

BRADY. I liked the salad, too.

CLARE. Jicama. I'll pack you some. Eat it soon, though, it'll spoil.

PAUL. What about when you combined technical and Mexican and were calling it "TechMex"? Played up the whole molecular gastronomy thing. That was neat.

EZRA. No one will ever get that.

PAUL. I got it.

CLARE. After we explained it to you.

PAUL. No.

CLARE. Yes.

PAUL. I don't know if it made me want to give you a hundred thousand dollars, but I got the name.

CLARE. Here.

(She hands EZRA *and* BRADY *a bag with Tupperwares of food inside.)*

BRADY. You're the best. I hate cooking.

EZRA. And I hate washing dishes.

(EZRA *and* BRADY *do a little flirty something, like tapping each other on the nose.*)

CLARE. Ezra.

EZRA. Hm?

CLARE. You guys aren't even thinking about it? You know.

EZRA. Okay, one: subject-changer. Two: NO. Three: also no but less hostile.

CLARE. You've been together forever.

EZRA. Three years is forever?

BRADY. Not to me.

EZRA. Darling.

(EZRA *and* BRADY *kiss.*)

CLARE. See?

PAUL. (*To* CLARE.) We lived together for a couple of years before getting married.

CLARE. But we were on the path. Are you on the path? A path just opened up here, after years of legal battles and hard work. That's so exciting, right?

PAUL. I don't know that I was on a path. I just remember I was living with my girlfriend, and then, one day, she was my wife.

(PAUL *gets the wine and refills glasses.*)

CLARE. We planned for a future together. We considered—

PAUL. You told me we had to either get engaged or break up.

CLARE. I did not say it like that.

PAUL. Maybe not in so many words, but—

EZRA. Clare, that is an insane ultimatum which, no offense, only a straight person would come up with.

CLARE. So you don't want to?

BRADY. (*To* PAUL.) I'm good, thanks.

CLARE. You finally can, but you're saying you don't want to?

PAUL. That's a little personal. Everybody's relationship is—

CLARE. What's too personal? Ezra's my best friend. And, look, I don't mean to—. Whatever you decide, obviously, it's fine. I just think it's so beautiful, all those couples at City Hall, some of them have been together for fifty years, and the flowers and the cakes. I get choked up whenever I think about it.

(EZRA *gestures and* PAUL *pours him more wine.*)

BRADY. It's nice. It's nice to have the option.

CLARE. (*To* BRADY.) We had a thing, at our wedding, to commemorate marriage equality.

EZRA. A sign, by the jars of quince jam.

BRADY. It sounds very thoughtful.

CLARE. I figured it's the least we could do for the most fundamental civil rights issue of our time.

(*Small pause.*)

PAUL. Well.

CLARE. You're kidding.

PAUL. I don't want to—

CLARE. Yes, you do, you do want to. What?

PAUL. I just think, all right, I think being able to arrest and indefinitely detain American citizens without charging them with a crime, I think maybe that's a little more severe.

CLARE. But nobody's actually doing that.

PAUL. Yet. That's the thing, nobody does stuff until, you know, the day they do it. That's why you make laws, and when someone changes the law, like with wiretapping or drones, we're all at risk. What if Obama doesn't win reelection? You really want to think about Michele Bachmann reading your e-mail?

EZRA. Maybe she'd learn something.

BRADY. You guys, they can both be very big deals.

CLARE. No, you think the hypothetical risk of someone being detained, which will never happen, is worse than the actual fact that millions of people can't legally marry the person they love?

BRADY. (*To EZRA.*) Help.

PAUL. "Never happen"? You're in a dream world. This is what happens when you buy the paper once a week and then only read Sunday Styles.

EZRA. Brady's right, we don't need to rank atrocities.

PAUL. Clare started it.

CLARE. That's not true.

EZRA. You did, actually. "Most fundamental"?

PAUL. Look, all I'm saying is I think we have to include Guantanamo in any conversation about civil rights.

CLARE. But that's completely different, it's in a different category.

EZRA. No flowers, for one thing.

BRADY. No cakes.

CLARE. You're all ganging up on me. I like weddings. I like marriage. Is it wrong for me to want to share the wonderful opportunity I have? How could it be wrong? You know, we almost didn't get married to protest—

EZRA. That is not true, you know that's not true.

CLARE. I thought about it.

EZRA. How hard?

BRADY. I like weddings, too. They're fun. And I like Sunday Styles. Please excuse me.

(BRADY *heads to the bathroom.*)

CLARE. It's such a mess in there. I meant to clean it before you came but—fig foam!

BRADY. Don't worry about it.

CLARE. Just—. I know there's toilet paper, at least, so.

(BRADY *exits.*)

I meant to clean, I did. He's going to be appalled. It's like some pornographic Wild West in there—all the tumbleweeds made of pubic hair.

PAUL. Clare.

CLARE. I didn't say it was *your* pubic hair.

(CLARE *hums a little Ennio Morricone and mimes a tumbleweed.* EZRA *joins in.*)

PAUL. We need more wine.

(PAUL *goes to the kitchen.*)

EZRA. Clare, honey. Could you stop planning our wedding?

CLARE. Fine.

EZRA. Thank you. Listen, we can't wait until we find the perfect name for the truck, we have to start talking with potential investors now. I've got a couple of meetings set up.

CLARE. With who?

EZRA. My neighbor does the website for the Food Network, and I met this guy who's a friend of a cousin of Mario Batali.

CLARE. Ezra, no, he's not.

EZRA. He might be. He said he was one of the first people to invest in Babbo. Will you come? He's free on Thursday.

(PAUL *returns with wine.*)

CLARE. I have to check with work.

EZRA. The whole point of the meeting is to get things going with the food truck, get an angel investor so you don't have to work at work, and you can work at making tacos and quesadillas and salsa all day.

PAUL. What rhymes with Mex? Tex-Mex? Rex-Mex?

EZRA. Sex-Mex?

PAUL. Sex-Mex.

CLARE. If we added Eastern European food, it could be Czech-Mex. Get it?

(PAUL *pours himself a glass of wine.*)

EZRA. Call in sick.

CLARE. If I can.

EZRA. Make me samples to bring, at least?

CLARE. If I can.

EZRA. You can.

CLARE. You really don't want to ask Brady to marry you? He's cute and smart and gainfully employed. His face lights up whenever you enter a room. And he treats you so, so much better than—

EZRA. I know.

CLARE. He's a good guy, Ezra.

PAUL. He's a great guy.

EZRA. I'm glad you've noticed. I love him so much it's embarrassing. And I politely reject your assumption that I need a piece of paper to tell me my relationship matters.

CLARE. That's not what I'm saying.

PAUL. And *we're* not together because of a piece of paper. It's not like if we weren't married we wouldn't be together.

EZRA. You said Clare told you "get engaged or break up."

PAUL. Yeah, but—

EZRA. So you're together because of a piece of paper. And that's fine, that's perfectly valid—

CLARE. I will try to attend the meeting with this Mario Batali guy, all right? I will try to stop making you so pissed at me.

EZRA. Thank you. Make your video.

CLARE. I will. Marry your boyfriend.

(BRADY *comes back in.*)

BRADY. I like the basket in there.

CLARE. Thanks. It's left over from a shoot I was arranging food for. There used to be kumquats in it.

BRADY. Huh.

(*Pause.*)

PAUL. Well, thanks for coming over.

BRADY. Yeah, we should split. I've got an early day tomorrow. And every day.

EZRA. You'll make this meeting?

CLARE. I will try to. Promise.

(BRADY *and* PAUL *shake hands.* EZRA *and* CLARE *hug.*)

EZRA. You'll look fine in the video. Go to the MAC counter at Macy's. They'll do you for free.

(*She touches her face, a little self-consciously.*)

CLARE. Okay.

PAUL. Thanks for bringing the wine.

BRADY. It was nothing, three-buck Chuck from Trader Joe's.

CLARE. It was good. They have good stuff there, it's like the Target of foods.

EZRA. We could pitch them, you know. After the food truck takes off, once we've got brand recognition and a loyal following.

CLARE. Target?

EZRA. Trader Joe's, get your churros in the frozen food section, next to the dumplings.

CLARE. Good night, Ezra.

EZRA. Dream big!

CLARE. I'll call you later.

EZRA. "Sing out, Louise!"

(BRADY *and* EZRA *exit.* CLARE *and* PAUL *start to clean up.*)

CLARE. I know about Guantanamo.

PAUL. I know you know.

CLARE. I don't think you can compare gay marriage to Guantanamo.

PAUL. You're right. After all, you can leave a gay marriage.

CLARE. Very funny.

PAUL. All I'm saying is gay marriage gets a lot more attention, and if everyone who posted a picture on Facebook of a rainbow took two seconds to learn about—

CLARE. You don't really think we're married because of a piece of paper, do you? It's not why we're together.

PAUL. No. We're together because we want to be together, right?

CLARE. Right.

PAUL. And I think the piece of paper matters for all of the reasons that it matters, but it's not like the paper is the marriage. We're the marriage, we're here because we want to be.

CLARE. What about if we don't want to be?

PAUL. (*Laughing.*) Uhh…

CLARE. No, God, of course I want to be, now. I just mean, when you say those things "richer, poorer, sickness, health" it seems like it's including when you don't want to be, right? I mean, would you really want to be married to a poor, sick person?

PAUL. How sick and how poor?

CLARE. I'm serious. The promise includes when you don't want to be.

PAUL. Or, maybe what you're promising is to want to be.

CLARE. Okay. That sounds nice.

PAUL. Good. The other thing to keep in mind is that's not actually what we said. "Richer, poorer."

CLARE. Because we wrote our own vows.

PAUL. Exactly.

(PAUL *takes a stack of dishes into the kitchen.*)

CLARE. Do you think Ezra and Brady have sex with other people?

(PAUL *re-enters with the dishes.*)

PAUL. Come again?

CLARE. I was thinking about our wedding and how Ezra was best man and hooked up that night with your cousin, and I wondered.

PAUL. Ezra was single when we got married. He had just broken up with the old guy.

CLARE. Right, I know, but right now, do you think they have sex with other people?

PAUL. No.

(PAUL *exits with the dishes.*)

CLARE. It's a thing people do. Gay men.

PAUL. Not all gay men. Not most, I bet.

CLARE. Of course not.

(*Small pause.*)

Dan Savage.

(PAUL *comes back in with Tupperware.*)

PAUL. Is Dan Savage the spokesman for gay people?

CLARE. Kind of.

PAUL. I don't think they do that, not those two.

(PAUL *starts putting leftovers into the Tupperware.*)

CLARE. Ezra found photos on Brady's computer of him having sex with another guy. Brady's kind of a player.

PAUL. That was years ago. Ezra found those photos before they even lived together.

CLARE. Still, though, if I found photos of you having sex with another woman, I would throw you out on your ass, you know I would.

PAUL. Old photos or current photos?

CLARE. Any photos!

PAUL. Good to know. Just making a mental note.

CLARE. When they were first dating, they didn't always go home together. Sometimes Brady would meet somebody, at like a bar or whatever.

PAUL. What about now?

CLARE. I don't know. Brady started coming for dinner and I stopped hearing stories.

PAUL. Did you tell stories to him?

CLARE. Old stories or current stories?

PAUL. Any stories!

(*A shared smile.*)

CLARE. Watch that, that's going to spill.

PAUL. I am watching it.

(PAUL *puts the lid on.*)

Look, the most important thing about their deal—whatever it is—is that they both agree to it.

CLARE. So if Brady steps out, it's okay?

PAUL. It's not stepping out if they're both okay with it. Maybe Ezra and Brady each have outside partners or one-night stands. Maybe they have threesomes, but whatever they do, it's done with respect and integrity. People have different sexual needs, but communication and patience, that's what matters.

CLARE. Right, I agree. Of course.

(PAUL *takes a small pill from a bottle.*)

Oh. I didn't realize——. Old man gut acting up?

PAUL. Dinner was a little spicy, so—yeah.

CLARE. I used fewer chiles than last time, and poblanos not jalepeños—

PAUL. Sorry, it just happens.

CLARE. You need water.

(*She hands him a glass of water. He swallows the pill.*)

PAUL. Thanks.

(*A moment, something shifts in* CLARE. *Then, with renewed vigor—*)

CLARE. You said "threesomes." Do you think they have threesomes? You think they do stuff, like bondage or whatever? You think they tie each other up? Or maybe the third guy, the new guy, ties up both of them. No, that doesn't seem safe, that way he could rob them. Probably the new guy should be tied up first. There's got to be a protocol, like Robert's Rules of Orgies.

PAUL. I don't know. I don't think about it.

CLARE. Me neither.

(CLARE *brings some dishes to the kitchen, then returns.*)

You think they look for a guy online and then bring him home? Or there's an app for it, like Grindr but only for threesomes. Trindr. Maybe they don't do certain things with the new guy, maybe it's only non-penetrative encounters. Maybe they have it all spelled out in an agreement, what's okay, what's not okay. Penis-to-hand, penis-to-mouth, penis-to-penis…

PAUL. I don't know, Clare. If you're really curious, you could always ask Ezra.

CLARE. Are you insane? That would be so rude.

PAUL. Or don't ask.

CLARE. That's what Dan Savage does, bring a guy home. A third. Occasionally. And he's gay-married and has a kid and everything. It's called being "monogamish."

PAUL. What does any of that have to do with Ezra?

CLARE. Nothing. I just want him to be happy, and I think being married to Brady would make him happy, and I'm trying to figure out why he won't even consider—

PAUL. It's still early, it's a new law. Probably, someday, he'll get married like the rest of us.

CLARE. Would you? Would you have gotten married to me if I hadn't nudged you?

PAUL. Bringing home bridal magazines is nudging?

CLARE. Answer me.

PAUL. How can I know that? I never really thought that much about marriage, it never seemed like a big deal.

CLARE. It didn't seem like a big deal to promise to stay with someone forever and be faithful to them? Are you nuts?

PAUL. I don't know. It didn't, not the ceremony part or the legal thing. I mean, I'm glad we did, but—

CLARE. I'm glad we did, too. Duh.

PAUL. But I didn't want all that, beautiful and magical and delicious as it was. I just wanted you. And technically, I'm not trying to weasel out of anything here, but technically, we didn't actually promise to stay faithful. We didn't say all that stuff about "forsaking all others" or "death do us part" or whatever.

(CLARE *approaches him.*)

CLARE. (*Tenderly.*) Because we wrote our own vows.

(She taps his nose, in an unconscious imitation of EZRA's *earlier gesture.)*

PAUL. *(Tenderly.)* Because we wrote our own vows.

(He taps her nose. The room is more or less cleaned up.)

CLARE. Hey. Nice party. We did good.

(She goes in for a kiss, but subtly, almost as if by coincidence, he avoids her touch.)

PAUL. Long day. I'm going to read and then pass out.

CLARE. Right.

PAUL. You coming to bed?

CLARE. In a bit.

PAUL. Don't get all hung up on Ezra's wedding. If they don't want it, then it's just a piece of paper, right?

CLARE. Just a piece of paper.

(PAUL leaves. CLARE sits at the dining room table, and goes through the mail. She opens an envelope and reads a letter.)

Hey, Paul? Can you—? Do you have time to look at something?

PAUL. I'm really tired, honey. Can it wait till morning?

(CLARE nods.)

Clare? I can't hear you when you nod.

CLARE. Sorry, yeah, everything's fine. No big deal. I'll be there in a sec.

(Carefully, she returns the piece of paper to its envelope and puts the letter in a drawer.)

Scene 2

EZRA *and* BRADY's *bathroom, also in Brooklyn, but nicer and tidier.* EZRA *and* BRADY *are getting ready for the morning: shaving, brushing teeth, etc.*

EZRA. How much money do you think they make? Clare and Paul.

BRADY. I don't know. Enough?

EZRA. I want a number. Guesstimate.

BRADY. I'm bad at that. When I was a kid, I would be off by a factor of ten when I had to guess the jellybeans in the jar. Why do you care?

EZRA. She's being so squirrely about taking time off to meet the investors, and I don't understand it. So she misses a day of work, it's not like she makes that much money anyway.

BRADY. When you're freelance, you feel paranoid turning down a client. You were the same way when you were taking people's headshots.

EZRA. Still. What do you think she makes?

BRADY. Thirty thousand dollars a year. Forty.

EZRA. I think less. I bet it's like $500 a week, arranging food for photo shoots. Plus overtime, if she gets overtime.

BRADY. No way. You made more than that waiting tables.

EZRA. On a good night. I could have a table full of dicks or Europeans and come home with 60 bucks in my pocket.

BRADY. Anyway, I'm sure Paul makes plenty of money.

EZRA. I don't know.

BRADY. At a fancy law firm?

EZRA. He's the assistant IT guy, not a fancy lawyer.

BRADY. Still. Over 100 grand a year, definitely.

EZRA. No way. Sixty. Under sixty.

BRADY. Seriously?

EZRA. If he makes 100 grand a year, why do they live in that shitty apartment? Why is her engagement ring so small?

BRADY. It is small.

EZRA. Plus, they're paying off her culinary school loans. And I don't think they have any savings.

BRADY. You could just ask her. If you're that curious.

EZRA. Oh yeah, I'm just going to call her up and say, "Oh hey Clare, I was wondering, how much money do you have because I need to assess how stingy you're being about this truck?" I can't do that.

BRADY. You're business partners, right? You need to know her finances.

EZRA. Not formally. We're friends who work together.

BRADY. So ask her as a friend.

EZRA. No, that's crazy rude.

BRADY. Then you'll never know.

EZRA. I don't think either of their parents help. I can't remember what his do, but hers don't help. They won't help with the truck either, Clare asked.

BRADY. Maybe they can't help.

EZRA. Sure, I know. Not everybody can be Dr. and Mrs. Jameson.

BRADY. Who miss you by the way.

EZRA. I'm sure.

BRADY. They do. Mom said—

EZRA. Brady, your parents hate me. They want you to be with an internist who looks like Taye Diggs. Dr. Fuckstable.

BRADY. You're not being fair.

EZRA. It's fine. If my parents ever met you, they'd hate you, too. Parents are the worst, I keep trying to make Mom and Ronny disown me to no avail.

BRADY. You don't mean that. Not about your mom at least.

EZRA. Are Clare and Paul broke or stingy?

BRADY. Probably neither, probably they're hanging in there like everyone we know. So she makes $500 a week, Paul's job covers her health insurance, so that's free.

EZRA. True.

BRADY. An advantage of marriage.

EZRA. Don't. Don't turn this—

BRADY. Health insurance. That's all. If we got married, then you'd be covered under my plan. If we even register as domestic partners—

EZRA. I'm all right. I'll be fine.

BRADY. I wish you would consider, a catastrophic plan alone—

EZRA. It's expensive.

BRADY. Lots of things are expensive.

EZRA. What's that supposed to mean?

BRADY. I just think it's worth pointing out that you have the new iPhone, but no health insurance.

EZRA. Every single person I know has an iPhone and nobody has health insurance. If Williamsburg is hit by dengue fever, we'll perish together.

BRADY. I care about you.

EZRA. I know. I'll look into it.

BRADY. Thank you.

EZRA. And I think Paul was kind of conflating "civil rights" and "civil liberties."

BRADY. What's the difference?

EZRA. I'm not sure, but they're different.

(BRADY *grabs* EZRA *around the waist and kisses his neck.*)

Do you think they own stock?

BRADY. Ezra, baby, please drop it.

(BRADY *stops kissing.*)

EZRA. I'm just wondering, like if the law firm gives Paul a 401(k), did he join it? Do they own stock? Have I been friends this whole time with someone who owns stock, or whose husband owns stock, against my knowledge? Do they own bonds? I don't know what a bond is. Are they bondsmen? Bondspeople?

BRADY. I have a 401(k) at work. I own stocks. I think. I don't know, it's a mutual fund, I just signed up for it this year.

EZRA. Oh God, does everyone around me own stock? Is there like some secret stock party that you all go off to where you trade stocks and talk about it and watch *Wall Street 2: Money Never Sleeps* and make fun of me?

BRADY. Calm down, please. You always think everyone is at a secret party making fun of you.

EZRA. Because they are. One day you'll take me there. When I'm a real grown-up and not just a wooden boy.

BRADY. If Paul makes what you think he makes, then he has, at most, a couple thousand dollars in his company's retirement plan and they couldn't access it for your food truck, anyway. The whole point about putting money away is that you can't take it out.

EZRA. Lame.

BRADY. You sign a thing saying that you promise not to withdraw or else there are penalties. I should go.

EZRA. Have a good day with our nation's future.

BRADY. I always do.

EZRA. I'm proud of you for teaching fuck-ups, you know that?

BRADY. I know. And I'm pretty sure we're supposed to call them "at-risk youth." Something about self-esteem.

EZRA. Whatever, at my grade school, everyone was a fuck-up.

BRADY. Not everyone. You got plans for—?

EZRA. Prep for this meeting on Thursday. Research, budgeting. I'll temp double hours next week to make up for it.

BRADY. Stop that. We're fine. I told you, worry about the truck right now, not about rent.

EZRA. Thank you.

(BRADY *gives* EZRA *a peck on the cheek.*)

This is a real business. I don't want you to think I'm, like, Countess LuAnn.

BRADY. How is a Countess named LuAnn?

EZRA. I love you.

BRADY. I love you, too.

(BRADY *exits.* EZRA *looks in the mirror at his reflection and profile.*)

EZRA. I hate that you're younger than me.

Scene 3

CLARE *shows up to the café where* EZRA *has been waiting for her.*

CLARE. Shit.

EZRA. Hi, Clare.

CLARE. How late am I?

EZRA. You have a phone. You know how late you are.

CLARE. I got here as soon as I——. Work was crazy, and then I missed a train, and——

EZRA. Sure.

CLARE. I'm sorry. I suck, I'm a sucky partner. Don't hate me.

EZRA. A question: When you picture Mario Batali's cousin's friend, are you picturing him roughly the same size and shape as Mario Batali?

CLARE. I guess.

EZRA. And when someone of these dimensions comes to a meeting with you, to talk about, for example, a food product and announces that he is hungry, what do you want to be able to say in response?

CLARE. The samples.

EZRA. I had to buy him a scone, Clare. An apricot scone.

CLARE. I'm sorry. I'm the worst, I'm the lowest rung on the evolutionary ladder.

EZRA. You're not. Look, I'm mad at you, but——

CLARE. I'm chlamydia. I'm bedbugs. I'm Donald Trump.

EZRA. Clare, look at me. I know what's going on.

CLARE. What do you mean?

EZRA. Self-sabotage. You've been doing this since the day we met.

CLARE. Have not.

EZRA. September, freshman fall. You picked at your pores the night before your big date with that guy——

CLARE. Byron O'Brien.

EZRA. Your skin had been fine, and then you started extracting every blackhead.

CLARE. I meant to stop after a few but——

EZRA. You treated yourself like human bubble wrap. Because you thought Byron O'Brien was too good for you and you were afraid of rejection.

CLARE. He was too good for me. He played lacrosse.

EZRA. And then you looked awful and he never called again. But you don't have to ruin this one preemptively, Clare. You deserve to be happy, you know?

CLARE. Yeah. Ezra, I wanted to—

EZRA. It's like that Nelson Mandela quote—"Our deepest fear is not that we are inadequate. Our deepest fear is that we're powerful beyond measure." We are powerful. We can do this.

CLARE. Ezra.

EZRA. What?

CLARE. That quote. It gets misattributed a lot. It's not Nelson Mandela. It's Marianne Williamson.

EZRA. Who's that?

CLARE. Not Mandela.

(*Her phone rings, and she checks the name, then rejects the call.* EZRA *grabs her phone.*)

EZRA. "Michael?"

CLARE. It's no one. A guy. No one.

EZRA. Okay.

CLARE. Not like that. I don't meet guys like…

EZRA. Like…?

CLARE. No, I mean, there are people you hear about, you know. Monogamish?

EZRA. Uh huh.

CLARE. But this—. He's just someone from work, it's a work thing.

EZRA. So shouldn't you get it?

CLARE. No. Look, I'm sorry—really sorry—I was late to the meeting.

EZRA. I know you are. Do better next time, okay? Okay?

(CLARE *nods.*)

Come here.

(EZRA *hugs* CLARE, *then holds her face in his hands.*)

Um, did you know your skin looks amazing?

CLARE. No, it doesn't.

EZRA. Yeah it does. What'd you do? Hit the spa, with Michael?

CLARE. Michael's from work.

(CLARE *pulls away.*)

I haven't been doing anything. I'm having a good day, I guess.

EZRA. You're sure you're not getting facials?

(*He comes closer to look at her face and she moves a bit out of the way.*)

CLARE. That reminds me, can I tell you a gross story?

EZRA. You have to ask?

(She settles farther away from him.)

CLARE. So there's this thing I realized like a month ago, and I can't now un-realize it. I was trying to pop this pimple, and the skin on my cheek was swollen and pink and sort of hard to the touch and I kept at it, every angle, and the pressure was building, you know, but it still wouldn't pop. I was so frustrated, and finally, I moved my fingers in exactly the right way and this thick white goo squirted out on the bathroom mirror and I realized, this is what masturbation is like for men. The pressure, the release, the sticky substance left over. When girls masturbate, there's no evidence, no proof of accomplishment. You're done, but you could maybe go again? But when I squeeze a zit, I go from utter fullness to utter emptiness. That's why it feels so good.

EZRA. That's. Jesus.

CLARE. I told you. I told you it was gross.

EZRA. No. I—I appreciate your honesty. Also, just as a man, I have to weigh in that those two sensations are very different.

CLARE. God, I could never tell Paul that. I'm so disgusting.

EZRA. So am I. I keep hoping Brady finds it endearing, like those two-legged dogs in wheeled carts.

CLARE. Ezra.

EZRA. Do you ever feel like we only have a few more mistakes to make before we've officially squandered our potential?

CLARE. Not until you phrased it that way.

EZRA. Oh good.

CLARE. Ez, you have tons of potential. You're very talented. You were such a great artist.

EZRA. You're very talented. I was a beautiful 22-year-old with supple nostrils.

CLARE. That's a kind of talent.

EZRA. Listen, gorgeous. I love you, but this adorably insecure thing is getting really old. I will set these meetings, but you have to show up—on time—with food.

CLARE. I know.

EZRA. And you have to film your video.

CLARE. I know.

EZRA. *(Singing.)* "I had a dream. A dream about you, baby." Don't you think about what will happen when we get the truck up and running? I think about it like every second. What it would be like to pay off my credit cards and student loans and shop for a winter coat in October instead of February when they go on sale. To buy a pair of shoes that costs over $200, that would be heaven. To buy Brady something classy, like a watch that I had engraved. My gifts for him are always so inventive and creative, and I just want to say, "No baby, it's not a scavenger hunt. It's a motherfucking watch." I'm going to try real hard not to get all The Secret on you, but you have to imagine the things that you want. And you want this truck, right?

(CLARE*'s phone rings again. She looks at the name.*)

CLARE. I'm really sorry. It's weird that he's calling again. Can I?

EZRA. Go ahead.

CLARE. Hi Michael, is everything okay? Oh, right, no, I understand. Give me a second.

(*She covers the phone with her hand.*)

I should go. I'm sorry. Work. I feel like shit doing this to you.

EZRA. No problem. I get it.

CLARE. Can you guys come over to dinner? Soon? I'll make some new recipes.

EZRA. Very soon.

(*She gives* EZRA *a quick hug goodbye and then leaves, putting her phone back on her ear.*)

CLARE. What's going on, Michael?

Scene 4

CLARE *and* PAUL *are getting dinner ready in the dining room.*

CLARE. Can I see?

(PAUL *shows her the cutting board.*)

PAUL. Here.

CLARE. Oh.

PAUL. I'm doing it wrong. I'm cutting the radishes wrong.

CLARE. Slicing. I asked you to slice, actually almost to shave—

PAUL. They're too thick.

CLARE. A little. I can. Can I?

(*She takes the cutting board.*)

PAUL. Fine.

CLARE. Just a little. Just to—.

(*She re-slices the radishes.*)

It's my fault. I wasn't specific enough. I'm never specific enough.

PAUL. You don't need to get global. You can just apologize for one thing, without making it a referendum on your entire character.

CLARE. I wasn't—. I was actually expecting that if I apologized for not being specific enough, you'd apologize for slicing them wrong. It was an opening apology in an imagined two-apology sequence.

(*She waits for it.*)

PAUL. I'll wash lettuce.

(PAUL *starts to get the lettuce from the kitchen.*)

CLARE. I washed it already. Sorry.

(*He gets a pill from the bottle.*)

Reflux? Already?

PAUL. It's better sometimes if I take it before the meal.

CLARE. Good to know.

PAUL. I know the medicine can make me a little low-energy, low-enthusiasm, but—

CLARE. It's fine.

(*He takes the pill and watches her slice for a few moments.*)

PAUL. Clare. I was paying our Visa bill today.

CLARE. I thought it wasn't due till the end of the month.

PAUL. I like to pay early. I saw a charge for a Dr. Azvadian.

(CLARE *keeps slicing.*)

I checked with insurance and he's outside of our HMO. Even with a referral, I don't think we could get reimbursed, and it was like $250 for the visit. All on the Visa.

CLARE. Huh.

PAUL. What's going on, Clare? Are you sick?

(*She puts down the knife.*)

CLARE. No.

PAUL. Good. Then what's—

CLARE. Dr. Azvadian is a dermatologist. I'm getting treatment for my skin, for my acne and the scarring—

PAUL. Clare—

CLARE. You noticed I look better, right? You did notice that?

PAUL. $250 per visit is a lot of money. You don't make, you haven't been making—

CLARE. I know.

PAUL. I feel like maybe you don't understand.

CLARE. I can afford it.

PAUL. I'm the one who keeps track of our spending, and I'm glad you're getting medicine for your skin—

CLARE. Are you?

PAUL. Yes, but I don't know—

CLARE. I got. I got some money.

(*She wipes her hands on a towel and goes to get the check from a drawer.*)

It's two hundred thousand dollars. Two hundred and eight thousand dollars.

(PAUL *stares at the check.*)

It's a settlement for—. I told you about this, I know I told you about this.

PAUL. No, you didn't, believe me—

CLARE. The blood thing.

PAUL. When you were a kid? You had anemia, right? So?

CLARE. Yeah. No one knew why, but my blood couldn't store any iron, and so I had to get transfusions at the hospital.

PAUL. And you still get weird around your period.

CLARE. Weak, yeah, I get weak.

PAUL. I don't understand why you get two hundred thousand dollars for weird periods.

CLARE. This transfusion I got at the hospital. It was supposed to have been screened, even in 1988 they understood, but it wasn't. They found out later that the blood I was given, it hadn't been screened for HIV. Other people at the same hospital, they got AIDS.

PAUL. Oh my God.

CLARE. I was lucky. I was fine. My batch, or whatever, even though it wasn't screened, it was okay. But the families of the people who got these transfusions, they sued the hospital, for pain and mental suffering, for the HIV tests I had to get as a kid. And it was this long, drawn-out thing, because the hospital got sold, so then they had to sue a different company, and it's been going back and forth for years, and I think we all kind of gave up and figured that, you know, it probably wouldn't ever amount to anything. But then it did.

PAUL. You have to cash this.

CLARE. I know.

PAUL. You can't just be sitting around with this in a random drawer, tomorrow morning, we are walking over to the ATM, no, we shouldn't do it at the ATM, at the actual bank, we'll go to the actual bank.

CLARE. Okay.

PAUL. Did you tell your parents?

CLARE. I wrote them an e-mail. They're on a cruise.

PAUL. What'd they say?

CLARE. My mom said "Be good to yourself." I'm never sure what she means by that.

PAUL. Clare.

CLARE. There's this guy, Michael, he's a financial consultant the lawyers set me up with, he's going to advise me on how best to—

PAUL. This is incredible.

CLARE. I know.

PAUL. I mean—

CLARE. I know. Anyway, when I got the letter, I thought, what's the thing I always said I would do if I had money, and I went to the dermatologist.

PAUL. I didn't know that's what you would do.

CLARE. Yeah. I don't really talk to you about my skin. How do you think I look?

(*Without really looking at her—*)

PAUL. You look great.

CLARE. Now or before?

PAUL. Both.

CLARE. Thanks. It's, there's a prescription cream, and he says I might also benefit from lasers—our insurance wouldn't cover it, but—

PAUL. This is so exciting, Clare. We could buy an apartment with this kind of money. We could leave the city and buy a house.

CLARE. I know. I haven't really—

PAUL. We could have a kid.

(*He takes her hand.*)

CLARE. Paul.

(*He cups her face and kisses her.*)

I thought we weren't going to even talk about kids until our careers were—. We said mid-30s.

PAUL. I don't mean that we have to, just that we could, we could afford to, I could go back to school—

CLARE. For what?

PAUL. I don't know. Anything.

CLARE. What do you want to study? You never mentioned—

PAUL. I don't know. Stop interrogating me for a second.

(*Knock at the front door.*)

EZRA. (*From outside.*) "Who's there?" "Hungry hordes!"

CLARE. I didn't finish slicing the radishes.

PAUL. Did you tell Ezra about the money?

CLARE. No.

PAUL. Are you going to?

CLARE. I don't know.

PAUL. The longer you wait, the weirder it will be when they find out.

CLARE. If I say anything, Ezra will want to use it for the truck.

PAUL. That's okay, we could put up a little seed money, if you wanted to.

CLARE. You think Ezra's going to be satisfied with—

EZRA. *(From outside.)* Now you say "Hungry hordes who?"

PAUL. Clare.

CLARE. The radishes look thick.

PAUL. What do you want to do?

CLARE. I don't know.

> (EZRA *keeps knocking.*)

PAUL. Well, for God's sake, at least put the check away.

> (CLARE *puts the check back in the drawer.*)

Not there. Somewhere safer.

CLARE. It's fine there. It's been there for a week.

PAUL. You waited a week to tell me?

CLARE. Get the door, please.

> (PAUL *goes to the door and* EZRA *and* BRADY *come in.*)

PAUL. Hi.

EZRA. Quite the dinner you're making.

CLARE. "Hungry whores"?

EZRA. Hungry hordes who are so grateful for the dinner invitation.

> (*Everyone hugs hello and gets settled.*)

What's tonight's experiment?

BRADY. It looks yummy.

PAUL. Deconstructed chilaquiles.

EZRA. Fig foam?

CLARE. Pork belly air.

EZRA. Pig foam. Fancy.

BRADY. Pig foam?

CLARE. These are, uh, radish garnishes. Help yourself.

> (*They pass the food and the garnishes.* PAUL *tries to get* CLARE's *attention.*)

BRADY. Really looks delicious. Clare, you've outdone yourself.

> (EZRA *takes a bite.*)

EZRA. This is insane. This is like cotton candy but bacon.

CLARE. I'm still tweaking it—

EZRA. Tweak away, but it's definitely on the truck menu. Future bestseller, right, Paul?

PAUL. Yeah.

CLARE. Thanks.

EZRA. Come on, you guys, I'm the only one eating the effervescent meat.

BRADY. I'm eating.

(CLARE *and* PAUL *look at each other, something's clearly unfinished between them.*)

EZRA. Were you guys fighting?

BRADY. Ezra.

EZRA. We can ask that, right? We're all friends. I'd tell you.

PAUL. You have told us.

CLARE. No. I'm just spacey tonight, I'm a little exhausted by the cooking.

BRADY. It's fine, relax.

(*Another pause.* BRADY *and* EZRA *look at each other.*)

EZRA. I met this woman today at the coffee shop. I went to this coffee shop in Park Slope to, I don't know, sear into my brain with hot lasers why I never want to have children, and the only other solo person there was this woman, and we were chatting, and she asked what I did, and I said I was an inventive foods entrepreneur and she said she was a poet and this moment passed, like this breath, and I could feel us both thinking so hard, but not saying, but thinking so hard: "How do you possibly make money? How are you here buying this tea latte and this pistachio macaroon when you are a poet? Do you have a patron in some archaic system of which I am unaware? Do you write poems for the Queen?" And I wanted to expand outward, to ask everybody from Flatbush Avenue to Prospect Park, "How are you doing it? How can I get to be a part of it, this magical economy where someone makes hand-stamped greeting cards and someone else makes hats of string. I mean, even if you bartered with each other, all you'd have at the end of the day is a card and a hat. Do you pay your landlord in jars of jam and bars of soap? How does this work? How, how, how, how, how?" But, you know, I just said I liked her legwarmers and then went away.

(*Pause.*)

CLARE. Huh.

PAUL. Yeah.

EZRA. Sorry, my fault, bad story.

PAUL. No. It's weird. Money.

CLARE. Yeah.

(Another pause.)

EZRA. Speaking of, how's the Kickstarter video coming, Clare?

CLARE. Good, I've been working on it.

EZRA. Remember Mandela. Nelson Mandela wants you to make this video.

CLARE. Ezra—

PAUL. Clare, how much is the Kickstarter for again?

CLARE. $100,000, I already told you.

PAUL. But what do you think you really need? What could you do with five, hypothetically?

EZRA. How hypothetically?

CLARE. Nothing. We could do nothing.

BRADY. You should put the pig foam in the video. Show the whole process, how the magic happens.

CLARE. I will.

EZRA. Do you want to give us $5,000?

CLARE. No. I mean we want to, but we can't.

(Pause.)

BRADY. How's work, Paul?

PAUL. Good. The same. How's work for you?

BRADY. Good.

CLARE. Tell us about teaching. I love your stories about the kids.

PAUL. Me too, they usually make me glad I'm in IT.

BRADY. They've got me judging the talent show this year.

EZRA. Don't, don't even bring that up. People want uplift.

BRADY. Okay, I know a good one, it's fun. I have this seventh-grader, Jayden.

EZRA. Oh, this is amazing. Jayden is who you'd get if you crossed Season 4 of *The Wire* with *Glee.*

BRADY. Look, I don't want to assume anything about him, but let's just say I wouldn't be surprised if he turned out to be gay. At all surprised. Which is tricky because I want to be a positive role model to him, but I also don't want my life, my sexuality, to be a big issue in the classroom. If I mentioned it, if I officially came out, it would be all anybody could talk about for weeks, and that's distracting, it could cause problems with the administration, and I don't know if it would even ultimately help Jayden who's actually pretty socially adept and has a lot of friends, girls and boys, and isn't teased or bullied or anything.

EZRA. So, he's perfect, just like you were.

BRADY. I did okay.

EZRA. He's too modest. Brady was the captain of the equestrian team at St. Adonis's School for the Genetic Elite.

BRADY. I was co-captain of the lacrosse team at Woodbridge Country Day.

EZRA. Country Day. Can anything truly bad ever happen in your life if you go somewhere called Country Day? It's like a fable. Country Day Mouse meets City Night Mouse—*et voila.*

CLARE. You played lacrosse? I dated a lacrosse player in college.

PAUL. Really?

EZRA. Embellishing.

BRADY. Back to Jayden.

CLARE. There's not so much asking, not so much telling.

BRADY. Right, but the thing is, he started asking. He'll ask me directly if I'm married or not. And I say, "That's not really what we're supposed to be working on right now, but no." And then he'll ask if I have a girlfriend and I'll say "Distraction, but no." And he'll look at me like, "There's more to this story," but meanwhile, I'm supposed to teaching him reading comprehension and about the American Revolution and stuff, so we're sort of talking past each other. And then one day last week, it was a Thursday, he comes into class and he's just completely different with me. I won't say he winks, but it's almost as strong, he gives me this look, like he's totally got my number, and when I call roll, he says, "Here, Mr. Jameson" and does this little chin nod, like, "I know. I totally know."

CLARE. Smart kid.

PAUL. Perceptive.

EZRA. No, but here's the crazy part. Brady comes home and tells me, because I have been following the saga of Jayden the whole time, and I'm concerned for him. As a former flaming twelve-year-old, I want him to know that it gets better, and so I ask him what's Jayden's last name.

BRADY. And it's the same as our cleaning lady. And she comes on Wednesdays. And I had just talked to her about teaching at Achievers' Academy. She outed me to her kid. And everyone's okay with it. Dolores Rodriguez-Garcia. Jayden Rodriguez-Garcia. I don't know, it seemed really beautiful.

EZRA. And then he stole Hot Cheetos out of someone's lunch and had go to the principal's office.

BRADY. He stole them from Kayla Prentiss. I don't think it was related.

(*Small pause.*)

CLARE. You have a cleaning lady?

EZRA. Yeah.

CLARE. How long have you had a cleaning lady?

EZRA. I don't know. A while.

CLARE. That's why your apartment is always so clean. Is because you have a cleaning lady.

PAUL. A lot of people have cleaning ladies.

CLARE. Isn't it expensive?

BRADY. It's not cheap, but—

CLARE. Does it feel weird to have someone touch your stuff?

EZRA. No.

CLARE. To have someone else's hands in your toilet?

PAUL. Honey.

CLARE. Do all our friends have cleaning ladies but they just don't talk about it?

PAUL. Yes. It's a sweet story. Good for that kid.

(*Another pause.*)

EZRA. So, speaking of expensive, I went to look at trucks yesterday.

CLARE. Oh. Great.

EZRA. There are some really lovely ones. We can either buy something that's already set up for food prep, like from a street vendor, or get like an existing mini-van or pick-up and retrofit it. I've also been talking to some folks who already do this about the permitting, and, like, whether it's worth it to just go rogue and start selling and build up a base of support, or whether we should try to get everything squared away legally first so as to avoid the hassle and fines.

PAUL. Interesting.

EZRA. Yeah. The thing is, we have to get going. Food trucks are really taking off, and if we don't get in early, so much of the ground game is just about setting up a presence, you know? We've got a social media strategy and I've been brainstorming ways to hold events and get into catering, but Clare, if we want to be up and running by summer, we have to tackle this fundraising thing now.

CLARE. Sure.

EZRA. How close are you with the video? Honestly.

CLARE. I've been busy. Work is—

EZRA. Look, you agree with me that this matters? That we have to do whatever it takes.

CLARE. I wouldn't say "whatever it takes."

EZRA. What would you say?

CLARE. I would say, it's important. It's important that we fundraise so we can start the food truck as soon as possible.

EZRA. And you don't have any brilliant ideas about how?

CLARE. I— No.

PAUL. Clare?

CLARE. What?

PAUL. Fine.

EZRA. All right. Here goes. Paul, give me your credit card.

PAUL. Um.

CLARE. What are you—?

BRADY. Ezra.

EZRA. I have totally thought this through. Paul, give me your personal credit card—not the one shared with Clare, okay?

PAUL. I don't—

EZRA. You trust me, right? I'm your wife's best friend and business partner.

PAUL. Sure. So could you tell me—

EZRA. Hijinks, that's all. I'm not going to put you at risk, I promise.

PAUL. Hijinks. Should we—

CLARE. It's okay, honey.

PAUL. I feel like we should mention—

CLARE. No. Not now.

EZRA. I told you you were fighting.

CLARE. Nobody's fighting.

PAUL. Come on—

CLARE. Paul.

PAUL. All right. Here you go.

(*He gives it to* EZRA, *who puts it in his pocket.*)

EZRA. Great, thank you. So, here's how it's going to work. I'm going to give this to my friend Stevie. He's going to get a giant cash advance that we can use for a down payment on a truck, and then buy a bunch of other stuff, like flat-screens at Best Buy or whatever, to make it look like credit card fraud. You're going to wait until the charges go through, then report your card stolen.

PAUL. What?

BRADY. What happens to Stevie?

EZRA. Nothing. He won't go anywhere where he's on camera and he's like totally generic looking and unmemorable, and besides, he doesn't know you and he can't be traced back.

BRADY. He knows me.

EZRA. We met him, like, a couple times, it's not a very established relationship.

CLARE. Who's Stevie?

PAUL. Ezra, that's illegal, we can't do it.

EZRA. How else are we going to get the money to make our dreams come true? This is our dream, right, we've been talking about it and talking about it and I'm fucking sick of talking about it. My friend Kevin made his first film this way, it's how he bought the camera and now he's going to Sundance. Come on.

(CLARE *looks at* PAUL.)

CLARE. Paul's right, it's way too risky. We'll find another way.

EZRA. Right, but there's not another way. Or, there is, but it takes like years and years of time, and in years and years there will already be inventive Mexican food trucks on every street corner and our moment will have completely passed us by. No one's going to find us, it'll take too much effort to track us down, the amount of money will be like a rounding error to the credit card company.

BRADY. That's how Kevin got his film made?

EZRA. It's not a problem.

PAUL. Please give me my credit card back.

EZRA. I'll give it to you tomorrow. Wink-wink.

CLARE. Ez.

EZRA. I'm not going to let you be your own worst enemy any more. I'm sabotaging your self-sabotage. "I had a dream…"

CLARE. Ezra, honey, this isn't the—

PAUL. Ezra. I mean it, I really want my credit card.

EZRA. Please, Paul, you're the one who's always railing on behalf of the dispossessed and the marginalized and, like, people in prison, right? We are the dispossessed and the marginalized. I have no money, I take crappy jobs, I have huge student loans to pay off, I can't get a small business loan because I have shitty credit, and I'm sick of it. I want to make something, to contribute my gifts. That's what we're put on earth to do, right?

BRADY. In a general sense, yes. But, honey, this is dangerous.

EZRA. Look, after we make enough money and we've franchised, we'll donate tacos to the Food Bank or something. We'll take money from Chase and give it to the homeless, you can't object to that.

CLARE. Please give Paul his card. And you're not the dispossessed, you have a cleaning lady.

EZRA. Brady pays for the cleaning lady.

(PAUL *stands up and moves toward* EZRA.)

PAUL. I don't want to get physical, I really just want you to give me my card back—

BRADY. You don't need to threaten him.

PAUL. I'm not threatening him, he took my property.

EZRA. I'll give it back tomorrow.

PAUL. Ezra.

EZRA. Calm the fuck down. We're at a dinner party.

(EZRA *takes a big bite of food. PAUL goes to grab the card from* EZRA's *pocket,* BRADY *intercepts him.* PAUL *moves past* BRADY, *and ends up shoving* EZRA, *who starts to silently choke on his food.*)

BRADY. Leave him alone.

PAUL. All right.

CLARE. Ezra, are you okay?

(EZRA *coughs and sputters.* CLARE *moves toward him.* PAUL *moves toward* EZRA *again.*)

BRADY. (*To* PAUL.) He's choking.

(BRADY *shoves* PAUL *out of the way and goes to Heimlich* EZRA. EZRA *snorts the food up his nose, and as* BRADY *tries to take him by the middle,* EZRA *bangs his head on the table and passes out.*)

PAUL. Shit.

BRADY. Is he unconscious? Ezra!

Scene 5

(PAUL *and* BRADY *at a café, a few days later.*)

PAUL. How often can they see that?

(*He waits.*)

Probably not often.

BRADY. No.

PAUL. Radish up the nose.

BRADY. Rare.

PAUL. Although my friend is a physician's assistant. They have a story for every orifice.

BRADY. I'm sure.

PAUL. Thanks for seeing me. Clare is getting a little loopy with concern. Did he get the flowers she sent?

BRADY. He did. They're nice.

PAUL. You know she's been calling him. She went by the hospital. They wouldn't give her any information.

BRADY. Ezra's home now. And he's not really in a place for visitors.

PAUL. Is he in a lot of pain?

BRADY. Not physically. Physically, he's doing fine. Emotionally, financially, spiritually…we'll see. He doesn't actually know I'm here.

PAUL. Ezra can't blame me for—

BRADY. I think he can.

PAUL. He was trying to take my credit card.

BRADY. Which is a piece of plastic. And my boyfriend is a human being.

PAUL. It was an accident. Look, I'm sorry for whatever my part was in hurting him.

BRADY. Your part was that you shoved him, but he's fine.

PAUL. He tripped.

BRADY. He tripped after you shoved him.

PAUL. I would never intentionally hurt Ezra. He's like family to me and Clare.

(*Small pause.*)

BRADY. Has Clare ever been hospitalized?

PAUL. When she was a kid. She had this blood thing.

BRADY. Was it expensive?

PAUL. I don't know.

BRADY. Ezra doesn't have any health insurance. I had been after him for months to get a catastrophic plan, something, but he never got around to it. It would have been like 150 bucks a month. The bill from the hospital was $14,000. Plus ambulance fees.

PAUL. You're kidding.

BRADY. They ran a lot of tests, just to be sure.

PAUL. For a radish up the nose.

BRADY. Think what they'd do if you really had a problem.

PAUL. What are you guys going to do?

BRADY. You mean, are we going to pay with your credit card?

PAUL. I didn't say that.

BRADY. But it's what you're doing here. Getting your card back.

PAUL. I came here to tell you that my wife misses your boyfriend and that since he's her best friend, maybe he could call her back sometime soon. She's going kind of nuts without him, it's like she's missing a limb. I'm sorry the bill is so much. That's a lot of money. That sucks.

BRADY. Yeah, and it's on top of his student loans and credit cards. They have programs to take away some of the hospital costs. If you're totally broke, you know. And, if you look at his income, if you don't consider us a family unit, he's basically living in poverty, so that's good.

PAUL. Well.

BRADY. What?

PAUL. He's living in poverty with someone who went to Woodbridge Country Day. I'm not sure he's exactly who those programs are intended for.

BRADY. Who is—"exactly?"

PAUL. I just mean—we don't all have the same opportunities.

BRADY. No. We don't.

(BRADY *reaches into his pocket.*)

I should be getting back to him.

(*He hands* PAUL *his credit card.*)

Here's what you came for. No shopping sprees.

PAUL. He wasn't really going to do that, was he?

BRADY. Now you won't have to find out.

PAUL. I didn't come for the card. I didn't e-mail under false pretences. I am genuinely concerned about Ezra. I love him.

BRADY. Me too.

PAUL. And, not that it matters but I cancelled my credit card days ago.

(*A beat.* BRADY *notices* PAUL's *shoes.*)

BRADY. I like your shoes. Those are nice.

PAUL. What do you mean?

BRADY. I mean I like your shoes. Are they new? Where are they from?

PAUL. You know, I can't remember. Target?

(*They're not from Target.*)

BRADY. Really?

PAUL. Target has some nice stuff.

BRADY. Those look really well-made for Target.

PAUL. Are we okay? Is there something I can tell you that will fix this? Because, yes, the accident was upsetting and traumatizing and—

BRADY. Expensive.

PAUL. Expensive, but it was mostly just chance, right? Radish in the wrong place at the wrong time?

BRADY. Something like that. It's funny, when I was watching the game yesterday—

PAUL. I always forget you're a football fan.

BRADY. Yeah. But in the game—

PAUL. It was a great game.

BRADY. Great game. And that last touchdown was crazy. The Giants shouldn't have even been near the endzone, but there they were. It can seem so random—who gets a concussion, who gets a huge signing bonus. Weather patterns, draft picks. Two guys get tackled the same way, one's back playing in five minutes, the other's out for the season, or worse. But it's not just randomness, is it? It's luck. Some people have good luck, some people don't.

PAUL. You have good luck, though, most of the time, right?

BRADY. I do.

PAUL. Ezra and Clare?

BRADY. They don't.

PAUL. Look, I just hope you understand how bad Clare and I feel about this, and if there's anything we can do to help—

BRADY. That's sweet, but, what could you do to help? Are you offering something specific?

(*A moment.*)

PAUL. Please, do give him a hug and a kiss from Clare and tell him we hope he's feeling better.

BRADY. Like I said before, he's feeling fine.

Scene 6

EZRA *and* BRADY *in the bathroom, getting ready for bed—brushing teeth, flossing, etc.*

BRADY. He had these great shoes.

EZRA. Paul had great shoes? The man has a goatee and uses a Bluetooth.

BRADY. He did. They were really nice.

EZRA. Weird.

BRADY. I think you'd like them.

EZRA. You're pouring salt in a wound?

BRADY. He said they were from Target.

EZRA. Too good to be true.

(EZRA *turns from* BRADY *and rinses his face.*)

BRADY. He also said you weren't calling her. He said she's upset, and Clare upset—

EZRA. Maybe she's not calling me. Maybe she's too busy.

BRADY. She puts food on top of other food, so someone else can photograph it.

EZRA. I'm not ready for her sympathy, okay? I don't want to see her big cow-eyes fill up with tears, or for her to tell me I'm brave.

BRADY. Okay.

EZRA. It's just—who am I, if I'm not the CEO of Malcolm X-Mex Tacos?

BRADY. You are not naming it that.

EZRA. Doesn't matter now.

BRADY. Hey. I'm glad you didn't commit credit card fraud.

EZRA. Thanks.

BRADY. I mean it.

(BRADY *kisses* EZRA *lightly*.)

I don't want you getting arrested. I want you here in our apartment and law-abiding.

EZRA. You're sweet.

BRADY. Look, I was thinking. What if you didn't apply for debt forgiveness for the hospital bills? What if we took them on together?

EZRA. That would be insane. You make $47,000 a year, I'm barely temping, and even with your parents' help—.

BRADY. I know, but I don't like the idea of your registering for something as an individual. I don't like thinking about you as an individual, as just an individual.

EZRA. Brady.

BRADY. Get mad at me, okay? I accept that you're going to get mad at me when I say this, but when you were in the emergency room, I was just thinking about the next time one of us ends up in the hospital.

EZRA. Which is going to be never.

BRADY. And when somebody asks who we are, I want to say more than, "He's my boyfriend." I want to say that we're family. We've been together for three years. I love you so much.

EZRA. I am so mad at you for doing this while I have a toothbrush in my hand. You have and have always had a flagrant disregard for ambiance.

BRADY. I want to get married to you. I want to get married and invite all our friends and look really gorgeous and I want you to look really gorgeous, and I want us to get lots of flatware and feed everybody small, wonderful appetizers in the Botanical Gardens.

EZRA. I'm crying. I hate you.

BRADY. I know. I didn't plan this, I've just been thinking about it. I want my money and your money to be our money. I want my things and your things to be our things. Forever.

EZRA. You mean it?

BRADY. I do.

(*They hug.*)

EZRA. And all because I lodged a vegetable in my nasal cavity. I should write a Modern Love column— "From Achoo to I Do."

BRADY. From noses to roses.

(*Beat.*)

EZRA. Hey—. Married means married, right? I'm probably being silly, but reassure me, okay?

BRADY. Honey.

EZRA. We're doing it traditional, like white flowers, string quartet, vows to keep our dicks in our pants.

BRADY. Ez, I love you so much.

EZRA. Not the issue.

BRADY. I—. Do you think people can really promise to be faithful forever?

EZRA. Yes. You want to propose to me, let's be real clear about what you're proposing.

BRADY. Fine. No. I'm sorry, I know monogamy is important to you, but I can't stand there and say that we'll be together for fifty years and I'll never slip up once. I just—I know myself.

EZRA. When was the last time? Tell me.

BRADY. Six months ago.

(EZRA *punches the air, then swallows.*)

EZRA. With who?

BRADY. You don't know him. I barely know him.

EZRA. You say it like it's a good thing. What did you do?

BRADY. Blowjob.

EZRA. Who on who?

BRADY. Reciprocal. He's clean. I would never put you at risk.

EZRA. That's my consolation prize?

BRADY. You said you didn't want to know, so—

EZRA. I said I didn't want you to do it.

BRADY. And I said I didn't think I could change.

EZRA. Not even for marriage?

BRADY. I don't want to start this by making promises I can't keep. That's probably why most marriages end, anyway, people set unrealistic expectations and then blame each other when they fail to meet them. We're better than that. We can do this better than that.

EZRA. My mom and my dad are divorced. My mom and my stepdad are divorced. My mom and Ronny aren't looking so good. I will not get divorced. I hate divorced.

BRADY. I know. I will try to be monogamous, I can promise that, but you have to try, too.

EZRA. What do I have to try?

BRADY. Accepting. Accepting me the way I am and that this is part of the way I am.

EZRA. I hate that.

BRADY. I know.

(BRADY *reaches for* EZRA. EZRA *pulls back.*)

You are the best thing that ever happened to me, you have to know that.

EZRA. Fuck. Okay, say we did this. Nobody hotter than me, or younger. No redheads. Nobody who's shirtless in their Facebook profile.

BRADY. Those guys are friends.

EZRA. Friends wear clothes.

BRADY. Do you actually want to draw boundaries? If you want to, I'll respect them.

EZRA. I want to draw a boundary of no. I want to be with someone who wouldn't hurt his husband.

BRADY. Everybody hurts the people they love. I'm trying to minimize—

EZRA. Really?

BRADY. Babe, it's not about you. This is my thing, it's about me.

EZRA. How can you say that? I get being a slut, okay, I had my time, but I am done with that shit, forever. Because you are enough for me. Why am I not enough for you? Tell me who you need me to be.

BRADY. I need you to be you. I need you so much.

EZRA. Then prove it. This isn't fair.

BRADY. I don't know what fair would look like. I'm not interested in keeping score.

EZRA. Says the guy who's always winning. God, there are so many ways you could destroy me, and I can't even think of one thing I could do to hurt you.

(*Small pause.*)

BRADY. You could leave.

(EZRA *walks out of the bathroom.*)

Scene 7

CLARE *and* PAUL *at the dining room table. They are doing their taxes.*
CLARE *has a shoebox of papers, and* PAUL *has his computer open.*

CLARE. Here's all my receipts for food and kitchen supplies.

PAUL. Are they organized?

CLARE. No. You want me to—

PAUL. It'll be better if I enter them in order, so—

CLARE. Okay. Chronological? I hate this. I hate paper. I would rather scrub a million toilets than get my receipts in chronological order. Not that I ever scrub the toilet.

PAUL. Hey, cheer up, it's our last year for receipts, anyway. Next year, because of the settlement, our taxes will be nuts. We'll probably need to hire an accountant.

CLARE. Who has accountants?

PAUL. The same people who have cleaning ladies. The Venn diagram is a circle.

CLARE. It's not like we have that much money.

PAUL. We do, Clare. It's, and I don't say this lightly, it's life-changing.

CLARE. That's a little extreme. I mean, we can't buy an island and retire there and eat grapes all day.

PAUL. No, but, think about it. If we follow the advice you got from Michael and invested this aggressively, aggressively and especially internationally, we could be making 6% a year on $208,000. That would be $12,480 a year.

CLARE. You just had that, off the top of your head?

PAUL. I have a calculator on my telephone.

CLARE. The future is now.

PAUL. I'm serious.

CLARE. What would we do with $12,480 a year? It's not actually that much, not when you think of it like—

PAUL. We could hire a cleaning lady and an accountant, for one thing. We could move to a nicer place. It would be the equivalent of one of us getting a part-time job that basically consisted of breathing. Or, we could be a little more strategic. Spend it in a lump sum, put a down payment on an apartment, buy a car, or—.

CLARE. Or donate it.

PAUL. Sure, we could donate some of it.

CLARE. To the ACLU, to stand up for civil liberties.

PAUL. That's fine, we can include charities and non-profits in our strategy.

CLARE. What does "invested aggressively and internationally" mean? The economy is shit right now, right? What do you think we'd have to do to make that kind of profit?

PAUL. Michael said Brazil or India—

CLARE. I think it means shady. I think it means Michael makes a commission on cutting down the rainforest.

PAUL. Okay, that's fine. We can look at socially responsible firms or green-energy companies.

CLARE. They don't earn as much do they?

PAUL. That's okay. We'll find something good together.

(PAUL *shows her something on his computer.*)

I—it's good that we're sitting down to do our taxes now, actually. I made a program that tracks our income and spending, and there's a little lever here where you can add more, you can kind of just drop the new money in and see what it does—

CLARE. You called it "blood money"?

PAUL. It was a joke. From your blood?

CLARE. Wow.

PAUL. If you want solar cells, we'll do solar cells. I want to make these decisions in a way that brings maximum benefit to everyone.

CLARE. That's exactly what Michael says. How much have you been talking to Michael?

PAUL. A little. Last week. That's all, to get the lay of the land, but I didn't do anything. We set up a regular check-in call.

CLARE. He's my consultant. It's my money.

PAUL. Well.

(CLARE *gets up.*)

CLARE. I want to make something. Make us a snack, a midnight snack.

PAUL. It's 9 p.m.

CLARE. What do you want?

PAUL. I don't care.

CLARE. You can have anything, peanut butter balls, cinnamon toast, cocoa, milkshake, popovers, anything.

PAUL. I'm not really hungry, but if it will make you happy to cook—

CLARE. Tell me, please. Name one specific thing I can do to please you.

(*Pause.*)

I gave away some of the money.

PAUL. Okay, Clare.

CLARE. I paid Ezra's hospital bill. You told me what Brady said it was and how it was adding to his debt, and I paid it as an anonymous benefactor, like in *Great Expectations.*

PAUL. That was very kind of you.

CLARE. It was $14,000.

PAUL. I remember. That's okay, that still leaves us almost 200 grand. It's a lot of money to spend on a gift for a friend, I think that it is, but I also think that given that we weren't uninvolved with the accident—

CLARE. You sliced the radishes too thick.

PAUL. That's a matter of debate.

CLARE. Paul.

PAUL. It was the generous thing to do. I think you are a very generous friend.

CLARE. What kind of snack do you want?

PAUL. I don't want a stupid snack!

CLARE. I gave away more money. I don't want to tell you about it, I know you're going to get mad, but you're going to find out the next time you talk to Michael and—

PAUL. How much?

CLARE. Don't you want to know to whom?

PAUL. Sure, how much to whom?

CLARE. It was to the Equality Project. They're trying to get marriage equality legislation passed in all 50 states, and also to take the cause all the way to the Supreme Court. I donated it to love.

PAUL. Clare.

CLARE. I gave away a hundred fifty thousand dollars.

PAUL. To gay marriage? To the abstract idea of gay marriage? Not even to any actually gay, married people?

CLARE. To education and legal fees and building awareness.

PAUL. Clare.

CLARE. They found this plaintiff, Edie Windsor—

PAUL. You gave away almost all of our money because you can't get over how adorable you think the idea of gay marriage is?

CLARE. I don't think it's adorable, I think it's important.

PAUL. Bullshit. You think it's cute, it's like when little girls have a wedding for their Barbie dolls or their pet rabbits or something, only in this case, it's their pet homosexuals.

CLARE. You don't believe in gay marriage?

PAUL. Of course I believe in it, it's like gravity, it's a fact of life and a good thing and I'd rather live in a world with it than without it, but I wouldn't take money from, I don't know, for example, my existing straight marriage and spend it on the theoretical concept of gay marriage, no I don't believe in it quite that much.

CLARE. This wasn't your money, you didn't get the blood transfusion when you were four, you didn't have to lie awake at night and wonder if you were going to die.

PAUL. No, but you didn't die, did you? And if repaying this money to gay people is an attempt to somehow atone for the fact that many of them died of AIDS and you didn't—

CLARE. Okay, so it's crossed my mind.

PAUL. I think another way of looking at it is that you wouldn't even have gotten your possibly tainted blood if it hadn't been for gay people to begin with.

CLARE. That's horrible. You don't mean that. Do you mean that?

PAUL. No, I'm sorry—

CLARE. Because that's horrible. Ezra and Brady are our best friends—

PAUL. And I am your husband, and you just yanked a pretty big rug out from under me.

CLARE. It's not your rug. It's my rug.

PAUL. Were you even planning to tell me? What if we didn't share a Visa or a checking account? What if I hadn't noticed the charges to Dr. Azvadian?

CLARE. I tried to tell you.

PAUL. How hard, Clare? Everyone knows you try, but how hard? We are supposed to be sharing something here, what's mine is yours, isn't it? But what's yours is apparently just yours, to be spent on frivolous political campaigns—

CLARE. Equality is not frivolous.

PAUL. And your alleged acne—

CLARE. I have acne. I give myself acne.

PAUL. On purpose? That's disgusting.

CLARE. Maybe I was hungry for a little personal attention. Maybe I stared at and touched my face because I like to be stared at and touched.

PAUL. Clare, it's a side effect of the reflux medication, I told you—

CLARE. You hadn't touched me in months. Months. I would think about other men as I walked down the street, I would imagine undressing them, playing with their chest hair, fondling their balls—

PAUL. I think every couple goes through a period of cooling off. And my pills—

CLARE. Sure.

PAUL. I just don't want to, sometimes, okay? I, there is no way to say this without sounding horrible, but sometimes I don't want to be with you, in that way. And I think you wouldn't want me to force something I don't want, right, so we don't do it. But sometimes I do want to be with you, really.

CLARE. So what's the difference?

PAUL. I don't know.

CLARE. Is it when I'm pretty?

PAUL. No.

CLARE. Is it when you know I'm rich?

PAUL. Clare.

CLARE. You only fucked me after you knew I had money. Did you have a threshold? $10,000? 50?

PAUL. I gotta say, credit where credit is due, if you wanted to sabotage our marriage, you certainly picked a creative way.

CLARE. I didn't—

PAUL. Clare. You did. This is how you break up with people, you just casually treat them terribly until they finally notice and leave.

CLARE. I—

PAUL. It's how you left the guy before me. Why we never see your old roommates. It's what you're doing with Ezra.

CLARE. Ouch.

PAUL. You don't really want to run a food truck with him, do you? Really? But you're too scared to quit, so instead you're destroying that taco company slowly, like you're trying to destroy us.

CLARE. I don't want to destroy us, I want us to have a beautiful relationship where we gaze at each other constantly with devotion and desire, where we love each other and fuck passionately at regular intervals.

PAUL. No one has a marriage like that.

CLARE. Ezra and Brady would.

PAUL. No, they wouldn't. You took that money from us, from a thing we could do together, like a house or a car or graduate school—

CLARE. In what?

PAUL. Not the point.

CLARE. What are you even interested in?

PAUL. I don't know. But I was really looking forward to finding out. My dad supports my mom, and I'm supporting us and I guess I figured that's the way it would be until—

CLARE. Stop this bullshit guilt trip. I never asked you for money once, I said 50/50 from the beginning. Rent, Con Ed, everything. You offered, you always offered.

PAUL. Yeah. I did.

CLARE. God, you're so perfect, aren't you? How are those shoes working out?

PAUL. My new shoes are very comfortable and I like them, but I did not buy a hundred and fifty thousand dollars' worth of shoes. I bought one pair.

CLARE. Two pair.

PAUL. Fine, two pair!

CLARE. I hate your fucking fancy shoes.

PAUL. So, you didn't buy shoes, instead you paid for other people's marriages, which seems pretty weird and it seems pretty alienating and it makes me feel alone and it makes me wonder if you want to make me feel alone.

CLARE. You make me feel alone, too. When you don't look at me or touch me, when you don't say I'm pretty, you make me feel alone.

PAUL. Maybe that's what being married is. Maybe it's being alone next to someone else who's being alone.

CLARE. That's the most depressing thing I've ever heard.

PAUL. Do you want to be married?

CLARE. Paul.

PAUL. If you could, if you could, without hurting me, without any of the pain and unhappiness and paperwork and expense, if you could just magically not be married to me, would you?

CLARE. That's a pretty well-formed hypothetical.

PAUL. Would you do it?

CLARE. Would you?

(PAUL *doesn't answer.*)

I'm making Rice Krispie treats.

(CLARE *leaves the room.*)

PAUL. I miss my girlfriend. I used to have the awesomest girlfriend named Clare.

Scene 8

EZRA *sits on a park bench with* CLARE. CLARE'*s skin is now blotched and scabby.*

EZRA. You look like shit.

CLARE. Yeah. But I'm empty, you know. Everything squeezed out. Pore nirvana.

EZRA. Ew.

CLARE. I know I should use the cream and forget my pores, it's just—. Other women my age, their skin is always so flawless. I see them on the street and it sends me into these horrible spirals of despair.

EZRA. Honey. Other women your age wear makeup. Like, all of them wear makeup. Any woman your age you see who doesn't look like she's slowly dying of an undiagnosed illness? That's makeup.

CLARE. Oh.

EZRA. It's cute what you don't know, but it won't be forever. Don't look so hurt, I'm the same way, vast pockets of adult life bewilder me. I think I'm mentally about 17.

CLARE. How long do we have?

EZRA. While it's still cute? I don't know. Thirty-five?

CLARE. That's not a lot of time.

EZRA. Tell me about it.

CLARE. You're looking great. No trace of radish nose.

EZRA. Supple nostrils. So good for partying, so bad for garnishes.

CLARE. I'm sorry about that whole night.

EZRA. It's funny, the hospital said that an anonymous benefactor paid my bill.

CLARE. Wow.

EZRA. Yeah. It actually said that on the bill: "anonymous benefactor."

CLARE. How cool.

EZRA. I think whoever paid it was a big fan of *Great Expectations.*

CLARE. Ezra—

EZRA. Brady called Paul, to tell him thank you. I didn't want to say it myself, I didn't want to say, "If you have $14,000 for my hospital bills where in the hell is a deposit for a truck?" That seemed rude, and ungrateful, so I let Brady say thanks. Thanks.

CLARE. You're welcome.

EZRA. Brady said Paul had moved out.

CLARE. Separating. We're separating? I don't know. We're starting counseling this afternoon.

EZRA. With who?

CLARE. Some place his insurance covers.

EZRA. Was he cheating?

CLARE. No, it wasn't that. He wants to get a graduate degree and move upstate. He wants to study forestry, apparently.

EZRA. Huh. You doing okay?

CLARE. I will be, I guess. Glad I could be helpful.

EZRA. Big changes.

CLARE. Yeah.

EZRA. I got us a contract.

(*He takes out a manila envelope, gives it to her.*)

I asked this lawyer friend of Brady's, frat brother if you can believe it, to draw us up a contract, stipulating our relationship as business partners, documenting who owes who what. Are you free to sign it now? We should get it notarized.

CLARE. Ezra, I—

EZRA. It's very thorough and very fair, I think you'll see that your interests are protected.

CLARE. Paul told Brady about the money, right? About all the money that I didn't spend on the truck.

EZRA. He did. And the donation.

CLARE. I gave it to a really good cause, huh?

EZRA. How much do you have now?

CLARE. Not much.

EZRA. How much?

CLARE. Around $40,000.

EZRA. I'm entitled to half of that.

CLARE. That's what this contract says?

EZRA. I'm your business partner and I deserve $20,000 for all the work I put into building this company. I've invoiced the months I spent working for free, on the assumption that we were both broke—

CLARE. I didn't ask you to—

EZRA. Yes, you did. When you don't do something, you're asking the other person to pick up your slack.

CLARE. That's not always true. Honey, I'm not giving you $20,000, I already paid you 14. If Paul and I split up, I'm going to need it, I'll need a new apartment and legal fees and to cover me while I look for a restaurant job. I can't afford to keep arranging food if I'm on my own—

EZRA. Do you want to run this truck with me?

CLARE. Ezra—

EZRA. Tell me no.

CLARE. I—

EZRA. It's okay. Just say it.

CLARE. I don't want to be an entrepreneur. And I think a Latin-fusion taco truck is a bad idea.

EZRA. Thank you.

CLARE. It felt so hollow, being rich. And gross. I was always on the verge of vomiting.

EZRA. The emotion you're looking for from me—is it sympathy?

CLARE. I'm not describing—. Like, I have these wool socks, right, and I wear them until they grow holes in the heels and they're special. But, when I was rich, I kept thinking, now my socks are pointless because I can just buy every pair in the store. In all the stores.

EZRA. Uh huh.

CLARE. I don't want something I didn't earn.

EZRA. That's very noble.

CLARE. Well—

EZRA. Another way of looking at it is that you are terrified of adulthood and you use poverty as an excuse to basically be an overgrown undergrad.

CLARE. I am not.

EZRA. And that when faced for the first time with the real possibility that you could grow up, start a business and even have a fucking kid, you did whatever it took to prevent your own maturity.

CLARE. That's not what—

EZRA. You have zits. By choice.

CLARE. I have adult acne.

EZRA. You think you're still a teenager.

CLARE. My husband wouldn't make love to me.

EZRA. I didn't know that.

CLARE. Yeah, well, I figured Paul didn't tell Brady everything. I don't know if I want to have a kid with Paul. I don't know if I want to have a kid, period.

EZRA. That's okay. That's what counseling is for.

CLARE. I guess.

EZRA. I still think the truck is a good idea.

CLARE. Ez.

EZRA. No, but I'm glad that you said you thought it was a bad one.

CLARE. I've been trying to say that for months. But you kept bursting into "Everything's Coming up Roses." You don't listen.

EZRA. You don't talk loud enough.

CLARE. Stop it.

EZRA. I'm trying to help you. You can be such a "Before Picture."

CLARE. I don't need your help. I'm not your project, okay?

EZRA. Okay.

CLARE. And I didn't give away the money because I'm afraid of growing up. You're the one who thinks you're still seventeen, not me.

EZRA. Then what the hell are you doing? You risked your marriage and your best friendship and the only excuse you've given so far is socks.

CLARE. I don't—. I know it wasn't fair to you or Paul. I know that. It was messy. And awful, but—. I don't know, necessary? When I was giving it, I felt powerful, and when it was gone I felt—. Free. I didn't want to be the person that money was going to make me.

EZRA. Who do you want to be?

(CLARE *tries to answer. She's not sure, but she really hears the question.*)

Open your envelope.

CLARE. I can't sign a contract with you. I don't think I can sign a contract with anyone for a long time.

EZRA. Just open it.

(*She pulls out an invitation.*)

CLARE. Oh my God! You guys are getting gay-married!

EZRA. Married, Clare. We're getting married.

CLARE. Right. That's wonderful.

(*She gives* EZRA *a hug.*)

EZRA. You don't feel, I don't know, any less enamored of marriage now that yours is collapsing?

CLARE. Not really, no, not for you guys. This is so great.

EZRA. I'm pretty nervous and terrified about the whole thing, but that's *de rigeur* for a groom, I've heard.

CLARE. I'm so happy for you. Is your family handling it okay?

EZRA. Yeah, my mom is actually like ridiculously excited about it. Since my sister's such a weirdo, this is probably her only chance at a legally married child.

CLARE. That's not nice.

EZRA. Clare, my sister is a hirsute traffic cop, this is a one-time event.

CLARE. (*Reading the invitation.*) You're getting married at the Woodbridge Country Club? Fancy fancy.

EZRA. We had wanted the Botanical Gardens, but since Brady's parents are paying for it—

CLARE. I didn't know they were so generous.

EZRA. They maybe pay for our cleaning lady. And our accountant. They won't invest in the truck, though, or any of my entrepreneurial business ideas. They only give money to Brady.

CLARE. Right, but now you're going to be married so—

EZRA. So what does that mean?

CLARE. I don't actually know. How'd you propose? Or, did he propose? Who proposes?

EZRA. He did. It was simple. Sweet.

CLARE. You're underselling, I bet it was beautiful: flowers, candles. You can tell me, was it everything you've ever wanted?

(EZRA *shrugs.*)

Honey?

EZRA. The proposal was a compromise, so I'm either settling down or giving up. I'm still working out which.

CLARE. You're being silly. You guys will be perfect husbands.

EZRA. That's what I told you and Paul.

(CLARE *gets something from her purse.*)

CLARE. Here. These might be useful, I don't know. Paul wanted me to bring them to counseling.

EZRA. "I promise to always respect your ideas. I promise to provide a space for your individuality." These are your wedding vows?

CLARE. "I promise to support you in all your endeavors. I promise to nurture your creativity."

EZRA. This sounds like the mission statement for a progressive prep school.

CLARE. "I promise to honor your spirit. I promise to foster open and attentive communication."

EZRA. I think you got married to Dalton.

CLARE. "I promise to approach every day as a new opportunity."

EZRA. "I promise to celebrate our accomplishments together and share our disappointments."

CLARE. What terrible vows. I didn't realize it at the time, obviously, but these are terrible vows. Who lets a 25-year-old come up with this crap?

EZRA. They're not that bad.

CLARE. But they're useless. They don't cover any of the stuff that comes up, do they?

EZRA. I don't know. I don't know what comes up. I'm so scared of getting married, Clare. I'm scared he's going to break my heart. I'm scared he's going to fall in love with someone else. I'm scared he's going to realize that he's a world-saving Abercrombie model and I'm a prospect-less mole-person, and he'll stay out all night with some other guy and I'll pickle in my own jealousy and then set fire to all the linens we've registered for.

CLARE. Sweetie, no. You'll grow old together and do crossword puzzles and grow dahlias.

EZRA. We might not.

(*A loss.* CLARE *lets something go.*)

CLARE. You might not. If I rip this paper up, does that mean our marriage is over?

EZRA. Honey.

CLARE. It's not like it's the original copy—I just printed it off the computer.

EZRA. I don't think you should rip up your wedding vows.

CLARE. Fine.

(CLARE *starts to fold the paper.*)

EZRA. Probably you should make new ones.

CLARE. What should they say?

EZRA. Whatever you want them to.

CLARE. Fuck.

EZRA. Come here.

(*He holds her.*)

CLARE. Stay friends with me, please? I'm sorry I don't want to work together, but I really do want to stay friends, I want to promise that, we can even get it notarized. And we'll never share money or sex and that will make it all right because without money and sex nothing can ever be too hard.

EZRA. I promise.

CLARE. I promise, too.

(CLARE *has made her vows into a paper airplane. She flies it offstage.*)
Whooosh.

End of Play

THE GROWN-UP
by Jordan Harrison

ABOUT *THE GROWN-UP*

This article first ran in the January/February 2014 issue of Inside Actors, *Actors Theatre of Louisville's subscriber newsletter, and is based on conversations with the playwright before rehearsals for the Humana Festival production began.*

"I'm really glad that we don't have a crystal ball," says playwright Jordan Harrison, reflecting on how inscrutable and strange the places we land in life would probably seem to our younger selves. This imagined sense of wonder and profound disorientation—and the ever-increasing velocity of time as we get older—are part of the theatrical spell that the playwright casts in his funny and sad adventure, *The Grown-Up*.

As Harrison describes it, the play started as a journey inward into memory, begun during a silent retreat for playwrights led by fellow writer Erik Ehn. "You're not allowed to speak or make eye contact the whole time, so you end up cooking and eating an entire meal without any human interaction. You only hear everyone else chewing and slurping," recalls Harrison. "And there's no Internet, no research books—you're cut off from your usual tricks and tools, with nothing but your own experience to draw upon." He traces the catalyst for *The Grown-Up* to a particular creative exercise in which participants were asked to pass through an imaginary door into a room they once occupied, where they would find themselves in a memory of another time. "We all had our eyes shut, all these thirty- and fortysomethings crawling around on the floor like kindergarteners," laughs Harrison. "It was only meant to be a starting point, but for me it became the engine for the *The Grown-Up*. I just kept compulsively opening doors to see what was on the other side."

The odyssey through which *The Grown-Up* travels, then, is set in motion by an object that's at once seemingly ordinary and tinged with metaphoric possibility: a crystal doorknob. As the play begins, a ten-year-old boy named Kai listens to a story at his grandfather's feet, the tale of a sunken pirate ship whose sole survivor washed ashore with the crystal eye of the mermaid on the doomed vessel's prow. That old sailor built the relic into the family's house, and it's now the unassuming doorknob to the linen closet. But here's the secret, Kai's grandfather confides: "It's a doorknob to anywhere." The charmed object, he claims, creates a portal to other times and places—but its user can't control when or where it takes him. Unable to resist testing this magic, Kai steps over the threshold and tumbles forward into his own life, as the play charts a quantum-leaping course that's both a madcap adventure and a sober meditation on the fleeting nature of experience.

The play's fantastical frame gave the playwright permission to fill that container with some of his own (very real) preoccupations about approaching middle age, and Harrison acknowledges that the piece became a sort of "slanty memoir." And so, for example, his recent experiences in Hollywood while pitching a television show inspired one of the threads in Kai's shifting reality. "There's a dissonance between the object's magic and the kind of quotidian, workaday places that it takes Kai," Harrison says. "Rather than jumping back to the age of dinosaurs or Henry VIII or something, he travels further into his own life—and not even the greatest hits of his life for the most part, but everyday scenes that are heightened by being seen through the eyes of a ten-year-old." Kai discovers that he's a writer—an inventor of stories as well as a passenger on the open waters of this bewildering one. Narratives within the story dovetail and merge with Kai's shifting reality, like a Möbius strip that circles forward, twists and loops back at the same time.

The transformative agility of this world is "not unlike a radio play," writes Harrison in the script's introductory notes. "We can go anywhere…because we don't have to see these places realized." With second-person narration supplied by an ensemble of players who also portray multiple characters, *The Grown-Up* unfolds on a nearly bare stage, its humor and energy supplied by nimble performers and the audience's imagination. "The special effects in my newest plays are the actors themselves, and the language," the writer explains. "I think maybe I needed a break from harrowing tech rehearsals!" Harrison also notes that he can separate all of his work into "plays with furniture" and "plays without furniture," borrowing terms coined by theatre scholar and writer Bert O. States: "Plays With Furniture are in the Chekhov camp, where the characters are described by and bound by the history of their things. Whereas Shakespeare is the quintessential Play Without Furniture playwright—lots of scenes, lots of settings—and all you know about his characters comes from the language."

This latter brand of formally inventive, linguistically driven storytelling makes *The Grown-Up* both a theatrical and an existential adventure. Sending the audience hurtling through each door with Kai, the play evokes the dizzying sense of how fast life goes, how remarkably difficult it is to construct a satisfyingly complete narrative out of our time on Earth. For who among us can outsmart the crystal doorknob's powers? As one of the colorful characters who crosses Kai's path warns, "Magic is so arbitrary."

—Amy Wegener

BIOGRAPHY

Jordan Harrison's plays include *Marjorie Prime, Maple and Vine, Futura, Doris to Darlene, Amazons and their Men, Act a Lady, Finn in the Underworld, Kid-Simple, The Museum Play, Standing on Ceremony* (written with Paul Rudnick, Doug Wright, and others), and a musical, *Suprema*. His work has been produced at American Conservatory Theater, American Theater Company, Berkeley Repertory, City Theatre, Clubbed Thumb, Curious Theatre, the Mark Taper Forum, Minetta Lane Theatre, NAATCO, Next Theatre, Playwrights Horizons, Portland Center Stage, SPF, and Theatre @ Boston Court, among others. Five of his plays have premiered in the Humana Festival at Actors Theatre of Louisville. His children's musical, *The Flea and the Professor*, won the Barrymore Award for Best Musical after premiering at the Arden Theatre. Harrison is the recipient of a Guggenheim Fellowship, a Hodder Fellowship, the Kesselring Prize, the Roe Green Award from Cleveland Play House, the Heideman Award, the Loewe Award for Musical Theater, a NYSCA grant, and an NEA/TCG Playwright-in-Residence Grant. A graduate of Stanford and the Brown University M.F.A. program, he is a recent alumnus of New Dramatists. Harrison is an Associate Artist with The Civilians, Clubbed Thumb, and The Playwrights' Center. He currently writes for the Netflix original series *Orange Is the New Black*.

ACKNOWLEDGMENTS

The Grown-Up premiered at the Humana Festival of New American Plays in March 2014. It was directed by Ken Rus Schmoll with the following cast:

ACTOR A	Matthew Stadelmann
ACTOR B	Brooke Bloom
ACTOR C	Paul Niebanck
ACTOR D	Tiffany Villarin
ACTOR E	Chris Murray
ACTOR F	David Ryan Smith

and the following production staff:

Scenic Designer	Daniel Zimmerman
Costume Designer	Janice Pytel
Lighting Designer	Paul Toben
Sound Designer	Lindsay Jones
Stage Manager	Katie Shade
Dramaturg	Amy Wegener
Casting	Zan Sawyer-Dailey, Meg Fister

Properties Master...Mark Walston
Directing Assistant ....Cara Phipps
Assistant Dramaturg...Sam Weiner

The Grown-Up was commissioned and developed by Clubbed Thumb and supported by the 2012-2013 Clubbed Thumb Writers' Group. The commission of *The Grown-Up* was made possible by the New York State Council on the Arts with the support of Governor Andrew Cuomo and the New York State Legislature.

CHARACTERS

ACTOR A: Kai *(rhymes with eye)*

ACTOR B: Anna Bell / Lane Heatherette

ACTOR C: Grandfather / First Mate / Barry / Minister

ACTOR D: Grandma / Rosie / Wedding Guest / Paula

ACTOR E: Mr. See / Wedding Planner / Award Ceremony Emcee

ACTOR F: Josef the Fisherman / Steven / Cater Waiter / Miss McGinn

NOTES

There is a strange kind of blindness to this play, not unlike a radio play. Hopefully this can be liberating: we can go anywhere – a tallship in a storm, a crowded ballroom – because we don't have to see these places realized. We can be any age. I suspect that there is very little on stage.

All of the actors do narrating duty. Narrated lines are *set in italics* for the sake of readability, but they are very much within the action and momentum of the scene. They are not a step outside; they are not direct-address.

Because the costume changes are minimal and the characters plentiful, the actors are always actors in a sense – which is maybe why it seemed right to identify them as Actor A, Actor B, etc.

Matthew Stadelmann, Tiffany Villarin, Paul Niebanck and Brooke Bloom
in *The Grown-Up*

38th Annual Humana Festival of New American Plays
Actors Theatre of Louisville, 2014
Photo by Bill Brymer

THE GROWN-UP

A. It doesn't *look* very valuable,

B. *you say.*

A. Looks like glass.

C. Crystal,

B. *your grandfather says, running his fingers over the doorknob.*

C. You can tell by the way the light is trapped. How it's split into rainbows, here?

A. Oh yeah,

B. *you lie. You don't want him to know you can't see. There's something wrong with people who can't see magic.*

C. It's older than this house. It's older than me. It's even older than your grandma.

D. Older than Grandma? Impossible!,

B. *Grandma says. And back to her knitting.*

C. I reckon it's older than this whole country.

A. How do you know?

B. *You squint but it still looks like glass.*

C. The man who built this house – When I was your age he was my age, if you follow. Real geezer, with one bad eye the color of an iceberg.

B. *Grandfather's eyes pass over the old ship's wheel mounted on the wall.*

C. He was just an ordinary fisherman, but long before, he'd been a cabin boy on a tallship. That's how he came across it.

A. The ship was carrying doorknobs?

C. Treasure, from the Silk Road. Spices, incense. *Jewels,*

B. *he adds, strategically. Spices are abstract to a ten-year-old, but jewels—*

C. (*To A.*) They figured to make a fortune, but half of them died on the way here, from scarlet scurvy.

D. Fever.

C. What?

D. Scarlet fever.

C. You weren't there.

A. Does scarlet scurvy make you scarlet?

C. Not anymore, thank god. They put an end to it long before you were born.

B. *And you're glad to hear it, though the idea of a disease disappearing altogether is somehow troubling – like your favorite TV show ending, or a whole species ending, or you ending.*

C. Anyhow—

B. *Grandfather lights his pipe—*

C. The old sailor said the doorknob was part of his ship, once. You know all those ships had a lady on the prow, a chesty lady.

D. A mermaid—

C. A chesty mermaid.

D. George, don't say chesty.

C. What should I say? Popular?

B. *Grandma drops a stitch.*

D. Look what you made me do.

C. Now this ship wasn't just any ship…

A. It was a pirate ship.

C. How do you know?

A. Why else would it have a story about it.

B. *Grandfather doesn't like how certain you are.*

C. Maybe it wasn't a pirate ship after all.

A. No, it was!

C. Maybe it was a tugboat.

A. *(Pleading.)* It *was* a pirate ship, it was!

C. *(Relenting.)* So it was. But before they could reach Portsmouth – when they were out in the deepest part of the ocean, the ship was eaten whole by a great wave.

D. I thought you said scarlet fever.

C. First fever, then the wave.

D. Very unlucky pirates,

B. *Grandma says.*

C. The unluckiest.

B. *Even at age ten, you sense there's something fun for them in these little battles.*

C. Can't you just imagine all those silks and doubloons sinking to the ocean floor? What a goddamn waste. And the hell of it was—

D. George—

C. The heck of it was, the only part of that whole great ship that survived, the only thing that washed ashore was the big round crystal in the eye of the chesty mermaid on the prow. And do you know where that eye ended up?

B. *You look over at the doorknob.*

A. No way!

B. *And he's got you now. There's a little itch down the back of your neck like the fingernail of a ghost.*

A. What's so special about a doorknob?,

B. *you say, covering.*

C. (*With mystic intrigue.*) It's a doorknob to anywhere.

A. A doorknob to anywhere? What's that supposed to mean?

C. It means if ever you're feeling a little bored with your smart-ass ten year old self; if ever you're getting tired of playing gin rummy with your sister; if ever you're feeling like summer is going altogether too slow, then you just go over and grip that doorknob very hard with both hands—

D. George, he'll think you're serious.

C. Just pull 'til it pops clean off. Then you stick that knob on any door you want, and the second the door opens you'll be someplace else.

A. Where?

C. That's the catch.

A. There's *always* a catch,

B. *you say, flopping back onto the couch in a way that makes Grandfather narrow his eyes, wondering if you aren't a future homosexual.*

C. The catch, since you asked, is that you can't choose where the doorknob will take you. The doorknob doesn't care about time and space, life or death. Death doesn't trouble it. You could end up a thousand miles away, or a hundred years ago. You could end up somewhere that will make you beg for your little sister and gin rummy.

D. Stop scaring the boy.

A. I'm not scared.

B. *Yes you are.*

C. You're very young. You could stand to be a little scared.

B. *Some of the light and love seems to leave his eyes, but you're not sure what's replaced it.*

A. If it's a magic doorknob, then how come I've seen Grandma open that closet a million times and there's nothing in it but placemats and napkins and stuff?

C. That's on account of it's the Safety Door.

A. The Safety Door?

C. Like neutral for a car. It's the one door where you can put the doorknob when you want it to be just a doorknob. The one door where its powers don't work.

D. How convenient,

B. *Grandmother says. She looks up from her knitting, hearing footsteps.*
   (ACTOR D *looks at* ACTOR B *for the first time.* ACTOR B *is now* ANNA BELL.)
D. Well look who's here, Kai. If it isn't your poor little sister, looking for a friend.
B. Gin rummy?
A. Not now.
E. *Anna Bell always wins at gin rummy. Always.*
B. Why not now?
A. I'm talking to Grandpa.
B. What about?
A. You're not old enough.
B. (*A second opinion.*) Grandpa?
C. I'm afraid he's right.
E. (*To A.*) *You and Grandfather share a look. You are never so close as when you're leaving Anna Bell out.*
B. Whatever it is, I bet it's stupid.
D. Yes, dear. It is stupid.
B. Why does Kai keep looking at that door?
D. Never mind that.
Sit down and I'll teach you the garter stitch.

II.

   The FISHERMAN *stands under a lamppost. It is raining lightly.*
   ACTOR A *stands outside of the light as he narrates:*
A. *An old Fisherman squints into the darkness.*
F. Hello?
A. *There's someone out there, just beyond his vision. He could see who if it weren't for his one bad eye the color of an iceberg.*
   (*The* FISHERMAN *tunes a little pocket radio that plays a sea chanty:*)
RADIO. Are you missin' the sea?
Sometimes like your mother
Are you missin' the sea?
Sometimes not at all
Are you missin' the sea?
Like a limb that you lost

Are you missin' the way
It makes you feel small.
> (*He turns the knob on the radio and finds a different station.*)

RADIO. Oh you batton the staysail and gaze at the stars
And wonder, are we meant to see that far...
> (*This one seems to stir up bad memories. He turns the knob. Another song:*)

RADIO. Storm a-coming tonight,
Let every man know.
Swing left, swing right
Hitch your hammock up tight
Swing high, swing low
Sweet dreams of a girl in a red trousseau.
> (*The* FISHERMAN *tries to see who's out there in the darkness. Squinting in the direction of* ACTOR A:)

F. Anybody out there?

A. *No answer.*

F. Come say hello if you want.
> (*Beat.*)

(*Muttering, giving up.*) Be a nice change.

III.

B. Gin!

E. *cries Anna Bell. She's won the last six games.*

A. I don't believe you.

E. *She shows you her cards.*

B. (*Showing him the win.*) One, two, three.

E. *She smiles. Her teeth are black with licorice.*

B. Play again?

A. Let me win this time?

B. No.

A. Then no.

B. (*Whining.*) There's two whole hours to dinner.

A. We could play something else.

B. Like what.

A. How about *Grossest Thing You Can Think Of.* Or *Where Did My Eyelids Go.*

B. You always win those games.

A. Or *Find My Booger.* I'll give you a hint – it's under your pillow.

B. Mom, Kai won't play normal!

A. (*To* B.) Shut up!

E. *It might be the most penetrating thing she's ever said: Kai won't play normal.*

B. Mom! Kai told me to shut up!

A. Shut up!

E. *You peek into the doorknob room, which is also your grandparents' sitting room. Empty now.*

D. *Grandma is cooking supper.*

C. *Grandfather is puttering around the garage.*

B. I'm bored.

E. *You get an idea.*

A. How 'bout we play hide-and-seek? You can hide first.

B. That's how you always get rid of me when you want to get rid of me.

A. I promise, Anna Bell,

E. *you lie.*

A. Anna Bell, my favorite only sister, I promise I'll come find you.

B. Okay, count to a hundred.

A. Fifty.

B. That's too short!

A. One,

E. *you say, and she's off and running. Off to the toy chest in the attic, her favorite hiding place. Never mind you've found her there before.*

B. (*Heartbreakingly, all she really wants is to be found.*)

E. *And there's nothing worse than giving her what she wants.*

A. Two, three, four…

E. *You make your voice a little louder to cover the fact that you're slipping into the next room. Reverse Doppler.*

A. Five! Six!

C. *Your hand on the crystal doorknob now, the doorknob to anywhere.*

E. *Does it give off a faint glow, or is it just your imagination?*

D. *You pull it off the safety door with a satisfying pop.*

A. Seven! Eight!

C. *Pick a door, any door…*

D. *Front door?*

C. *Nah*

A. No

E. *Maybe.*

D. *The front door has little glass windows. You can see the sunny day beyond, the climbing tree, Anna Bell's purple plastic ponies mouldering on the lawn.*

C. *Yes,* <u>*this*</u> *door. Not a crooked little gnomish door, but an everyday door: The perfect test for a magic doorknob.*

A. Nine! Ten!

E. *You put the knob on the door—*

D. *It slides over the real one with magic ease—*

C. *The knob turns in your hand, and the door opens*

B. Kai? You were up to ten and you stopped. Kai?

C. *And you step on through.*

　　　　(Continuous into...)

IV.

E. *(Cordial.)* Kai!

F. *You enter the bright office.*

E. Welcome.

F. *Big desk with a man behind it. Sun in your eyes not his.*

E. Sorry to make you wait.

A. Oh no, it wasn't – It was actually good to have a little breather after the traffic, which was—

E. Yeah, welcome to L.A. How long were you waiting?

A. It was my fault, I got here early, so.

E. Yeah you shouldn't do that in this town.

A. I shouldn't?

E. Looks low on the totem pole.

A. Trying too hard.

E. Something like that. Another thing you shouldn't do is pace outside the TV executive's window for twenty minutes practicing your pitch to thin air.

A. You saw that?

F. *Shit.*

E. I was trying not to.

C. *Shit.*

E. Relax, Kai. Can I call you Kai, Kai?

A. Sure.

E. Just relax. Bonnie warned me I was getting an 18-carat New York City neurotic.

A. 24-carat.

E. Hah, whatever. Bonnie sure can pick 'em.

A. Bonnie's great.

E. She's got a real eye for writers. Or is it an ear.

A. Both maybe.

E. She said you were like the new Woody Allen but more, you know...

A. Waspy?

E. No. Woody Allen but with more...

A. (*Off his gesture.*) *Cojones.*

E. What? What's that?

A. Balls in Spanish.

E. That's it – Woody Allen with balls.

F. *Silence.*

A. Yeah, Bonnie's great.

E. So you wanna go ahead and tell me this thing of yours? Bonnie says you're cookin' up something special.

A. Actually, do you guys have any coffee?

E. (*Preposterous.*) "Do we have coffee." (*Into intercom, but not miming this:*) Rosie, our writer friend wants to know if we have any coffee. (*Back to A:*) We have a freezer full of Acid Reflux Roast from Intelligentsia. Know that place?

A. No.

E. You should never admit to not-knowing in this town.

A. Oh, sorry.

E. And never apologize. Kidding!

A. Ha

D. Milk and sugar?

A. Oh, no thanks

E. Thanks, Rosie

A. Thanks.

E. So now you're all parked, you're all coked up on that—

A. Getting there—

E. And you've done a little dance outside my window. Any more stalling you wanna do?

A. Well I just – ha, that's good – I would really just love to hear what you guys do here first. I have a few different ideas so I don't wanna just throw spaghetti against the wall, you know? I wanna hear what you guys are into.

E. First of all, there's no "into," okay? That's what you literary types have to remember. This isn't personal. We're not "into," we're "about."

A. What are you about?

E. Cops, doctors, and lawyers. That's the brand, that's what works for us. You can slice up the series in syndication, shuffle it every which way and Judy Housewife doesn't care if she's watching season 3, 9 or 17, so long as there's a guy in a trench coat looking at some bones. His haircut might change but that's about it. We call it counter-context programming. Say it for me.

A. I'd rather not.

E. *("Really?")* You're not gonna say it for me.

A. Counter-context programming.

E. See? That wasn't so bad.

A. Great. So, should I just?—

E. No time like the present.

A. Ha. *(Three descending notes:) Duh-dah-dum.*

E. Yeah, I know that, that's *Psycho.*

A. Actually I think *Psycho* is *Ree-ree-ree-ree.* I was doing more like classic Lon Chaney horror I guess, with a soupçon of *Jaws.*

E. This guy's a real movie buff.

A. Well, yeah.

E. *(Lightly condescending.)* No, it's great.

A. So I've been rolling this idea around in my head a lot

E. Good, good…

A. And I mean it's kind of a guilty pleasure but highbrow. Kind of a *Pirates of the Caribbean* meets *Quantum Leap,* but not at all '80s. Very current, good hair… Bonnie told me period is out, so.

E. Period's the worst. Isn't it, Rosie.

D. Hate.

A. Is she gonna keep listening in?

E. That a problem?

A. I guess not.

E. So: *Quantum Leap* plus pirates

A. Well the hero is this guy who's like the opposite of a pirate. Like the guy from *Sideways,* whatshisname

E. Oh I love him

A. But with more sex appeal

E. (*Obviously.*) Yeah.

A. But still, you know, normal

E. Rick something

A. (*"No."*) Something like that

E. What's the guy's name Rosie

D. Paul Giamatti

E. *Giamatti.* Tip of my tongue.

A. And he plays this guy who gets time-jumped back

E. *There's* Quantum Leap

A. He has to right a wrong from his family's past or something

E. (*Liking this more.*) Okay, okay. Revenge is stupid right now.

A. Revenge is "stupid"?

E. Oh sorry, that means "hot." I see how that could be confusing.

A. So our guy, he ends up back on a 19th century pirate ship—

E. Why a pirate ship?

A. (*He realizes he doesn't know.*) I guess I just like pirates.

E. Stop. (*The best idea ever:*) What if they were *modern* pirates, like Somali pirates.

A. I don't think so

E. But you said not period

A. Just trust me on this. So our hero finds himself in this life that's not his own— He has to man the crow's nest, he has to survive a shipwreck, maybe he gets himself a parrot

E. This is TV we're talking about?

A. Yeah, why

E. Feels Feature to me. Does it feel Feature to you Rose?

D. Feels feature.

E. See?

A. Feels feature why?

E. Time stuff is easier to pull off on the big screen. Big canvas, bright colors. Like *Jacuzzi Time Flux*, you see that?

A. (*Politic.*) I saw the ads.

E. That thing set records. (*Significantly.*) On the big screen.

A. I was kind of seeing one-hour drama. Well, drame*dy.*

E. That's a word we like. That's a good word here.

A. As I was saying the pirate is kind of a sad-sack, like an office worker, a janitor

E. (*Helpfully.*) A writer

A. Yeah – *Hey*

E. Kidding, go on.

A. Say, what's that on your desk?

E. What, the paperweight?

A. Is it glass?

E. Crystal, I think. My last assistant gave it to me.

A. I saw something like that once. I don't know where.

E. Nice girl, totally burned out on me. That's how it goes with these girls. They come in all ready to grab the world by the – what was that word?

A. *Cojones*

E. Ready to kick the world in the *cojones*, but then they just (*He makes a gesture for disappearing in a puff of smoke.*). You still listening in, Rose?

D. Sure am, Mr. See.

E. Don't burn out on me, 'kay Rosie girl?

D. Not the plan, Mr. See.

E. Isn't she great?

A. Mr. See, how old do I look to you?

E. Early-late twenties I'd say, but your skin's good for a writer. Bonnie said you could pass for late-early twenties, and she wasn't wrong.

A. (*Almost to himself.*) I was talking to my grandfather – it was yesterday. It was today. I was ten.

E. You okay, Kai? You look confused.

A. What did he tell me. "If you're ever bored…"

E. Could be the coffee – Not everyone can handle the Reflux Roast. Right Rosie?

(ROSIE *is strangely paralyzed – like an actor who's forgotten her lines.*)

Rosie, you make the coffee too strong again?

(*Still no answer.*)

A. (*With new resolve.*) I know what this is.

E. Again with the paperweight.

A. It's not a paperweight.

E. Are you *trying* to throw this meeting? Or do they like bullshit back in New York?

A. I went through a door. How did I forget?

E. Don't touch that!

A. That must be part of it – the forgetting

E. This isn't coffee. Lemme guess: you're the new kid in town, you snort a few uppers, don't know how to handle it—

A. (*Piecing it together, in his own world.*) I'm a boy, I'm ten. I'm playing gin rummy with my sister.

E. Rosie, get security. Rosie?

A. I'll go back. Maybe if I turn it the opposite way—

E. Put the doorknob DOWN.

A. I thought you said it was a paperweight.

F. *Silence.*

E. Kai, / listen—

A. (*Overlapping.*) Stay away from me.

C. *You move toward the door.*

E. Whatever's on the other side of that door, it's not your sister playing gin rummy. It's not your grandfather and his pipe. It's farther down the path – infinitely worse.

A. How can it be worse than here,

F. *you say, turning your back*

C. *And he's up from his desk, his hands reaching for you*

F. *But you're faster, you're younger*

C. *You're twisting the knob and you're safe*

F. *You're safe*

C. *You're gone.*

E. Rosie!

V.

> *The old* FISHERMAN *stands under the lamppost listening to the radio. Another sea song:*

RADIO. Still haven't got your land legs
Still got your hands on deck
Salt in your hair, salt in your shorts
And you're a doggone wreck.
Ohhhhh, still haven't got—

> (*The* FISHERMAN *changes the station – a little too close to home. Static, nothing but static. Finally he picks something up. The voice of an eight-year-old girl:*)

B. Kai? You promised you'd find me.

Kai? This isn't funny.

>(*The radio starts to weep. The* FISHERMAN *turns it off.*)

F. Poor kid.

>(*He climbs the lamppost like the mast of a ship. As he gets higher, we hear the sound of the ocean. A voice from out of the darkness:*)

C. Boy!

>(*The* FISHERMAN *closes his eyes and light slowly rises on* ACTOR C *as the* FIRST MATE.)

A. *With your eyes shut, the past rushes in—*

C. I said Cabin Boy!

F. (*Eyes shut.*) Up here!

A. *The First Mate takes shape – first his body, then his handlebar mustache, and finally his black-toothed pirate's mouth – like the Cheshire cat in reverse.*

>(*The light on* ACTOR C *completes.*)

C. What do you see up there?

>(*The* FISHERMAN *opens his eyes on the horizon.*)

F. Nothing, Sir!

A. *The First Mate narrows his eyes.*

C. If you're gonna man the crow's nest, you have to learn to see better. Nothing is ever nothing.

F. What do you mean?

C. The clouds. Cirrus or altostratus?

F. Sky's clear, Sir!

C. Moon. Gibbous or crescent?

F. No moon!

C. *New* moon. Sign of land?

F. Middle of the ocean, Sir.

C. Waves?

F. Still as a bathtub.

C. That's it, I'm coming up.

A. *He scales the mizzen like a monkey up a tree.*

C. Well I'll be damned.

F. What?

C. Looks a whole lot like nothing.

Except—

F. Where

C. See that red ribbon where sea meets sky?

F. What is it?

C. Could be nothing. Could be a mean squall headed our way.

F. Is it ever a friendly squall?

C. (*Unsmiling.*) You're a funny kid. You got a mom or a dad?

F. Dead, Sir.

C. Well you've got me now. I think I'll call you Josef. It sounds better than Cabin Boy.

F. Josef.

C. Never had a son,

A. *The First Mate says. His eyes are wet, but they stay fixed on the sky.*

F. Sir? Is this really happening?

A. *The image of the First Mate starts to swim a little. You shut your eyes tight, holding onto the memory.*

C. What do you mean, really happening?

F. Because I miss you – but you're right here.

C. 'Course I'm here,

A. *he says, eyeing the red ribbon on the horizon.*

F. It's getting wider. Is that good?

C. It's not good.

A. *You watch it grow 'til it eats half the sky.*

C. Feel that wind?

F. Yeah.

C. That wind's bringing rain.

VI.

When B, C, and F speak for ROSIE, they look directly at her.

B. *Eff me,*

D. Rosie says to herself as she presses her brand-new espadrille slingbacks on the gas and merges across four lanes of traffic to the carpool lane of the 405. She's propped up the mannequin torso her sister got her from the SkyMall catalog for the purpose of masquerading as two people in the carpool lane. Cut her commute nearly in half. Thanks, Sis.

Rosie presses harder with her espadrille slingbacks. She speeds. Trying to outrun the stinging awareness that she's let down Mr. See. It is the job of the

assistant not merely to brew delicious coffee and deflect unwanted calls and
to sparkle like a fine hard gem, but also to maintain whatever reality is called
for on any given day, with any given subject.

C. *Dammit,*

D. Rosie says, pulling into the driveway.

F. *Eff me,*

D. she cries as she washes the kale, juliennes the jicama slaw and brings the
quinoa to a slow boil all at the same time.

B. *Effing eff!,*

D. she shouts as she pulverizes two Adderall with a spoon and sprinkles the
Adderall dust on top of the kale, and puts the kale in her mouth.

B. *That*

C. *Effing*

F. *Doorknob.*

D. It's true, the real effover of this job is that the magic totem in question has
to be present in each reality, present like DNA. Be it wand, broom, enchanted
flute, or in this case, magic doorknob, the object has to reside out in the
open. Hidden in plain view. Magic is so arbitrary – it can be very annoying.
Still, a more seasoned assistant would have hidden it better, in plainer view.
Right under his nose maybe. (In the coffee mug? On the seat of his seat?)

At the very least she might have furnished Mr. See with a diversion as the
subject, Kai Shearwater, started to get his bearings, to remember his base
reality. That was known to happen from time to time – they covered it in the
training manual. Instead she froze up. She hasn't froze up like that since the
time Lane Heatherette spilled her 'tini on her on purpose at the Palm Springs
New Gen Networkathon.

F. *Dammit Rosie you're better than this.*

D. At least Mr. See knows her heart is in it. How does he know her heart is
in it? The other day he was asking her, Rosie, what's it like being on Adderall.
And Rosie said she didn't want to sound *conceited,* but one time she was in the
finals of the Miss Junior Executive of Arkansas Pageant?

E. *Rosie, you hick!,*

D. Mr. See joked.

E. *I knew you had a little southern twang, but Arkansas? You fucking backwater hick!*

D. They were always joking like that. And Rosie went on to explain how she'd
been in the Final Five Round, the question round, after doing her utmost-
most in evening wear, swimwear, and her stand-up routine with Lazy Sue her
ventriloquist dummy who likes rabbi jokes, and how the judges asked her,

F. *Rosie, here in the final round of the Miss Junior Executive of Arkansas Pageant, what* *would you like to give the world if you become Miss Junior Executive?*

D. and how they meant not just giving to Arkansas but to the non-Arkansas world also, and how she replied first with "I'm glad you asked that question," which is a time-honored time-buying strategy, and then how she calmly answered, "*Me,* Sir. I would give the world all of me, down to the capillary, down to the hot-oiled hair follicle," and the crowd was on its feet, all except for her nemesis Lane Heatherette.

And *that,* long story short, is what it's like to be on Adderrall, when every second is like, I'm gonna give all of me, me, me to you, Mr. See, See, See. I'll give my all to Arkansas, and to non-Arkansas, and to the sad runners-up of the pageant, and even to that poor confused man with the crystal doorknob. The whole world is going to get all of Rosie, and then someday, although she doesn't like to sound conceited, someday the whole world will be hers in return.

E. *You're gonna shine Rosie,*

E & C. *Shine Rosie,*

E & C & B. *Shine girl,*

E, C, B & F. *Shine.*

VII.

B. *On the other side of the door from that bright office, it's the middle of the night.*

E. *You kick off the sticky covers.*

F. You awake?

A. No. You?

F. It's too hot to sleep.

B. *You can just make out the glow of the sad little Milky Way someone stuck on the ceiling, its charge almost gone.*

A. I was thinking about what happens when we die.

F. What did you figure out?

A. It doesn't look good.

> (*Beat.*)

F. What made you think of that?

A. I'm going to be *forty,* Steven.

F. In a year.

A. A year is nothing. (*Beat.*)
…Also my grandpa.

F. I thought your grandpa died when you were in college.

A. He did, but – Have you ever known someone who always seemed so alive that it's weird that they're not?— I'm too tired for this conversation.

E. *You look out the window.*

      (ACTOR C *comes out of the darkness, looking like* GRANDFATHER.)

C. *There's an old man coming out of the 24-hour bodega who looks like he could be your grandfather.*

A. He'd be over a hundred now.

F. How old was he when he died?

      (ACTOR C *putters back into the darkness, an anonymous old man again.*)

A. Eighty-seven. He had a good life.

F. Buddhists think death is just another beginning.

A. Buddhists are bullshit.

F. It's kind of sexy when you're a dumb mouth-breathing thug.

A. Steven.

F. What.

A. It's too hot.

F. You smell good.

A. I don't feel like I smell good.

F. Well I don't mean like a *rose garden*. You smell like the cigarette you thought I wouldn't notice you had earlier but it stuck to you.

A. So: dumb, thuggish and guilty. That's really a – that's quite a mandala of desire you have going on. Why not throw in some whips and chains just to lighten things up?

F. No objections here.

B. *There's an invitation in this which you don't accept.*

E. *Still he's moving toward you across the bed, this full grown man is on you, his mouth on your neck, his weight on your cock, your cock growing— You're a grown man too, it turns out.*

B. *The cat runs from the room, terrified. You hadn't noticed it 'til now.*

E. *And you're not sure what to do – Have you done this before? Is this your body? – But Steven knows what to do and his mouth is on you and the world*

falls

away

OK you're back. The room is even hotter now.

A. What's wrong.

F. Nothing's wrong.

A. If you want me to do something different just say so.

F. I don't want something different.

A. I'm too old.

F. No

A. I'm too old for you.

F. I like too old for me, so lucky you.

A. Did you ever think you'd be with someone who could be a grandfather?

F. You couldn't

A. Sure I could – if I had my kid young, and my kid had a kid.

> (*Beat.*)

I can feel my bones. That can't be good.

F. What kind of a name is Kai?

A. I see what you're doing

F. What am I doing

A. Distracting me. We've been together, what / now

F. Fifteen months

A. And all of a sudden you're asking about my name?

F. We can still small-talk, can't we? Or do we have to just talk about death.

> (*Beat.*)

A. It's Scandinavian. It's the name of the boy in *The Snow Queen*.

F. Hans Christian Andersen.

A. Ja.

F. Remind me how it goes?

A. Um, there's this evil queen

F. *You're* an evil queen

A. (*Facetiously, exaggeratedly gay.*) Werq!

F. Werq!

A. There's an evil queen, and she breaks this mirror, on purpose or not I forget, and the pieces go flying out into the world. But it's a twisted mirror, a fun-house mirror that makes everything look dark and mean. There's a little boy – Kai – and his sister.

F. What's the sister's name?

(ACTOR B *is close by right now.* ACTOR A *looks right through her:*)

A. I don't remember. So the little boy gets a piece of mirror stuck in his eye and everything looks dark and mean. And he becomes like the disciple of the evil queen, like he drives her carriage or something.

F. If it's snow then it's a sleigh.

A. Fine, a sleigh. And he's her footman or whatever, he doesn't even remember his sister. It's like his childhood is stolen. They never say that in the story exactly but it scared the shit out of me as a kid. The protagonist is just suddenly...not the protagonist anymore – It's kind of radical actually.

F. That's such a writer thing to say.

A. Poor you. Boyfriends with a writer.

B. *The cat has returned. She runs her wet nose along your hand.*

F. How does it end?

A. His sister goes looking for him— (*Maybe we notice* ACTOR B *hearing this.*) And she like beats the Snow Queen and wins him back in the end.

F. Of course.

A. "Of course"?

F. It's a fairy tale.

A. Hans Christian Andersen is different. It's, like, bleeding mermaids

F. Oh yeah

A. So happy's a departure.

F. (*Absently trying this phrase on.*) "Happy's a departure."

(*Beat.*)

A. (*Grave news.*) Picador doesn't want the book.

F. What? They told you?

A. This afternoon.

F. You didn't say anything

(*Beat.*)

What did they tell you?

A. They want more fantasy stories, they don't want memoir. Never mind the writing's gotten better.

F. Nadra didn't fight for you?

A. Not enough, apparently.

F. Oh baby.

A. What if I'm not supposed to do this, Steven.

F. Don't be crazy

A. What if I was really supposed to be in data entry but too many people told me I *had* something but they were just being nice and now it's too late—

F. It's one rejection

A. It's a mountain of rejection.

B. *All of a sudden, you feel something under your pillow*

E. *What is that*

A. What *is* that?

F. What's what.

A. There's like a rock. Under my pillow.

F. It's like a cheesy new age crystal.

A. Turn on the light.

F. Maybe it's your crazy ex, casting a spell on you.

A. Who, Richie?

F. I don't know his name.

A. Yes you do.

F. He never got over you.

A. It's not Richie. (*Beat.*) How the fuck did this get under my pillow.

F. It's really weird.

A. Is it a doorknob? I can feel the screws.

> (KAI *closes his eyes tight. Warm light rises on* C *and* D *playing* GRANDFATHER *and* GRANDMA, *as before.*)

D. *With your eyes shut, you can see your Grandma knitting and rocking, knitting and rocking.*

C. *You can see your Grandfather, lighting his pipe for dramatic emphasis.*

A. It was yesterday. It was today. It just happened.

F. What just happened, baby?

> (KAI *opens his eyes and* C *and* D *disappear.*)

A. I'm not your baby.

F. Kai, what the fuck?

A. What if you're just like him

F. Him who?

A. That TV executive, Mr. See. What if you're trying to keep me from remembering?

F. I'm getting your Lexapro.

A. How old am I, Steven?

F. Settle down.

A. How old am I!

F. 39.

A. I was in my twenties.

F. Weren't we all.

A. I mean – this morning.

F. (*Re: the medicine.*) Did you skip a day again?

A. (*Not re: the medicine.*) I skipped more than a day.

F. You know you can't do that.

A. I was this kid going to L.A. for meetings…

F. Baby, everybody gets old.

A. Pitching some awful show with pirates

F. You had a bad day, that's all. Here, swallow.

A. (*Preoccupied.*) It was today. It was this morning.

F. Swallow.

A. (*He doesn't.*) He had a crystal, just like this one. Not a crystal – a doorknob.

E. *You eye the door to the closet.*

A. What happens if I go through another?

F. Another what?

A. (*To himself.*) He said "farther down the path"

F. I'm calling your therapist

A. What if it only goes farther, not back

E. *Your hand on the doorknob*

F. (*Trying to talk reason.*) Kai. This is me. That's you. That's our cat. This is our life.

A. Then why does everything feel wrong?

(*Beat.*)

Goodbye, Steven.

E. *The doorknob turns*

F. What do you mean, goodbye? That's the closet.

A. Wish me luck.

(*Light shifts. Continuous into:*)

VIII.

ACTOR F *is suddenly a young* CATER WAITER *with a tray of hors d'oeuvres.*

F. (*Pronouncing it wrong.*) Canape?

B. *Bright green meadow. Everyone dressed in white.*

A. (*Dazed.*) I'm sorry?

F. (*Holding up a tray.*) Canape.

A. (*Correcting him, lightly.*) Oh, canapé.

F. (*Not realizing he's being corrected.*) Yeah. Make sure you get one with lots of roe.

A. Oh, I'm actually a little queasy?

F. (*Putting it together.*) You're the one getting married.

B. *It occurs to you this is true.*

A. Guilty.

F. Is it your first time?

A. Yeah, why do you ask?

F. Oh I just mean you're not – I mean you're not exactly…

A. A blushing bride?

F. Well

A. It's okay. I'm fifty-five.

F. (*His mind is blown.*) Wow.

A. Yeah. It kind of hits you like a truck.

F. I'll watch out. (*Beat.*) For the truck.
I'm gonna— (*He moves to go.*)

A. Off you go.

(BARRY *enters, played by* ACTOR C.)

F. Canape?

C. No thanks.

(*The* CATER WAITER *exits. The following a kind of game. Deadpan-flirty:*)
Say. Aren't you the one getting hitched?

A. That's right.

C. Who's the lucky guy?

A. Some shmo from the Bible Belt. Trying to pass as a New Yorker.

C. Bible gays – better watch out.

A. It's okay, I'm into guilt. His mother though, she's a piece of work.

C. He's worth it, though?

A. Sometimes.

C. Well if it doesn't work out, you just give me a call.

A. Forward.

C. I knows what I likes.

A. What do you likes?

C. Neurotic, fifty-something writers with a little meat on their bones and a healthy aversion to the outdoors.

A. Keep talking.

C. Especially writers whose short stories were once overlooked by a mainstream literary culture that looks down its nose at *genre*, but are finally starting to attract a passionate following.

A. That is a very specific fetish.

C. Lucky you.

       (D *floats by, an unidentified* WEDDING GUEST. *She squeezes them.*)

D. You two look so handsome – Congratulations!

       (*And she's gone, as quickly as she came. They drop the game:*)

A. Hi husband.

C. Hi husband.

       (*They take each other by the hand.*)

You nervous?

A. Not yet.

       (ACTOR C *sees* ACTOR E *rushing in as the harried* WEDDING PLANNER:)

C. Brace yourself.

E. We're out of champagne. I'm not gonna say your friends are lushes, but—

A. They are, they're lushes.

E. Open the Prosecco?

A. Yeah.

       (*The* WEDDING PLANNER *is already heading out – maybe he never broke his stride. Shouting to an unseen underling:*)

E. Do it!

       (A *and* C *survey the guests.*)

A. (*Nervous.*) People aren't eating, why aren't they eating.

C. They're eating.

A. Maybe the mini *banh mi* were too exotic.

C. I don't know, I don't care, it's our wedding. There's my mom. We should probably—

A. Hide?

C. (*"You're terrible."*) See how she's *doing.* She's a harmless old lady who wants you to feel comfortable with her.

A. Comfort. From the woman who wears a sequined gold sheath to a daytime wedding—

C. I know, it's a lot—

A. She's like an Emmy Award with a Tampa accent.

C. Well, you're not marrying *her.*

A. I sort of am.

C. (*Taking him by the arm.*) C'mon.

A. Barry wait – can we just stay here a moment? Just 'til the world stops spinning?

C. We could be waiting a long time.

B. *You take a mental snapshot of Barry. What's left on top of his head is grey, and his eyes disappear when he smiles.*

A. I'm just trying to – hold onto this.

C. That's why we hired a photographer.

A. I'm serious. The present is so – fast.

(*The* CATER WAITER *is here again.*)

F. Short-rib lollipops?

A & C. No thanks.

(*The* WAITER *exits.*)

A. He looks just like one of my exes.

C. Yeah?

A. It's kind of unnerving.

(*The* WEDDING PLANNER *rushes back in:*)

E. Okay people, we're five minutes away.

A. Wow. Wow.

C. (*To* E.) His head just exploded.

E. (*To* A.) You'll be fine.

A. (*To* C.) I'm gonna just – pee preemptively. (*To* E:) His mom's reading like half of Corinthians.

(*Classical music starts to play – not Pachelbel's Canon, but something that says the ceremony is imminent.*)

C. Hurry.

A. I am!

C. Don't try to escape out the bathroom window.

A. Ha ha.

B. *On the way to the bathroom, you pass everyone you ever met.*

A. Hi. Hi. Hey there.

F. *Your palms are sweating. Hand on the bathroom door.*

E. *As soon as the doorknob's in your hand, you know you've held it before*

D. *But you can't think where—*

> (*Lights shift. Continuous into:*)

IX.

C. *On the other side of the door is darkness. Darker than any room you've ever been in.*

D. *Somewhere far away, a radio plays a mariachi song.*

A. Hello?

> (*He listens a moment as the song plays.*)

Hello out there?

C. *There was something in your hand. Something many-edged and cool. Something you were supposed to remember...*

X.

E. Come in.

D. *Same bright office. Same big desk.*

E. Sorry to keep you waiting. I'm between secretaries – obviously.

D. *A row of girls just like her lined up outside.*

B. Oh god, don't even think about it – I'm just so pleased for this opportunity to meet you.

E. Well you didn't brave rush hour on the 405 just to *meet* me. If you want the job, you should say it.

B. I want the job.

E. You can't be coy in this town, Miss Griggs.

B. That's sage advice, Mr. See.

E. You can call me Mr. See.

D. *A moment of confusion.*

B. Okay.

E. Are those Louboutins?

B. You like?

E. (*"Yes."*) That's test number one – a well-turned out foot. Pity 'bout your nails though.

B. I'm not really a pedicure kind of girl.

E. You work for me, you're a pedicure kinda girl.

B. Yes sir.

D. *The girl's eyes pass over a bald spot on his desk. Little circle of unfaded wood, as though it housed an object gone missing.*

B. Maybe you should tell me what you'd expect of me as your assistant.

E. I'll decide what to tell you.

B. Yes, Mr. See.

D. *He looks at her resume.*

> (*Actually he keeps his eyes fixed on her – there is no resume.*)

E. Phi Beta Kappa.

B. I worked hard.

E. Overseas program. Istanbul?

B. My minor was Byzantine art. You know, offset the whole cynical Communications pre-MBA—

E. Smart. Do any drugs?

B. I'm sorry?

E. Do you do any drugs, Miss Griggs.

B. You mean like medication?

E. You know what I mean.

B. No sir, I'm clean.

E. (*Disappointed.*) I see.

B. (*Trying to recover.*) I tried mushrooms once. Tasted terrible. I spent most of the afternoon hugging a tree. So on the nose, right? (*Getting a bit lost in it again:*) The moss was like a whole world.

E. You might wanna think about acquiring some uppers. That's pretty much how things get done around here.

B. Long hours.

E. Yes ma'am. My last assistant, sometimes she spent the night here. Right over there on her yoga mat. Good for the back, Rosie would say.

B. I bet she was a real ace.

D. *This hangs in the air.*

B. A reeeal ace.

D. *Is she mocking him?*

E. *(To B.)* She sure was, until last Friday she just up and never came back. Just *(He makes the "poof" gesture from the earlier scene.)* – into thin air.

B. My brother disappeared like that,

D. *she says, taking a little risk.*

B. We were playing hide and seek. *(Tragic:)* He won.

E. I'm sorry.

B. I haven't given up yet.

D. *The hint of a challenge in this.*

E. I see.

D. *Mr. See takes one more look at her unpedicured toes.*

E. Who are you, really?

B. Jane Griggs, like it says on the resume.

E. I don't think so, Miss Griggs. You know what I think? I think you're as fake as those Louboutins.

B. What do you mean, these / set me back—

E. Louboutins have red soles. Those, as you see, are taupe.

D. *Shit.*

E. Plus, your Vuitton bag only has one "t."

D. *Shit.*

E. Clear Chinatown knock-off.

  (Beat. Then, coming clean:)

B. Sixteen years, Mr. See, and not a trace of my brother.

D. *She kicks the fake Louboutins across the room and puts her feet on his desk, like a lazy cop.*

B. Sixteen years. Then out of the blue, on my Google Alerts: "Firelight Pictures Reaches First-Look Deal With Kai Shearwater." So you see, I just *had* to meet the man in charge.

E. Rosie didn't really burn out, did she. You've done something to her.

B. All I did was put some more Adderall in her Adderall.

E. Jesus.

B. I just gave her more of what she wanted. She's tied up in her closet, babbling about the Miss Arkansas pageant.

E. Impressive. Maybe I *should* hire you.

B. I'm just here to find my brother, Mr. See – or take you down trying.

E. He must've been a good brother.

B. He wasn't good or bad – he was just my brother.

E. Could it be you've made him perfect in hindsight? The way we do with dead people?

B. You don't know he's dead.

E. (*Crafty.*) Do you even remember him? Or do you just think you do?

D. *Anna Bell steels herself for the counterattack.*

E. Is it even him you miss? Or do you miss the way things were when he was alive? The way you were.

D. *Anna Bell rips one of the legs off his desk.*

E. Jesus!

(*A low, frictive sound underneath the following, like metal on metal.*)

D. *She takes the leg and scratches one long, terrible wound around the wall of the room, like someone keying a car.*

E. What the hell are you doing?

B. You don't ask the questions anymore you piece of shit.

(*Thunder. Continuous into:*)

XI.

The FISHERMAN *atop his lamppost.*

C. *Cabin Boy!,*

A. the First Mate shouts from the wheel. The whole sky red now.

C. *Josef!*

(*Another clap of thunder.*)

A. Before you can take a single step, a great wave knocks two good men overboard.

C. *Lash yourself to the staysail or you're next to Davy Jones!*

F. *Which one is the staysail?*, you shout, drinking a gallon of salt water.

C. *Port side of the skysail!*

F. *Which one's the skysail!*

C. *Just shy of the moonraker!*

F. By now you've drunk another five gallons, but you bolt for the nearest staysail, the ground alive under you; the ground drunker than the First Mate that night he called you Nancy by mistake, "Pretty Nancy from Norwich" you remember as you lash the rigging round your ankle. Faster than you can finish the thought, the staysail snaps free of the mizzen and you're taken like a leaf in the wind, shooting high over the ship, stomach in throat. It would be almost fun if your life weren't about to be over. Then *splash,* you're down in the drink, under the ship, a keel-hauling performed by nature; lucky you know enough to swim down deeper so the barnacles don't cut you to ribbons. And just like that you're airborne again, the water flying off your hide like a wet dog getting dry; hand at your boot, on instinct, where it finds your favorite dagger for cutting you free. Headfirst falling now you jack out your right arm hoping anything will stop your fall and you end up with a handful of mermaid breast. Not a warm, welcoming mermaid breast but a hard wooden mermaid breast that nearly snaps your wrist; your left hand finds her right breast and you're dangling from the prow by both breasts, a picture that would go down in seafaring lore if anyone lived to tell. And now the prow liberates itself from the stern – she's shaking you free, that wily mermaid! – and your last fumbling grab as you freefall frees the great round crystal in the mermaid's eye; you're falling together now, you and the crystal, and you don't let go when you hit the water, and you don't let go all night. The great ship lost beneath the black water along with the First Mate, your only friend, your only father, your something else. (You never even learned his name for calling it out.) And still you hold onto the crystal, which gives off a faint light of its own even in the new-moon night. And the sea creatures come and nibble at its edges – long-eyed viperfish and luminous jellies who think they've found a mate, but you fight them off; and the waves churn and the salt in your mouth but you don't let go.

XII.

The faint mariachi music returns.

C. *Still you're sitting in the dark. Those faraway notes raining down on you like Chinese water torture.*

B. *Creak of a floorboard.*

A. Hello? Why can't I see anything?

D. Don't be a smart-ass, Mr. Kai.

A. No, really – I can't see my hand in front of my face.

D. You've been blind for five years.

A. Who are you?

D. This isn't your best day, is it.
(*This is pronounced "Pow-la".*) I'm Paula. I look after you.

A. We're not related?

D. God no.

A. I can tell. You have a bit of an accent.

D. I'm from El Salvador but my English is good. Some people can't even tell. They think I'm just formal.

A. No, I can tell.

D. Sure, Mr. Kai.

A. My last name is Shearwater.

D. Yes, but to me you're Mr. Kai. I like to be different.

A. Why can't I feel my legs?

D. You lost them.

A. Lost them where?

D. They cut them off.

A. They who?

D. Doctors.

A. Why'd they do that?

D. To save you.

> (*Beat.*)

A. Do I have anything left?

D. (*Chuckling a little.*) Two arms, to write. Two ears.

A. I'm a writer?

D. Oh yes.

> (*A longer beat.*)

A. Do you go through this with me every day?

D. (*Gentle.*) Most days you remember a little more. Things come back to you. Gutting a fish with your father, when you were a boy. Your grandfather's pipe. Your wedding day. I think the far-back things come easier. Or maybe that's just where you'd rather be.
Hold still now—

A. Ouch!

D. This won't take long.

A. Ouch! What are you doing?

D. Just plucking your ears – you don't want hairy ears, do you? Not on your big day.

A. My big day?

D. You don't remember? You're getting an award today, for writing.

A. An award for not being dead yet.

D. Something like that.

A. I have a lot of those?

D. You put them on the shelves above the toilet. That way all / the guests can see

A. (*Overlapping.*) All the guests have to see. Yes, it's coming back to me.

D. We should get going – if you're up to it. There's a luncheon.

A. Oh no

D. Overcooked salmon and German wine. That's what you always say.

A. Do I have to give a speech?

D. You recorded it, on video. On one of your good days.

> (*Beat.*)

A. Do I have any kids?

D. No.

A. But I have a wife?

D. (*With a little laugh.*) I don't think Barry would've let you call him that.

A. Barry. Are you saying I'm a gay?

D. Oh Mr. Kai, sometimes you just slay me.

A. "Would've." Past Conditional. So Barry is...

D. Dead, yes. You had thirty-three wonderful years together and now he's dead.

A. What got him?

D. He was just old.

A. Like me.

D. Like you.

A. How old am I?

D. Eighty-eight.

A. Eighty-eight. That's older than Grandpa was when he told me— When he told me—. What did he tell me?
Why can't I remember?

D. Mr. Kai, you're crying.

A. What did you say your name was?

D. Paula. Like "Pow."

C. *You can't see how she punches the air with her fist to illustrate "pow."*

F. *She's done it so many times since moving here that she doesn't realize it's lost on a blind man.*

D. You try.

A. *Pow*-la.

D. Good.

Now let's get you into your tux.

XIII.

C. *Mr. See keys in a secret code and the heavy door swings open.*

E. Satisfied?

D. *Anna Bell removes the table leg from between his ribs.*

B. Very.

D. *And she steps into the room.*

B. It has to be zero degrees in here...

E. On account of the active molecules. The cold air keeps them tame. I think of flies, the way they hibernate in the cold.

B. (*Contrary.*) I don't think of flies.

D. *As they walk, Anna Bell takes in the shelves, high above their heads.*

B. (*Awed.*) You can't see where they end even.

E. You're a lucky girl, Anna Bell. No civilian has ever laid eyes on this before. Some real Area 51 shit.

B. Look but don't touch.

E. You can touch whatever you like. I just can't guarantee your safety.

B. Is it ever just a straight answer with you?

E. It is and it isn't.

D. *Anna Bell gives the wall a frustrated kick. A Chinese mask rolls forward, toppling an ancient Egyptian top.*

E. Careful!

B. Sorry.

E. I am a custodian of magic forces, Anna Bell. Totems and talismans especially. You look at me and all you see is a bad-ass executive with the world between his teeth, but in a realer sense I am a humble custodian of magic. The threads that surround your life – that surround all lives? – they can get awfully twisted when you start playing cat's cradle. It takes a lean, hard, bottom-line-minded mind to maintain order. It takes a quick fuse. It takes a sharp bullshit detector. It takes an interest in supply and demand – In the market and what it can bear.

B. I thought magic was supposed to be—

E. Fun?

B. Well, magical.

E. Not when it's your job. (*Beat.*) I'm a busy man, Anna Bell. You have one minute. Within this hall, there is a duplicate of every magical device anyone ever used.

B. There's two of each?

E. We keep the doubles for tracking. Whichever object you pick will lead you to its twin. Pick correctly, and it may even lead you to your brother.

B. You mean I have to guess?

D. *Running her hand along a shelf, Anna Bell touches a scepter topped with an onyx, a horn of plenty, a purple crayon that ever so slightly glows, and a robe made entirely of snakeskin.*

E. We think of magic things as mute, like animals. But like animals, they talk to each other. They say, *How long have you been waiting for a new adventure? Will you cause trouble this time? Will you be helpful?* And the answer is always *I don't know, I don't know…*

B. What happens if I pick wrong?

E. Don't think too much. That's good advice for most situations.

C. *Anna Bell closes her eyes and some of the fear goes away.*

Her hand touches something metal, then something like fur—

B. Ew!

C. *—then something light as cotton candy, and finally something many-faceted. Cool but not cold, familiar but not intimate. Something she might have had in her hand before without even thinking about it, fetching the table linens for her grandmother—*

B. This one. I want this one.

E. Are you sure?

B. Of course not.

C. *Her hand closes on the crystal.*

XIV.

A. *The crystal is still tight in your fist when you wake, half-dead, on a bed of brown kelp.*
        (ACTOR F *looks into the darkness.*)

F. Sir! Are you out there?

A. *A chorus of birds answers.*

F. Sir!

A. *You walk 'til you no longer see the ocean. You build a house there. You build the crystal into the house.*

C. *Still you can hear the ocean.*

        (ACTORS D *and* C *appear as* YOUNG GRANDMOTHER *and* GRANDFATHER.)

A. *Fifty years go by and you sell the house to a young man and his wife, who will one day be grandparents.*

F. I was once a Cabin Boy on a ship,

A. *you tell them.*

C. On a pirate ship?

F. On a pirate ship.

A. *...in the hopes that in telling the story you will be free of it. But instead you pull other lives in with you, down in the drink.*

F. Mind the doorknob,

A. *you say, on your way out.*

> (ACTORS C *and* D *look at each other, puzzled, as their light goes out.*)

You walk until time slows down. You find a lamppost to stand under. You pick the lamppost because it's less like the ocean, man-made.

F. (*A small defeat in this:*) Like the mast of a ship.

C. *Still you can hear the ocean.*

> (*It starts to rain lightly.* JOSEF *looks into the darkness towards* KAI, *just as he did in Scene II.*)

F. Hello?

A. *You wait for your story to end, but it isn't ready.*

F. Hello out there?

XV.

D. Rosie lies bound and gagged on the floor of her walk-in closet, feeling quite forgotten. She has tried and she has failed to wriggle out of Anna Bell's cruel girl-scout knots. She takes an emotional inventory of her closet to keep herself entertained:

> (ACTOR B *appears in a pool of light as* LANE HEATHERETTE. *She holds up each item as it is described, with cool detachment.*)

D. Putty-colored Manolo Blahniks, worn the night she heard that Lane Heatherette got the Yarbrough Mentorship...

Raspberry beach cover-up, worn to the Brentwood pool party where Lane Heatherette made the biggest splash...

And who could forget the Swarovski-encrusted Vera Wang column she wore that storied night she lost the Junior Miss Arkansas Executive crown by the smallest margin ever to the likes of – wait for it—

B. *Lane Heatherette.*

> (LANE HEATHERETTE *smiles slightly, enigmatically, as her light goes out.*)

D. While she *seems* immobile, something is afoot in Rosie on a micro-
biological level: Her pupils un-dilate; her eyelids un-twitch; that dry patch of
skin on her elbow goes unscratched by nervous fingers. And as the Adderall
and Acid Reflux Roast drain from her system for the first time in years, Rosie
starts to lose her razor's edge, her killer's instinct – and somewhere, another
Rosie who is half an inch taller and two percent twinklier silently surpasses
her, taking her place as a strong second behind Lane Heatherette.

And a strange thing – Rosie doesn't care. She has been supplanted, yes, and
yet the world still spins and the demon lights of Los Angeles still burn and
little girls in Little Rock still practice with their ventriloquist dummies. And
right about now, Rosie, still gagged and bound in a closet in a condo on a
side street in Silver Lake, floats out of herself and advances one rung on the
spiritual ladder they learned about in fifth grade Social Studies – Gandhi and
Jesus on the top rung, Ted Bundy in the basement. The past rushes in and
Rosie is back at her desk at the front of Miss McGinn's fifth grade classroom:

> (MISS McGINN *comes out of the darkness, holding a single sheet of paper.
> She is patient and dowdy and faintly angelic in a real way – even in this drag
> manifestation.*)

F. Class,
I am your teacher, Miss McGinn
Or was it Miss McGann.
Why am I holding a blank sheet of paper?,
you might be asking yourselves.
Pretend that this is a picture of your soul.
Everyone begins their life with a smooth new piece of paper.
Some of you, if you're very lucky, might still look like this on the inside. But
you see, every time someone says something a little unpleasant to you, a little
discourteous, this is what they're doing to your sheet of paper.

> (*She crumples the page.*)

And you try your best to smooth it back, to make it good as new, but you'll
never be entirely smooth again.

> (*She carefully smoothes the page.*)

D. At the time, Rosie thought this was any old Do-Unto-Others lesson. It
didn't occur to her that her teacher Miss McGinn or Miss McGann had
already had her own piece of paper crumpled countless times. She wasn't
just giving them a lesson on how to treat people – she was giving them
permission to get hurt.

> (MISS McGINN *shows us the page and its faint creases.*)

F. Every day, someone crumples your sheet of paper, and every night you
try to get it smooth again. We'll never be done, but that's the balance we

strike between innocence and experience. That's the effort that will make us human. (*Beat.*) Any questions?

D. And her wrists remain bound and the gag in her mouth, but Rosie is free.

XVI.

B *and* C *speak in the direction of* A.

B. *Still can't feel your legs. Still can't see a damn thing.*

C. *Rustles and whispers, a roomful of bodies.*

B. *Silverware.*

(*We hear microphone feedback.*)

E. Ouch – sorry folks. I just wanted to say how most of us in the room have been touched in some way by Kai Shearwater – even if it was just him telling us our writing was crap. Some of us he even had to tell twice.

F. *Polite laughter.*

E. This was a man with no patience for precious little observations of everyday life.

C. *"Was." Even as you sit here they're past-tensing you.*

E. Here was a man who believed in righteous fabulism – who believed you better fabulize or get the hell out of Dodge. After his one bitter taste of the Hollywood hack factory, he ran screaming back to his subconscious and that's pretty much where he stayed. His peers marveled at his childlike access to invention – like a kid making up whole worlds in his backyard. The purpose of writing, he once said, is to

make

shit

up.

F. *Polite laughter.*

E. And nobody made up more shit than Kai Shearwater.

Well, Mr. Shearwater. This award is for making the world a little more like the inside of your head.

D. They're standing, Mr. Kai.

A. Isn't that nice.

D. Everyone is standing for you.

A. At least that idiot isn't talking anymore.

D. I know.

A. Somebody should tell him the Beats are dead.

D. I know.

A. "Access to invention," what does that even mean?
All I did was rip off my grandpa's tall tales.

D. Here's your award, Mr. Kai. Careful, it's heavy.

A. Is this glass? Cheap bastards.

D. I think it's crystal.

A. You sure I haven't won this before? Feels familiar.

D. I think you can only get it once.

A. Ah yes, the Not-Dead award.

B. Excuse me, ma'am?

D. Yes?

B. This is going to sound kind of crazy, but I really have to talk to Kai?

D. If you want me to have him sign something for you, / I can—

B. No, I have to talk.

D. And you are...?

B. I'm his sister.

D. You're just a girl.

B. I told you it'd sound crazy.

D. (*Dismissing her.*) Thank you for paying your respects. I'll tell him you said hello.

B. Hey, what's that big bird over there?

D. What big bird?

B. Kai, it's Anna Bell!

A. (*Disoriented.*) Anna Bell?

B. I was hiding in the toy chest and you never found me.
Remember? You were counting but you only got to ten.

A. I had a sister named Anna Bell. She was almost my age.

B. This might sound a little crazy, but I came here through a door in the office of a Mephistophelian studio executive using an exact duplicate of the doorknob that stole you out of our grandparents' sitting room 78 years ago, the very doorknob that's sitting there in front of you, disguised as a lifetime achievement award. That's how it works – it stays with you every time you pass through a door. It's there to remind you, but that's not always enough.

A. You seem like a sweet girl, and I'm sure you're somebody's sister. But what you just described is the plot of my short story, "The Crystal Doorknob."

F. *What the*

C. *What?*

A. It's an early work. To be honest, it sounds a little plotty to me now.

B. That doesn't mean it's not true.

A. Sometimes people take my stories too seriously. Unfortunately they tend to be my best readers – the ones who lack boundaries.

B. Please, we were playing hide and seek—

D. I think you should stop bothering Mr. Kai. / This is a big day for him—

B. Just let me show him how the doorknob works.

A. I'm very old, I'm not looking for adventures.

B. This is the opposite of an adventure. This is going home. (*Beat.*) What if it could take us all the way back? Back to Grandpa and his stories, and Grandma's endless scarf, and Find My Booger?

A. (*Faintly familiar.*) "Find My Booger..."

B. And Gin Rummy! I'll let you win this time. I'll always let you win.

D. Please, don't confuse him. He has trouble with reality as it is.

B. (*To* A.) Please—

F. *Anna Bell takes your used-up old hands and places them on her face.*

A. What are you doing?

C. *This is not a surefire plan:*

F. *Coming to blindness late in life, and being a natural cynic, your stomach always turns at this particular brand of blind-person scene.*

C. *But your fingers find her strong, stubborn chin; the wide, Nordic planes of her cheeks, now trimmed of their baby fat; and the eyes a little too closely set, the first lines of permanent concern between them.*

A. Anna Bell. It *is* you.

B. Told you, stupid. Let's get you out of here.

D. Mr. Kai, where are you going?

A. Thank you for everything, Paula!

C. *Your chair already speeding, the crystal in your lap, your long-lost sister breathing down the back of your neck as she breaks into a sprint.*

F. *You can hear the women jumping to their feet, sequins flying; the men in tuxedoes falling away like dominoes.*

D. Help! She's kidnapping Mr. Kai!

E. Stop her!

B. Door, door, there must be a...*There!*

F. *The chair makes a hairpin turn.*

B. I've gotta send you through first. I'll be right behind you.

A. What if I lose you again?

B. Then I'll find you again.

E. Stop!

B. There's no time. Go! Go—

XVII.

A. On the other side of the door is nothing. Not darkness, but nothing. Far as the eye can see. Where there was Kai there is nothing but nothing. Nothing isn't all bad, of course. Your joints don't ache anymore, and you don't have to think about the effort of your next breath. You are beyond fear. Beyond the sea creatures who inhabit the edges of old maps.

XVIII.[1]

D. *Crisp autumn day in Green-Wood cemetery. A young Minister, who didn't know the deceased, addresses a small crowd.*

C. Thank you, Mrs. Juarez, for that lovely remembrance. And now we will hear a few words from Mr. Shearwater's own sister, Anna Bell.

(ANNA BELL *comes into the light – she is an old woman with a walker now.*)

E. *The crowd makes way for a very old lady.*

B. Sorry, this is as fast as I go these days.

E. *Her eyes cataracted, but still somehow bright.*

B. Sorry. This is Mach 10 for me.

(*She's at the front now.*)

Well. I was never the speechmaker in the family, my brother was. But I thought it might be nice to read a passage from his story "The Crystal Doorknob." The bit near the end, after the girl pushes her brother through the last door.

(*The minister takes out a paperback and sets it before her. On the cover: "Firelight Tales, by Kai Shearwater."*)

Thank you, dear. (*To the crowd again:*) This was one of Kai's first stories to get any attention. I think it embarrassed him a little when he got older – too much *plot*, he said. And he wasn't maybe as fancy as the author in the story, he wasn't collecting lifetime achievement awards. But it's always been one of

---

[1] *Note: A new feeling of reality in this scene. Maybe we see a degree of visual detail we didn't see before. (In the Humana production, for example, autumn leaves were scattered on the stage.)*

my favorites – maybe 'cause he put me in it. And anyway too bad, big brother, you can't stop me now.

(*To herself.*)

Is that the page? Yes.

(*She starts to read.*)

"*On the other side of the door, you feel a weight has been lifted…*

(*As she reads, the crystal doorknob, lying on the ground somewhere, starts to glow.[2] In its light, we can just make out* JOSEF THE FISHERMAN, *standing under his lamppost, and* KAI, *a boy again, standing a way's off. The way we first saw them, way back in Scene II.*)

Your joints don't ache anymore, and you stand taller, and you don't have to think about the effort of your next breath.

A. Am I a boy again?

B. *you ask, out loud, to no one in particular. To your surprise, somebody answers:*

F. At long last, he speaks!

A. What do you mean, at long last? I just got here.

F. You've been standing there in the shadows long as I can remember.

A. (*Disoriented.*) I came through a door. I was in a chair. My sister was pushing me.

F. I haven't seen her.

A. She was right behind me.

F. How old are you?

A. Ten, I think. Or Twenty-seven. I've been a lot of different ages today.

F. I see.

A. Are you a sailor?

F. In another life I was.

A. (*Childlike.*) On a pirate ship?

F. On a pirate ship.

(*Beat.*)

A. Are we dead?

F. (*The best he can answer.*) I think…everything has already happened to us.

(KAI *looks at the doorknob. Maybe he moves to pick it up.*)

My mermaid's eye.

A. Do you think, can it take me back home? Back to where I started?

F. Think of how many doors there are in the world.

A. (*Sad.*) I know.

---

[2] Note: I suspect that this is the first time we've actually seen it.

F. Think of how much you know. No little boy can know that much.

(KAI *looks down at his feet.*)

Hey now, don't look so sad. Let me tell you a secret – Something that helps me when I get to missing the way things were.

A. What is it?

F. Lean close, I have to whisper it.

(*As* JOSEF *whispers into* KAI's *ear,* ANNA BELL *speaks for him – she doesn't need the book anymore:*)

B. *We can be innocent twice, the Fisherman whispers. The first innocence we are given; the second we have to fight for.*

A. Fight how?

(JOSEF *starts to lean in again.*)

Can't you just say it out loud?

B. *From up close, the old fisherman smells of fish and his whiskers are wet.*

F. Some things are easier to hear if you whisper.

(JOSEF *whispers in* KAI's *ear.*)

B. *We must smooth our page, the Fisherman tells you, every night and every day, until all the wrinkles are gone. Until it looks like the page of a ten-year old boy a little bored on a distant summer afternoon, wishing his life would begin."*

(ANNA BELL *closes the book. The light of the crystal goes out, and* JOSEF *and* KAI *are gone. She takes in the audience at the memorial service.*)

Smooth our page. I don't know what my brother meant by that, but I kind of like it.

(*She smiles sadly.*)

Maybe when I'm older.

(*Light fades.*)

End of Play

POOR SHEM
A TINY PLAY FOR THREE CHARACTERS
AND PHOTOCOPIER
by Gregory Hischak

BIOGRAPHY

Gregory Hischak's short plays *Hygiene* and *Poor Shem* have been produced as part of Actors Theatre of Louisville's Apprentice/Intern *Tens* program and both were restaged as part of the Humana Festival of New American Plays (2010 and 2014, respectively). His full-length play, *The Center of Gravity*, won the 2009 Clauder Prize and premiered at Portland Stage Company (Portland, ME) in 2010, and was recently staged at the Cotuit Center for the Arts (Barnstable, MA) in 2014. His plays have also been staged by A Contemporary Theatre (Seattle, WA), A Theatre Under the Influence (Seattle, WA), City Theatre (Miami, FL), The Source Festival (Washington, D.C.), Salem Theatre Company (Salem, MA), The Pan Festival (San Francisco, CA) and the Boston Theater Marathon, among others. Hischak lives in Yarmouth, MA where he is the Associate Director of the Edward Gorey House.

ACKNOWLEDGMENTS

Poor Shem was produced at the Humana Festival of New American Plays in April 2014. It was directed by Meredith McDonough with the following cast:

KENDEL	Andrew Garman
KAITLIN	Jackie Chung
KYLE	Matthew Stadelmann

and the following production staff:

Scenic Designer	Dane Laffrey
Costume Designer	Kristopher Castle
Lighting Designer	Seth Reiser
Sound Designer	Christian Frederickson
Stage Manager	Stephen Horton
Dramaturg	Jessica Reese
Directing Assistants	Cara Phipps, Jacob Sexton
Production Assistant	Suzanne Spicer

Poor Shem began as a spoken word piece for three voices, performed by Staggered Thirds (Anna Mockler, Doug Nufer and Gregory Hischak) in Seattle, Washington. It was subsequently staged in the Boston Theater Marathon.

CHARACTERS

KENDEL. A dominant male, 35 to 55

KAITLIN. A woman of easily diluted compassion, 25 to 55

KYLE. A less dominant male—probably younger than Kendel, 30 to 40

SETTING

The setting is an office copying room. Present day.

TEXT NOTE

Tabbed type in the script indicates where an overlap—that is, a stepping on of—the previous line of dialogue begins.

Andrew Garman, Matthew Stadelmann, and Jackie Chung
in *Poor Shem*

38th Humana Festival of New American Plays
Actors Theatre of Louisville, 2014
Photo by Bill Brymer

116

POOR SHEM

Machinery sounds—these are performed by the characters.

KENDEL. Shicka shicka shicka shicka… (*Continues as* KAITLIN *joins in.*)

KAITLIN. Fwoosha ha fwoosha ha fwoosha ha fwoosha ha… (*Continues as* KYLE *joins in.*)

KYLE. Kahlakala kahlakala kahlakala kahlakala kahlakala kahlakala kahlakala KLAHK.

 (*All stop.*)

KAITLIN. Of all the things you give in your life, none is more precious than your labor.

KYLE. The job you are paid to do.

KENDEL. The job you dedicate your best, most productive years to.

 (*Beat.*)

KENDEL. Shicka shicka shicka shicka… (*Continues as* KAITLIN *joins in.*)

KAITLIN. Fwoosha ha fwoosha ha fwoosha ha fwoosha ha… (*Continues as* KYLE *joins in.*)

KYLE. Kahlakala kahlakala kahlakala kahlakala kahlakala kahlakala kahlakala KLAHK.

 (*Abrupt pained all stop.*)

KAITLIN. (*Taken aback.*) Ummm…

KYLE. (*Horror.*) For The Love Of G—

KENDEL. (*Annoyed.*) Jesus.

KAITLIN. (*Taking* KENDEL's *lead.*) For the love of Jesus.

KYLE. What happened?

KAITLIN. Jammed.

KENDEL. Jammed?

KYLE. Tell me what's happened?

KAITLIN. Jammed.

KYLE. Who jammed it?

KAITLIN. *Nobody* jammed it.

KYLE. It just jammed?

KENDEL. Yes, jammed.

KAITLIN. It *just* jammed.

KENDEL. Christ.

KAITLIN. Christ.

KYLE. There's an eight and a half by eleven stuck in the bypass tray.

(*Thoughtful beat.*)

KENDEL. An 8-1/2 x 11 stuck in the bypass tray?

KYLE.   It says so right here…

KAITLIN.   Try hitting Print again.

KYLE. Don't hit Print.

KENDEL.   There's an 8-1/2 x 11 stuck in the bypass tray.

KAITLIN. Push the Print Button.

KYLE. Don't push the Print Button, you'll kill us all.

KENDEL. Let's not panic, people.

KAITLIN. Christ.

KYLE. What do we do?

KENDEL. Open the front panel.

KYLE. What?

KAITLIN. Right. Open the front of the copier.

KYLE. *I'm* not opening the front of the copier.

(KAITLIN *and* KENDEL *speak together:*)

KAITLIN.   Do I look like I'm dressed to open copiers?

KENDEL.   It's not my job to open the front
of the copier to fix every goddamned paper jam…*Jesus.*

(*A beat after* KYLE *has opened the copier.*)

KAITLIN. For the love of…

KENDEL. I'll be damned.

(*Thoughtful beat.*)

KYLE. That's a jam.

KENDEL. That is *one hell* of a jam.

KAITLIN. What *is* that?

KENDEL. *One hell* of a jam.

KAITLIN. No, that.

KYLE. What?

KAITLIN. That.

KYLE. You mean right *there?*

KAITLIN. No, *that* right there.

KENDEL. There?

KYLE. There?

KAITLIN. Yeah, right *there.*

KENDEL. What *is* that?

KYLE. That?

KAITLIN. Yes, *that.*

KYLE. That's my abutments and drainage proposal.

KAITLIN. No. What's that wrapped around it?

KYLE. There?

KAITLIN. *THERE.*

KENDEL. That's a tie.

> (*Thoughtful beat.*)

KAITLIN. It's a necktie

KENDEL. Yup, that's a necktie all right.

KYLE. It's a yellow necktie with…a…

KAITLIN. So, what's *that* then?

KYLE. You mean right—

KAITLIN. There.

KENDEL. Inside the necktie?

KAITLIN. Right there inside the necktie.

KYLE. That would be…

> (*Beat.*)

KENDEL. It's a neck.

> (*Beat for examination.*)

KYLE. Yup, that's a neck all right.

KAITLIN. It's a neck.

KYLE. That's a neck in that tie.

KENDEL. Yup.

> (*Beat.*)

KAITLIN. So, it stands to reason that this…this *neck* is attached…to *something?*

KENDEL. Absolutely.

KYLE. No way around it.

KENDEL. Necks don't just *happen.*

KAITLIN. So, what's that attached—

KENDEL. to the neck—?

KYLE. That neck?

KAITLIN. Of course *that* neck.

KENDEL. Do you see another neck in there?

KYLE. It's Shem.

> (*Thoughtful beat.*)

KENDEL. What?

KYLE. Shem.

KAITLIN. That's Shem all right.

KENDEL. (*Addressing Shem.*) Shem?

KYLE. (*Addressing Shem.*) Shem?

> (*Thoughtful beat.*)

KAITLIN. Jesus

KYLE. Don't that beat—

KENDEL. Shit.

KYLE. It's Shem, all right.

KAITLIN. (*Addressing Shem.*) Shem?

KENDEL. Shem's in the copier.

KYLE. That's Shem's tie.

KENDEL. How do you know that's Shem's tie?

KYLE. I bought Shem that tie.

KENDEL. You *bought* him that tie?

KAITLIN. That's Shem's tie all right. Poor Shem.

KENDEL. What do you mean you bought him that tie?

KYLE. It was a present.

KENDEL. A present?

KAITLIN. How thoughtful. Birthday?

KYLE. Secret Santa.

KENDEL. Poor Shem.

KAITLIN.   Poor Shem.

KYLE.   Poor Shem. (*Addressing Shem.*) Shem?

> (*Thoughtful beat.*)

KAITLIN. He's dead isn't he?

KENDEL. Very much so.

KAITLIN.   Shem is dead.

KYLE. Crushed to death in the 8-1/2 x 11 bypass tray.

KAITLIN. Asphyxiated.

KENDEL. Decapitated.

KYLE. Mangled.

KAITLIN. Electrocuted.

KENDEL. Collated.

KAITLIN. Poor Shem.

KYLE.   Poor Shem.

> (*Respectful beat.*)

KAITLIN. How old was he?

KYLE. Thirty-four.

KAITLIN. *Only* thirty-four.

KYLE. His whole life ahead of him.

KENDEL. Apparently not.

KYLE. We should get him out.

KAITLIN. It's the right thing to do.

KYLE. He'd have done it for any one of us.

KENDEL. How do you know that?

KYLE. He was that kind of man.

KENDEL. *What* kind of man?

KAITLIN.   Did you say birthday?

KYLE. Secret Santa.

KAITLIN. It's very nice.

KENDEL.   Yes, nice tie, Kyle.

KYLE. Thank you.

KAITLIN. Stylish.

>   (*Beat.*)

KENDEL. So, why is it—?

KYLE. What?

KENDEL. Why is it—we don't have interns for cleaning up messes like this?

KYLE. An intern is an excellent idea.

KAITLIN.   On-the-job training.

KYLE. It develops those people skills.

KENDEL. Priceless skills for later…in life.

KAITLIN.   in life—poor Shem.

KYLE. Struck down in his prime.

KAITLIN. You just *never* know.

KENDEL. Know what?

KAITLIN. Life.

KENDEL. Oh, that.

KAITLIN. Blink.

KYLE. That's right, blink.

KENDEL. Blink?

KAITLIN. It's that quick.

KENDEL. (*Looking at his watch.*) Look at the time.

KYLE. How did it get to be lunchtime?

KAITLIN. Poor Shem.

KENDEL. It's...*really* not my job...I mean—scraping Shem from the copier.

KAITLIN. Do I look like I'm dressed for—

KYLE.   Drainage and abutments, that's my job. Poor Shem.

KAITLIN. Poor ol' Shem. We should call his wife.

KENDEL. We should call the copier repairman.

KYLE. Morrie?

KENDEL. Morrie.

KAITLIN. Yes, we should call Morrie.

KENDEL. Morrie will know what to do.

KYLE.   Morrie knows his copiers.

KAITLIN. Somebody should call Shem's wife. She'd want to know.

KENDEL.   It's not my job to tell people that their husbands were sucked into photocopiers.

KAITLIN. She'd want to know.

KENDEL. It's the right thing to do.

KYLE. Poor Shem.

KENDEL.   Poor Shem.

KAITLIN.   Poor ol' Shem.

(*Longer thoughtful beat.*)

KENDEL. Did Shem *have* a wife?

KYLE. No. I mean, I don't think so...

KENDEL. No wife?

KAITLIN. With a tie like that—and no wife?

KENDEL. Hard to believe, isn't it?

KYLE. It is.

(*Beat.*)

KENDEL. So then...

KYLE. Well...

KAITLIN. There you are.

KENDEL. Yup.

KYLE. Poor Shem.

KAITLIN.   Poor Shem.

KENDEL.   Poor Shem—you know...maybe...

KYLE. Maybe—?

KAITLIN. Maybe…what?

KENDEL. Maybe the 8-1/2 x 14 tray is working?

KAITLIN. (*Mild outrage.*) What?

KENDEL. I mean Shem is stuck in the 8-1/2 x 11 bypass tray—

KYLE. Tragically mutilated in an 8-1/2 x 11 bypass tray.

KAITLIN. (*Mild outrage.*) A co-worker is *dead* here.

KENDEL. Yes, poor Shem.

KYLE. Poor ol' Shem—you've got a point, though.

KENDEL. That's right

KYLE. The 8-1/2 x 14 tray *might* be working.

KAITLIN. A *co-worker* is dead here.

KYLE. We should call Morrie.

KENDEL. Hit the 8-1/2 x 14, people.

KAITLIN. Maybe we should call a priest.

KYLE. No, we should call Morrie.

KAITLIN.   Morrie is not ordained.

KYLE. Morrie knows his copiers.

KENDEL. No, hit the Reset first.

KAITLIN. We should call a priest.

KENDEL. Hit the Reset first.

KYLE. Maybe we should call Morrie *and* a priest.

KAITLIN. A co-worker is dead.

KYLE. I know. Do I hit Reset or call a priest? (*Beat.*) Do I hit Reset or call a priest?

(*Thoughtful beat for moral dilemma.*)

Reset, or a priest?

(*Thoughtful beat for moral dilemma.*)

Reset, or a priest, Kaitlin?

(*Thoughtful beat for moral dilemma.*)

Kendel, Reset, or a priest?

(*Longer thoughtful beat for moral dilemma.*)

KENDEL. Reset.

KYLE. Reset?

KAITLIN. Reset.

KENDEL. Close the front panel, Kyle.

KYLE. You close the panel, Kaitlin.

KAITLIN. Do I look like I'm dressed for closing the front panel?

KENDEL.   Close the front panel, Kyle.

KYLE. I'm closing the front panel then.

KAITLIN. Okay. Hit 8-1/2 x 14, Kyle.

KENDEL. No, hit the Reset first.

KAITLIN. Hit Print.

KENDEL. *Don't hit Print.* You waste your time hitting Print until the copier is warmed up.

KAITLIN. A co-worker is dead.

KYLE. He had his whole life ahead of him.

KENDEL.   Tragically mutilated in an 8-1/2 x 11 bypass tray.

KAITLIN. Of all the things you could give in your life, none is more precious than your labor.

KYLE. Your labor—

KENDEL. Hit Reset.

KYLE. —is the most precious. The job you are paid to do; the job you dedicate the best, most productive years of your life to. Nothing is more precious than that.

KENDEL. *I've* always believed that.

KAITLIN.   I've *always* believed that.

KYLE.   *Nothing* is more precious than that.

(*Thoughtful beat.*)

KENDEL. So, we'll wait for the Green Button to light up.

KAITLIN. And when it lights up—

KYLE. —we'll hit Print.

KENDEL. Wait for the Green.

KYLE. I'm waiting for the Green.

KENDEL. It's warming up…it's warming…

KAITLIN.   Let it warm up.

KYLE. I'm *letting it* warm up, already.

KENDEL. Wait for the Green.

KAITLIN. And when it turns Green.

KYLE. We'll hit Print.

KENDEL. Almost lunchtime.

KYLE. I'm starved.

KAITLIN. Wait for it.

KYLE. I'm waiting.

KENDEL. Wait for it.

KYLE. I'm waiting.

KENDEL. Wait for the Green.

KAITLIN. Of all the things you could give...

KYLE.   Nothing is more precious ...

KENDEL.   I've always believed that.

KYLE. I've always believed that.

> (*Beat.*)

KENDEL. Shicka shicka shicka shicka... (*Continues as* KAITLIN *joins in.*)

KAITLIN. Fwoosha ha fwoosha ha fwoosha ha fwoosha ha... (*Continues as* KYLE *joins in.*)

KYLE. Kahlakala kahlakala kahlakala kahlakala kahlakala kahlakala kahlakala klahk.

> (*All stop.*)

KENDEL. Poor Shem.

KYLE.   Poor Shem.

KAITLIN.   Poor ol' Shem.

> (*To black.*)

End of Play

THE CHRISTIANS
by Lucas Hnath

ABOUT *THE CHRISTIANS*

This article first ran in the January/February 2014 issue of Inside Actors, *Actors Theatre of Louisville's subscriber newsletter, and is based on conversations with the playwright before rehearsals for the Humana Festival production began.*

Twenty years ago, Pastor Paul's church was nothing more than a modest storefront. Today, he presides over a congregation of thousands, in a complex that includes classrooms for Sunday School, a coffee shop in the lobby, and a baptismal font as big as a swimming pool. The church is thriving, and its debts are finally paid; today should be a day of celebration. But Paul is uneasy. "There is a crack in the foundation of this church," warns the pastor in *The Christians'* opening sermon. "And I'm not talking about the building." What follows is an announcement that will shake the very bedrock of his congregation's belief.

The play chronicles the aftermath of that radical announcement—in which Paul unilaterally changes the church's stance on an essential article of faith—for the pastor and those who surround him. "For some time now," says playwright Lucas Hnath, "I've been interested in stories of preachers who decide to orchestrate some kind of major doctrinal shift. Such shifts can be profoundly disorienting." His fascination has roots in his own childhood; Hnath grew up attending a megachurch in Orlando, Florida. As a young boy, he occasionally preached "mini-sermons" in the children's church. When his mother, now an ordained minister and hospital chaplain, went to seminary, Hnath accompanied her to some of her classes, and throughout high school he imagined he would eventually attend seminary himself. Although ultimately his interests led him elsewhere, those early formative experiences stayed with him. "I've wanted to write a church play for a really long time," says Hnath. "A play that takes believers seriously, and that non-believers wouldn't smirk at. A play about Christianity whose point of view is not satirical, that isn't making fun."

Conversations with a childhood friend who became a preacher helped inform the conflict at the heart of *The Christians*. "He told me that one has to be really careful not to remake the Christian faith in one's own image," says Hnath. "Which for me raised the question, is that even possible? To actually get out of the way, to have an absolutely true doctrine that is in no way influenced by human subjectivity? That's what I'm trying to wrestle with." In *The Christians*, Pastor Paul's radical change seems to be the result of sincere soul-searching and rigorous theological examination. But as his friends and followers begin to question his motives, the preacher's own confidence is shaken. Does he know what he thinks he knows? *Can* he know it? And is a man with so many followers really free to change his mind?

While this story was inspired, in large part, by Hnath's own experiences of the church, the playwright drew formal inspiration from the Greeks. *The Christians* unfolds as a series of arguments between Paul and some of the people closest to him. "The tradition of the Greeks," says Hnath, "is to have these really great argument-counterargument scenes. Some sort of hotly contested problem is dropped into the room, and then you watch two or more people just argue it out." When asked if he himself still identifies with a church or ascribes to a set of religious beliefs, Hnath politely declines to answer. "I hope the play is dialectical," he reasons, "and that the opposing views articulated inside it are as evenly matched as possible."

In performance, the experience of the play is richly aural. Hnath's dialogue was written to be delivered almost exclusively into microphones, which draws attention to the tension operating in the play between the public and the private. "To me one of the most interesting, and sometimes sad, aspects of the life of a preacher is that you're constantly on public display," he muses. "The moment you make a mistake, people are very hard on you." Music also plays an important role, and the Humana Festival production, directed by Les Waters, featured songs performed by a large choir. "I tend to think in terms of arguments and flow charts and proofs," Hnath muses. "But there's this other realm that I really wanted to engage in the play, which is the antithesis of logic—the euphoric. And that's what music does."

Though he opted out of seminary, Hnath still traces his vocation back to his early experiences in Orlando. "Looking back, my first schooling in the theatrical took place in church," the playwright reflects. But if its ritual and performative aspects can make church seem like theatre, Hnath is quick to point out that theatre can also function as a kind of church—a public space in which to contend with the big mysteries of existence. "There is this thing that is very hard to see, that is slippery, and the moment you too rigidly define it, can become corrupt in some way," he says. "I think theatre's at its best when it's trying to momentarily make visible something that can't really be seen or pinned down."

—Sarah Lunnie

BIOGRAPHY

Lucas Hnath's plays include *The Christians* (2014 Humana Festival), *Red Speedo* (Studio Theatre, Washington, D.C.), *A Public Reading of an Unproduced Screenplay About the Death of Walt Disney* (Soho Rep.), *Sleep Rock Thy Brain* (2013 Humana Festival), *Isaac's Eye* (Ensemble Studio Theatre), *Death Tax* (2012 Humana Festival, Royal Court Theatre), and *The Courtship of Anna Nicole Smith* (Actors Theatre of Louisville). Hnath has been a resident playwright at New Dramatists since 2011 and is a proud member of Ensemble Studio Theatre. He won the 2012 Whitfield Cook Award for *Isaac's Eye* and the 2013 Steinberg/ATCA New Play Award Citation for *Death Tax*. He is also a recipient of new play commissions from the EST/Sloan Project, Actors Theatre of Louisville, South Coast Repertory, Playwrights Horizons, New York University, and the Royal Court Theatre.

ACKNOWLEDGMENTS

The Christians premiered at the Humana Festival of New American Plays in March 2014. It was directed by Les Waters with the following cast:

PASTOR...Andrew Garman
ASSOCIATE PASTOR...Larry Powell
ELDER...Richard Henzel
CONGREGANT...Emily Donahoe
WIFE .... Linda Powell

and the following production staff:

Scenic Designer...Dane Laffrey
Costume Designer.....................................Connie Furr Soloman
Lighting Designer...Ben Stanton
Sound Designer...Jake Rodriguez
Media Designer ....Philip Allgeier
Stage Manager ....Paul Mills Holmes
Dramaturg..Sarah Lunnie
Casting..Zan Sawyer-Dailey, Meg Fister
Music Director/Conductor..................................Scott Anthony
Properties Master...Joseph Cunningham
Associate Scenic Designer..........................Scott Tedmon Jones
Assistant Director...John Rooney
Production Assistant ....Jessica Potter
Assistant Dramaturg.. Sam Weiner

The Christians was commissioned by Actors Theatre of Louisville and was developed through a Creativity Fund at New Dramatists, as well as through a workshop at The John F. Kennedy Center for the Performing Arts.

Production supported by the 50th Anniversary NCTF/Ford Foundation Fund for New Work.

WHO

Paul, a PASTOR,
and his WIFE, Elizabeth,
the ASSOCIATE Pastor Joshua,
a church ELDER named Jay,
and a CONGREGANT named Jenny or Jennifer or Jenn.

WHEN

The 21st Century

WHERE

America

HOW

In church, a real big church.
and what we see is the stage, raised and carpeted,
in the center, a podium;
and further upstage, hanging, a cross;
surrounding, potted plants;
above, a screen for slides and stuff;
off to the side, two or three chairs in a row, chairs for the associate pastors;
and off to the other side, a church organ and organist facing upstage.
There could even be a church band with organ and guitar and percussion, but not necessarily.
And there are microphones, enough microphones for everyone in the play, and some microphone stands, whenever needed;
because everyone will always speak on mics, just the way pastors do,
or just the way congregants do when they testify.
The whole play is a kind of sermon.
Sometimes it's a literal sermon.
Sometimes it's made up of scenes that use the formal elements of a sermon.
And as such, even the most private scene has a kind of
declamatory, performative, sing-songy quality.

A NOTE ON SONGS

During the play, the Choir will sing four songs. Below are suggestions for what those songs could be. Even if you do not use the suggested song, the song you use should have that general tone. Additionally, the songs you use should not in any explicit way conflict with Pastor Paul's theological stance. Also note: it is the responsibility of the producing theatre to obtain the rights to any songs that are not in the public domain.

Song #1: Gospel, steady, comforting. "God's Unchanging Hand."

Song #2: Faster, rousing, revival music. "Catch on Fire."

Song #3: A bit anthemic, deliberate. "I Feel Like Going On."

Song #4: Bright, not-too-fast-and-not-too-slow. "Farther Along."

SPECIAL THANKS

Thank you to Sarah Lunnie, Les Waters and Amy Wegener for guiding the play; to Marc Bovino, Phillip James Brannon, Katya Campbell, Rick Foucheux, Marianna McClellan, Dominique Morisseau, Gordon O'Connell, Randy Rand, Thomas Jay Ryan, Kim Schraf, and P.J. Sosko for performing in various incarnations of this play; to Emily Donahoe, Andrew Garman, Linda Powell, Larry Powell, and Richard Henzel for premiering the play; to Darius Smith and Scott Anthony for musical guidance; to New Dramatists and the Kennedy Center for helping develop the play; to David Collins, Dana Higginbotham, and Mark Schultz for being my theological advisors; to Darlene Forrest and Denice Martone for their support and encouragement; and a very special thank you to Pat C. Hoy, II for the airplane story.

BILLING: I am a pagan and proud of it. Believe me, before long, we will all be pagans.

MORTEN: And then will we be allowed to do anything we like?

BILLING: Well, you'll see.

—Henrik Ibsen, *An Enemy of the People*

I feel an uncontrollable urge to communicate with you,
but I find the distance barrier
insurmountable.

—Pat C. Hoy, II

This play is dedicated to
Pat C. Hoy, II,
Sarah Lunnie,
and Les Waters

Larry Powell, Linda Powell and Andrew Garman
in *The Christians*

38th Humana Festival of New American Plays
Actors Theatre of Louisville, 2014
Photo by Michael Brosilow

134

THE CHRISTIANS

Pre-show into show: The music plays. An organist. Singers. Maybe even a full choir, the bigger the better. The Choir sings Song #1.

As this song goes on, enter PASTOR *and his* WIFE.

Perhaps the PASTOR *makes his way down a line of Associate Pastors and Elders seated on stage, on his way to his seat, having to shake hands and briefly speak to each one.*

And eventually, the PASTOR *sits, reviews his notes, as the Choir sings Song #2.*

Singing ends.

PASTOR *approaches the pulpit.*

Takes a microphone in hand.

PASTOR. Brothers and sisters...

Let's pray.

> (*Some music continues under the prayer.*)

Dear Lord,
bring us together today,
    bring us together
        in our hearts
           and souls
               and minds,

               make us one,
               make us a body,
                    because when we are one body,
                    we see something
                    we cannot see
                    by ourselves.

Make us whole.
Take away our fear.
Give us strength,

        and give us courage.

        Give us the kind of courage that helps us press on even though
        we know death is standing there

watching

waiting,

give us the courage to know,
to feel,
to understand,
that if we pass through that death, we will find

life.

ever
lasting.

In the name
and in the blood
of Jesus.

Amen.
            (*Pause.*
            Music ends.)
Today's sermon
has four titles.
If you're taking notes, I suggest you write them down.

They are:
            (*Titles appear on the screen above.*)
Where are we today?

A Powerful Urge

The Fires of Hell

and
A Radical Change.

Part 1:
Where are we today?

Well

We   are

            here.

Where is here?

"Here" is this
                      church,
                      this big,
                      enormous
                      building.

                      Thousands of seats, classrooms for Sunday
                      school,
                      a baptismal big as a swimming pool. In the
                      lobby
                      there's a coffee shop and a bookstore,
                      and out back, a parking lot so vast
                      you could get yourself lost in it
                      if you're not careful.

Where are we?
        We are here, today,
        a day of celebration,
        a day of freedom...

...because 20 years ago this church was
nothing more than a storefront church,
10, 15 people.

Then for the next couple of years every Sunday,
20, 30 people

                and then 50,

                and then 100, and 100 that seemed big—

                then 500.

                We had to move ourselves into a bigger space, a local
                gymnasium. But when 500 turned to three times
                that, then we started holding three services every
                Sunday: one at nine, one at 10:30, and one at noon,

                and then we grew to twice that,

                and then we just couldn't fit.

So,

            we built this,
            this sanctuary,
            built it from the ground up.

And how ever much we thought it was going to cost,
it cost that and many times over.

> And we were in
> way over our heads.

That
was ten years ago,
ten years from today.
And you stayed,
    and you paid,
       and together we prayed
           that someday we would finally free ourselves of debt.

> And that someday
>   is today.
> And today is the day
>   that debt is paid.

And ya know, today should be a happy day:
    We have, it seems, reason to celebrate.
    We have, it seems, reason to think that we are
       free.

> Sorta reminds me of the one about the man who
> turned 102,
> and at his birthday party,
> his friend asked him, do you think you'll make it to
> 103
> and he said "of course I will,
> because statistically speaking,
>   there are very few people who die
>   between 102 and 103."

But we all know, *a lot* of people die before that.

> And we all know, a lot of churches die
> before they make it to where we are
> but that doesn't mean
> we are as free as we think we are.
> There is a different kind of debt
> that we have not yet paid

    There is—there is a crack
in the foundation of this church,

and I'm not talking about the building.

> I'm talking about something like Isaiah talks about,
> Isaiah 30 verses 12 and 13
> "Because you have rejected this word"
>> "this word" that's God's word he's talking about
> "And relied on oppression
>
> and depended on deceit,
> this sin will become for you
> like a high wall,
> cracked
> and bulging,
> whose collapse comes suddenly
>>>> in an instant."

> There is a crack,
> and if we don't fix that crack,
> it doesn't matter how solid this building is,

>> we
>>> will

>>>> crumble,

>>> and we will
>>> fall in on ourselves.

so today we're going to talk a little about that crack
and we're going to talk about what we have to do
to save ourselves from collapse

> (*The title appears on the screen: "Part 2: A Powerful Urge."*)

PASTOR. Twenty-two years ago, I was a young man on an airplane flight from L.A. to Florida. I'm sitting in my seat, and I see a woman pass me by. I see this woman, and I think to myself: Lord, that is the most beautiful woman I have ever seen.

And the Lord said, that's right.

And I said to myself:

> Paul,
> that is the most beautiful woman you have ever seen.
> And my self said to its self: well you better do something
> about it.

And I looked back down the length of the plane and I saw her sitting on the aisle. She was far away, at the other end of the airplane. Had to lean to see her, could barely catch her eye. I took out a little scrap of paper, and took out a pen. And I wrote down,

> "I have a powerful urge to communicate with you,
> but I find the distance between us insurmountable."

I folded the paper, gave the note to the stewardess. I said, you see that woman in the pink pantsuit. Will you give this to her. And the stewardess said yes. And I waited. I watched and I waited and I saw,

I saw her lean,
into the aisle.

And she looked at me,
and she said:
(Waves.)
and I said:
(Waves.)
And that's all we needed to say, that was it, so easy, so easy you might call it

grace.

"I have a powerful urge to communicate with you but I find the distance between us insurmountable."
(Pause.

Another title appears on the screen: "Part 3: The Fires of Hell.")

PASTOR. I was—
oh about
two weeks ago, I was

at a conference for pastors of churches like this church,
it was a uh conference where you go and hear missionaries speak,
to hear about the "good"
work our church is doing in other places.

Now I go to these conferences because I am told to go to these conferences—
I get a little letter in the mail from the powers that be saying
you should go to this, and I go, I don't

think about it much—I just go.

And here I am at this conference at the Orlando Marriott,
and I'm eating my free continental breakfast,
and I'm listening to a missionary speak.

This missionary that's talking,
he works overseas in one of those countries
that we hear about on the news,
but if you were asked where it was
or what that country was all about, you probably
wouldn't be able to point to it on a map.

And this missionary, he's trying to start a church there
like the church we have here
in a place—a country—where there's
a lot of fighting, a lot of violence, a lot of chaos,
gun fights and bombs and
and
and
he talks
about one day,
he's in a market,
people going about their business,
shopping, buying food,
and a bomb goes off—I think it was a car bomb.
A grocery store lights on fire.
And people run, they scatter off into—

there's a boy, 16, 17 years old, a young man,
and instead of running *away* from the burning grocery
store,
he runs into it.
He runs *into* the fire.
And some time passes,
the store is still on fire,
and eventually the boy comes out of the store,
and his whole body is shielding a girl, maybe seven years
old, this girl—
he's helped her to safety, saved her from the burning
building,
but
his own body, is on fire. His clothes are burning,
his arms are burning, his face is

burning, his skin is melting.
He helps the girl to safety,
and she's okay. But
he,
the boy,
is dying.
And there's no one to put out his fire.
And he lies down on the street,
body gone into shock,
and he burns until he's dead.

The missionary tells us that the boy—
that that was his sister, that he ran into the store to save.
And the missionary tells us that this boy—he didn't know
him personally,
but talked to the boy's family enough to know
that the boy was not a Christian.
He did not believe in the God we believe in.
He did not believe in Jesus,
or the Holy Spirit.
He believed in a different set of beliefs,
and attended a church that did not talk about the cross,
and prayed a different set of prayers than the prayers we
pray.

And the missionary said: isn't it a shame
that we lost that boy, what a man of Christ he might have
been.
And and and I thought—
I thought that he meant
"what a shame the boy died," and I thought,
"yes, what a shame that boy died,"
but the missionary, he meant,
"what a shame, I didn't save this boy for Christ,
what a shame I didn't convert him into a Christian,
what a shame he went to Hell."

The missionary said, "We need help."
He said, "We need money
to save these souls,
we need people,
an' we need your prayers
to save these souls,
because without that,

they all go to Hell."

This boy, by all accounts,
was a good boy.
And yet, he went to Hell.
And what do we say, we say
Amen.
And all the pastors at the conference say—they said
Amen.

And here I am, thinking about this image,

that boy,
          the body on fire,

and the thought of him
going from one fire
                    into another.

I went back to my hotel room that night.
I sat on the toilet, and I cried.

          Convulsively.

              I cried.

I said,
God, I don't understand.
And He said, That's not your problem.
And I said,

          Well it kinda is.
And he said, Why?

And I said, Because I'm a pastor.
And he said, Oh you're a pastor, what does *that* mean?
And he said,

          No,

no, it's not your problem because you haven't made it your
problem,
you haven't gone over there and done anything,
you're just sittin' on the toilet.
And I said, you're right. I am. Just sittin' on the toilet.
And he said, what are you gonna do?
And I said, well after I'm done here on the toilet,

I'm gonna brush my teeth,
and then I'll go to bed.
And he said, why.
And I said—I said…
And he said,

        why.

And I said, because you have already done so much.
And he said

        exactly.

And he said that he's saved us, he's taken care of us,
       he said, "why don't you listen when I tell you that."

And he said, You think the Devil is a little man with horns.
He said, You think that?
An' I said, I don't know.
An' he said, You really think that?
        Do you really really really think that?

And I said, No
      not really.
And he said,
There is no little man.
There is only you
and your fellow man.
You wanna see Satan—?
      there's your Satan.
You wanna see Hell,
      you look around.

And he said, There is no Hell.
And there is no reason to tell people
that they're going to Hell.
Because they *are* in Hell.

They are already there.
You gotta take them out of the Hell they're already in.
That boy, the Lord tells me—he says,
that boy, he is standing next to me right now.
And anyone who tells you otherwise
                lies.

    I know
you *all* have a powerful urge to communicate.

I know it. I see it. Your urge
to communicate God's love,
to bring people into this church,
to help them,
to save them
to make their lives better,
and their after lives
                    everlasting.
                    You have that powerful urge to communicate.
                    But you are failing
                    because the distance between
                    you
                    and everyone else
                    is
                    insurmountable.

But I'm here to tell you,

        the distance

            is you.

            It's me.

            It's all of us.

            We put the distance there.
            When we shun our neighbors,
            when we judge our friends,
            when we look down at people
            from other places
            and other religions,
            we create

                        an insurmountable distance
                        where there is no distance at all.

Where are we today?
Where are we
today?
I say

            we are no longer a congregation that believes in Hell.
            A radical change: we are no longer a congregation that says my
            way is the only way.

We are no longer

that kind of church.

(*End of sermon.*
Nods to Music Director... Off microphone:)
Go ahead.

(*Organ plays. If there's a band, then the whole band plays.*
PASTOR *sits down.*
Music plays in silence.
A set of projected images play on the wall behind the PASTOR...
A lake.
Majestic mountains.
A dove.
A tree in a field.
The Grand Canyon.
A dove.
Another kind of dove.
The sky.
Music comes to an end.)

PASTOR. Associate Pastor Joshua will deliver the prayer for the sick, for those who can't be here today.

Brother Joshua...

(ASSOCIATE *Pastor Joshua stands, takes a microphone.*
Pause.
Then, reading from a list.)

ASSOCIATE. Please bow your heads in prayer.

Dear Lord,
We bring to you members of the congregation,
who are ill. Their bodies have failed them,
but even so, we know you will not.

We ask that you watch over,

Mary Rafferty,
Helen Mounts,
Abe Higginbotham,
Maxine Judson,
Peter Stanford,

Bethany Tallis,
Sandra Coleman,
Agnes Silver,
Amanda Stapp,
Tiffany Leveroux,
Rachel Stein,
and Earl Browne.

An' if there are others in our family, who are sick,
who we did not mention,
please look after them too.

In the name,
and the power—the cleansing power—
of the holy blood of Jesus...

Amen.

(Pause.
Goes to return to his seat.
But then, stops.)

PASTOR. And Associate Pastor Joshua just stands there at the pulpit.
I say to him,
Brother Joshua?
And he says

ASSOCIATE. *(Leans into the microphone.)*
... I find myself
wrestling with your sermon

I...

PASTOR. ...

ASSOCIATE. ...

PASTOR. *(Still very calmly.)*
Go on...?

ASSOCIATE. Because what you said in your sermon
seems to go against everything
our church believes.

PASTOR. What do we believe?

ASSOCIATE. We believe in Satan,
and we believe in Satan because the Bible tells us

Satan is real.

And we believe in Hell

because the Bible tells us Hell is there,
that Hell is the price we pay for sin

PASTOR. where?

ASSOCIATE. "where" what?

PASTOR. Where does the Bible tell us that Hell is waiting for us?

ASSOCIATE. uhhhhh, seriously?

PASTOR. Yes.

ASSOCIATE. ...

PASTOR. ...

ASSOCIATE. in the Bible

PASTOR. yes

ASSOCIATE. Christ says
"The wages of sin is death"

PASTOR. "Death" is not "Hell"

ASSOCIATE. means eternal death

PASTOR. says who? says you?

ASSOCIATE. no, the Word of God

PASTOR. show me

ASSOCIATE. when read in context

PASTOR. what context are you referring to?

ASSOCIATE. Luke 16:28

PASTOR. yes—?

ASSOCIATE. (*Fumbling with Bible.*)
talks about—Jesus he—

let me find it—says...

okay

"Let him warn them, so that they will not also come to this place of torment."

PASTOR. which is

ASSOCIATE. Hell

PASTOR. says "a place of torment"

ASSOCIATE. and that's not Hell?

PASTOR. wouldn't you call guilt, feeling bad about what you've done,
a place of torment?
Isn't that torment enough?

ASSOCIATE. then what about
Matthew chapter 10,

or, Luke 12
Matthew 5, verse 22
PASTOR. yes—?
ASSOCIATE. again and again and again, Jesus says, Jesus, he warns us of
Hell, of the danger of Hell, tells us again and again, about sinners getting
thrown into Hell.

Here it's:
PASTOR. but it
doesn't say Hell
ASSOCIATE. are you going to let me read it?
PASTOR. sorry
go ahead
ASSOCIATE. "Fear God, who has the power to kill you and then throw
you into Hell."
PASTOR. It doesn't really say Hell.
ASSOCIATE. didn't I just say Hell?
PASTOR. *you* said Hell. But it does not say Hell.
ASSOCIATE. ...
PASTOR. in the original language the word "Hell" is not used
instead it's Gehena and Gehena is the name of a
of a garbage dump, a a a place where they burned trash
just outside of Jerusalem.
He was just saying that bad people,
when they die,
often get thrown into that particular trash heap—
which was factually true, so that's
actually what he's talking about.
ASSOCIATE. ...
PASTOR. ...
ASSOCIATE. First Corinthians
PASTOR. Congregation please turn to First Corinthians so you can follow
along
ASSOCIATE. 15:22
PASTOR. Chapter 15, verse 22,
read along
ASSOCIATE. For as in Adam all die,
PASTOR. For as in Adam *all* die
ASSOCIATE. so also in Christ

PASTOR. so also *in* Christ

ASSOCIATE. shall all be made alive.

PASTOR. shall *all*...be made alive.

ASSOCIATE. yes

PASTOR. In Adam we die.

ASSOCIATE. that's what it—yes—it says

PASTOR. but of course we do die, we know that,
we die

ASSOCIATE. but then the "alive" means that it's different

PASTOR. different from whatever it is with Adam

ASSOCIATE. yes.

PASTOR. so clearly Christ does something

ASSOCIATE. It's saying that if you're going to live,
you need Christ.

PASTOR. sure

ASSOCIATE. so

PASTOR. so?

ASSOCIATE. And you say, you say this boy,
the boy in the missionary's story,
who uh doesn't believe the Word, doesn't
believe Jesus is the son of God,
doesn't come from a faith that believes in Christ

PASTOR. that is correct, he did not believe in Christ

ASSOCIATE. so yes, I'm sorry but:
it is certainly,
without a doubt,
a sad and moving story about
what can happen in a fallen world.
But it's just that: a sad and moving story.
It's a message that our work is not done,
and that we need to not be complacent
in these dark end days.

PASTOR. ...

ASSOCIATE. ...

PASTOR. So...

you're telling me that you would not—if you were—
imagine, you're on the throne, and you have love in your heart—
you say you have love in your heart, I believe you have love in your heart—

and this boy comes to you—you will send this boy
to Hell... ?

ASSOCIATE. I'm not God

PASTOR. no, you're not

ASSOCIATE. it's blasphemous to even pretend

PASTOR. I'm asking you
in front of this entire church,
these brothers and sisters,
would you
send that boy to Hell...?

...to look that boy in the eyes,
knowing what he has done,
knowing what he has given of himself

ASSOCIATE. ...

PASTOR. would you

ASSOCIATE. ...yes

PASTOR. you would

ASSOCIATE. I'd have no choice but to

PASTOR. because—?

ASSOCIATE. it's

PASTOR. what

ASSOCIATE. the law.

PASTOR. Whose law—?

ASSOCIATE. God's.
And God's law is just,
because we are fallen,
an' we are sinful, and we *do*
we *do* go into markets
and we *do* set off bombs,
and we *do* kill one another.

And in turn, what God asks of us—
all He asks of us—
is to just believe that He is there, and repent,
and that is so little to ask
to become cleansed—

to say yes, I accept that you sacrificed your son on the cross, and we are saved

from Hell.

PASTOR. But

that's not what the Bible actually says,
because according to the verse you just read,
First Corinthians
ASSOCIATE. it says
PASTOR. it says all, not some,

all
ASSOCIATE. who are in Christ
PASTOR. in Christ
ASSOCIATE. with the help of Christ
PASTOR. that he gives

freely.
ASSOCIATE. it says
PASTOR. "*in* Christ,"
interchangeable with "through Christ"
all
through
Christ.

The sentence means:

because of Christ

all are made alive.

First Timothy 4:10:

"we trust in the living God,
who is the Savior of all men,
especially believers."
ASSOCIATE. …
PASTOR. "especially believers." Which is to say,
you don't
have to
believe.
It says that—that's
what
it *actually*
says.

(A beat, a meaningful pause, almost as though JOSHUA *really is checking inside to see what God wants him to do.)*

ASSOCIATE. ...

PASTOR. ...

(And then.)

ASSOCIATE. The Lord is tellin' me to—in my heart deep down I feel the Lord right now feel the Lord telling me to—

reject what you're saying—I feel

PASTOR. yes—?

ASSOCIATE. the Lord is telling me that you are going against his Word

PASTOR. Yes, I got that Brother Joshua

ASSOCIATE. if you really believe what you say you believe, you are not my brother.

PASTOR. Then
you're free
to leave this church.

I release you.

ASSOCIATE.
...I don't think I'd be alone

I think there are many who would question your teaching this morning, who do question—who believe that it is fundamentally against what we believe.

PASTOR. ...If that is so,
then they can leave with you.

ASSOCIATE. ...

PASTOR. *(To the* AUDIENCE.*)*
And Brother Joshua
says:

ASSOCIATE. *(Never breaking eye contact with* PASTOR.*)*
Pass around the offering plates.
And have each member of the congregation write down
on a little scrap of paper:
Pastor Paul

or

Associate Pastor Joshua.

Okay?

PASTOR. Okay.

> (*Music, organ.*)
> And with that,
> the ushers pass around the offering plates
> to the members of the congregation.

> > Everyone is taking out pens and little scraps of paper,
> > and each one writes something down.

> > > And I wait.

> (*Pause.*)

> > > And I think.

> (*Pause.*)

> And it takes a long time for this whole process to take place.

> > And I pray.

> (*Pause.*)
> And the offering plates come back,
> and Associate Pastor Joshua,
> and Associate Pastor Ken
> and Associate Pastor Will,
> my Associate Pastors count the little bits of paper.

> > And we wait.

> (*Pause.*)
> An' Brother Joshua comes back,
> and he is flanked by the two other
> Associate Pastors.

> (*Music stops.*)
> Brother Joshua says

ASSOCIATE. we have counted the little pieces of paper

PASTOR. yes. And?

ASSOCIATE. …fifty

PASTOR. Fifty?

ASSOCIATE. there were fifty people

PASTOR. who said

ASSOCIATE. who sided with me.

PASTOR. okay.

ASSOCIATE. …out of the hundreds

PASTOR. okay

ASSOCIATE. Thousands

PASTOR. I see

ASSOCIATE. who have said
they want
to stay with you.

> (*Pause.*
> *The Choir sings the opening verses of Song #3, then switches into a soft vocalization as* BROTHER JOSHUA *speaks.*)

ASSOCIATE. ya know, Pastor Paul: many may have sided with you today, but I think there are many more who did not speak up

many who did not cast their vote, who stayed silent and who do not see things like you see them

and I imagine there are even people who said they side with you but maybe deep down, they don't.

They just don't want to see you topple, when they think you're the one holding up the roof over their heads

they don't want to see you fall, when they've given so much to you

given their time, their faith, their money, their trust

PASTOR. All right then

you've said what you wanted to say.

Now it's time to go.

> (*The music swells and the Choir sings the closing verses of the song.*
> *Silence.*
> ASSOCIATE *exits.*
> *All watch as he walks off.*
> *He's gone.*
> *Pause.*
> ELDER JAY *steps forward, takes a microphone.*
> PASTOR *pours himself a glass of water, drinks, and dabs his sweaty brow.*
> *Silence.*
> PASTOR *finishes his "rest-and-reset moment."*)

PASTOR. And Elder Jay walks into my office and he says

ELDER. Pastor Paul

PASTOR. Yes, Elder Jay

ELDER. On behalf of myself and on behalf of the church's Board of
Elders...

I'd like to take a moment
and reflect
on your sermon.

PASTOR. go ahead, Brother Jay.

ELDER. You've been a long-time family friend, godfather to my
grandchildren,
trusted confidante,
and spiritual mentor.

An' I just want you to know that
I think this new direction you're taking us is
exciting, it's a—you called it—a radical change and
it's an important change I think for the longer life of our church
and for the life of our faith.

The church board and I, we discussed the sermon, your message, and they
also find it very interesting uh very progressive
what you're doing here

PASTOR. so you're saying you're behind me

ELDER. yes

PASTOR. you support me

ELDER. yes absolutely

PASTOR. along with the board of this church

ELDER. ...yes.

PASTOR. well thank you

ELDER. but

PASTOR. oh there's a "but"

ELDER. It's just that as we're celebrating this new exciting direction for our
church community,
I'll be honest: we're really broken up about Joshua leaving this church.

PASTOR. Yes, I know.

ELDER. For the past five years he's been a blessing to our family, you do
agree that he's been a blessing?

PASTOR. sure,
in many ways, yes

ELDER. Let me remind you:
Joshua is your spiritual son.
You saved him.

he walked into this church
lonely and just looking for some friends,
I seem to remember he was thrown out of his home,
I forget what—some sort of family problems.

And I remember this boy came down to the altar,
saying "I need something
    I don't know what but I need something
    to help me
    to keep on
       goin' on."

An' that young man started coming to church,
every Sunday,
then every Sunday and Wednesday,
then Sunday Wednesday Saturday Friday every day of the week.

    and bit by bit,

you gave him more responsibility here at the church:
    a Sunday School class,
        then counseling responsibilities,
        the prayer line,
            then here and there,
            Bible reading,
                a testimonial in the Sunday service,
                and then you hired him on as an
                Associate Pastor.

And you'll agree,
he worked hard

PASTOR. he did

ELDER. he was honest and good and

PASTOR. no yes all of that is true Brother Jay

ELDER. he galvanized and organized and revitalized our youth ministries.
You cannot deny he is very charismatic, and gets folks excited
about our church and the work it does.
He became an outspoken member of the community,
going and reaching out
to the poor
and to the sick,
the disenfranchised
and the lost.

PASTOR. …
ELDER. So

What I'm getting at is:
did you have to be so quick to let him go?
Did you have to, need to—was it absolutely necessary to
cut him off?

While he may have failed to follow you, this time, yes he failed,
He's young, sure, he's got a little chip on his shoulder

still isn't there room for a second chance
and a third and a fourth and a fifth—?

Your sermon talked about being more accepting,
and so shouldn't that same acceptance be extended to Joshua?

…no, I've said what I have to say.
I'm going to stop talking and let you speak.

>   (ELDER *does so.*)

PASTOR. Thank you for that,
Elder Jay.

I hear you.

Ya know, it's kinda like a marriage
How in the Bible it says
that in a marriage
you cannot be unequally yoked.
A divided head cannot lead.
I welcome Joshua into this church.
But if he is going to lead it with me, under me, any way,
then we need to be
of one mind.
you talk about Joshua
reaching out
being the face of this church
out there in the world.
True: he does reach out.
But what does he show the rest of the world about this church.
How does he represent us?
Do you know how he represents us?

ELDER. I know he can be very uh passionate, sometimes a bit

PASTOR. last November

ELDER. right.

PASTOR. you know about this

ELDER. I think I do

PASTOR. Associate Pastor Ken came to me, told me
about how Joshua had gotten together
some of the college kids

ELDER. yes I know this

PASTOR. Saturday nights they'd go downtown,
a group of five or six, they'd
go up to people on the street,
call them out as sinners,
down where the bars are, the clubs,
they'd go up to people and tell them
they were going to Hell, tell them

ELDER. it was inappropriate

PASTOR. How do you think
it makes people feel
to be pulled aside
and told that they're sinners?

ELDER. We're all sinners, aren't we—?

PASTOR. To be told "hey—you're bad,
you're a bad person and you should feel bad about yourself"

Why do thieves hang out with thieves?

So they don't feel so guilty.

But shouldn't it be the church that makes a thief feel welcome.

ELDER. I don't disagree.

PASTOR. But then here we have Joshua and a gang of college kids calling
people sinners,
the world looks at us and says: who is responsible
for spreading around all that
contempt, that's what it is really—
and the world looks back at our church,
and the world looks back at me, me,
and they say: *he* is responsible for that.
and I don't want to be responsible for that,
that suffering.

What good is a good church
if all it does

is make everyone feel so bad.

ELDER. yes—but what good is a church that no one goes to?

PASTOR. only 50 people left

ELDER. Joshua was very popular, he had a different kind of relationship with the congregation than you, not better, just different, you're so busy running the church, writing your sermons, overseeing all sorts of—I understand that's hard, but that meant Joshua was the one who people came to, who listened, on a daily basis, to their problems. He was the one that people had a uh uh more personal relationship with—again you're busy, you can't be blamed, but I have to think that carries a certain weight, and people might have a stronger attachment to him than you'd think.

I just think that Joshua served a very important function and without him

PASTOR. you think

ELDER. yes

PASTOR. or the board thinks—?

ELDER. I'm just here to let you know their concerns

PASTOR. and I need you to tell the board that there's nothing to be concerned about.

ELDER. we can't afford a schism

PASTOR. afford

ELDER. yes

PASTOR. now you're talking about money

ELDER. among other things

PASTOR. the church has paid its debt

ELDER. only to incur another?

PASTOR. you and the board worry about the business of the church so that I don't have to.

ELDER. …well, you say that, Paul, but you have a board, a group of ten or so people who really like you a lot,
and care about you and your ministry,
and your family, and they wouldn't be serving on the board
unless they cared about you.

And keep in mind, we're—we're not business-minded,
I mean I'm a doctor, I give out flu shots; Jerry, our treasurer, runs a
local telemarketing firm, and
we have
no prior experience running something on this scale,
this church, you understand, it's a massive corporation, and

for the past several years while the church was in debt, that was scary,
for sure, and in the middle of it all, when Agnes got caught on
the church escalator, got her leg all cut up, turns out the Board of
Directors was personally liable, and we had to get lawyers, we're
in the position where we do have our necks on the line, in a way
that you don't. You understand.

PASTOR. I do

ELDER. But at the same time, we had a congregation that was here every
Sunday
and was growing, exponentially and so
slowly but surely, the place got paid off.

I worry, yes, I do worry, a little, about what happens when you tell a
congregation that they don't need to believe—then I have to wonder if that
makes them feel like going to church isn't so important.

PASTOR. so would you have me threaten them?

ELDER. no

PASTOR. would you have me tell them that if they don't come to church,
they're going to Hell—?

ELDER. no

PASTOR. would you have me tell them that if they don't tithe every week,
they'll burn?

ELDER. oh no of course not

PASTOR. then what would you have me say
that I'm not already saying?

Jay, you know I respect and value your opinion
and you know that I appreciate everything you've done for me and this
church.
If you would just give me your trust it would mean so much to me.

ELDER. You have my trust. You know you do.

PASTOR. and we hug
Elder Jay leaves my office
and shuts the door behind him.

> (*Abruptly, the Choir sings Song #4, ending the scene.*
> *At the end of the song…*
> *A member of the Choir steps forward, takes a mic.*
> *She looks to* PASTOR *and says…*)

CONGREGANT. Pastor Paul, I'd like to give a testimonial

PASTOR. thank you sister Jenny

CONGREGANT. I'm gonna read if that's okay

PASTOR. that's fine

CONGREGANT. (*She reads from a piece of paper.*)
Pastor Paul.
Sister Elizabeth.
I really wanna just thank both of you,
you two have been such a blessing to me and my family,
which right now,
consists really of just me and my son, Donny.

Over the past seven or so years you and this church family
has been there with me through some pretty tough times.

When I got divorced, you and your associate pastors
counseled with me.
And when my husband refused to pay alimony,
you helped us get food stamps.
You let us use the church clothing bin,
so that my son would have new clothes to wear
when school starts in the fall.

And when I feel sad and like I'm gonna collapse,
it does something for me to walk into this building,
there's a spirit in the building that is really something special,
like the spirit of God is in this place,
and it makes me feel like I can go on one more day.

It's been really great to sit here and listen to the testimonials that church
members have delivered in response to your sermon.
They said some really beautiful things.

and you know…

I've been thinking a lot about the sermon you preached,
and I think what you said about this church,
and the walls of this church, how we've built up walls,
how we have cut ourselves off from the world.

And what you said about distance and communication,
and what you said about Hell,
how the Bible says, in a lot of ways, that there is no Hell,
and that through Christ all are saved,
and yes,
all of that makes sense.

It makes me really sad that people left the church because of what you preached.

Some of those who left are really close friends of mine.

Those friends—I feel like they look at me differently than they used to look at me.

I call them up, ask them to get coffee with me, and they don't.

They're too busy.

And before they hang up, they say they're praying for me like there was something wrong with me.

PASTOR. ...sorry to hear that, sister Jenny

> (She nods, almost inaudibly says "thank you," maybe off mic. WIFE might even hand the CONGREGANT a Kleenex. She continues reading.)

CONGREGANT. an' it makes me feel judged and bad
and I think this is the thing you were trying to fix with your sermon,
but in some ways it made it worse.

> I don't know how to respond to them.
> when they ask me questions that I don't have answers to.
> A lot of us are getting asked a lot of the same questions from the people who
> left and went to the new church that Brother Joshua started.
>
> They point to other Bible verses where it doesn't sound like Hell is just a trash dump.
> Like for example, there's one where Jesus talks about your soul being burned in the thing you're calling a trash dump and it makes me wonder if it's a real trash dump then how does it burn a soul. It's as if you have a choice about how to read it.
>
> And my kid asks me questions, about how what we believe could just so suddenly change. And when he asks me, then I get nervous because I see myself as leading him. I pick the church we go to, and so in a way I'm really responsible for his soul. Our lives are hard enough already, I don't need to be jeopardizing the spiritual well-being of my son.
>
> And then this guy I was seeing, a guy I met last November in singles group, just last week he left and went to Brother Joshua's new church. He's been asking a lot of questions.
>
> I try to defend you when he asks me about it,
> He says things like well if there's no punishment
> why should we be good?
> And I say, we are good because we know that's right,

because if we're just being good because we're scared of getting in trouble,

that's not really being good.

And then he says, but if there's no punishment for being a sinner, isn't that a slap in the face to those who are good?

But then I'm like, that's not our problem—worrying about whether or not other people are getting punished.

PASTOR. I think that's a very good answer, Jenny, I

CONGREGANT. (*Takes the mic in her hand.*)

And then the guy, he asked me:

> what about someone like Hitler,
> if there's no Hell,
> then what about him.
>
> Where does he go?

That's a real question—I'm asking for an answer.

PASTOR. …

CONGREGANT. …

PASTOR. …

CONGREGANT. …

PASTOR. so

now see

if all are saved through Christ

all

then so is Hitler, so must even he be

Hitler is in Heaven.

The thief on the cross next to Jesus is in Heaven,
     Hitler is in Heaven,
          and everyone in between,
          and everyone who comes after.

CONGREGANT. see now, that's hard to swallow, I think,

PASTOR. if there is no Hell

CONGREGANT. can't he just go nowhere?

PASTOR. But then you have to figure out where the line is, how do you draw that line?

CONGREGANT. but according to you, it sounds like God doesn't even draw lines.

PASTOR. no yeah I don't think He does

CONGREGANT. What you're basically saying is that if someone were to murder my son

PASTOR. yes

CONGREGANT. and the murderer dies

PASTOR. yes

CONGREGANT. then both my son and the murderer would be in Heaven together.
And me too, when I die, all three of us
like a like a big happy family

PASTOR. ...yeah

that's right

But I mean...

think about it

wouldn't that be Heaven—?

CONGREGANT. no

PASTOR. a place where everything that was awful about earth is gone, where the wrong that one has done is washed away

isn't that Heaven?
Wouldn't you want that too: no matter what you've done, it can all be washed away?

CONGREGANT. I can't imagine it, that Heaven

and if I can't imagine it, I can't believe it,
and if I can't believe in Heaven,
then that makes me feel lonely
and scared.

PASTOR. ...But

why?

CONGREGANT. Why what?

PASTOR. I just...I don't understand
      your need to—
      please don't take this the wrong way but
      I don't understand why Heaven should be imaginable.

I think I would be disappointed if Heaven were something I
could imagine,
because what I can imagine is pretty dull, it's pretty uhhh
imaginable. I want the Heaven
        that my mind cannot fathom,
        that is better than what my human brain can handle.
I want a God who doesn't think like a man,
        who isn't as small-minded as I am,
        who is, in a way, unearthly and inhuman.
Because I'd be pretty scared and feel pretty lonely
if God were so
            imaginable.

                    You see?

                    So my advice to you
                    is to be patient.
                    To sit with it.
                    To pray.
                    To have an open heart.
                    And the understanding
                            will come.

                    Okay?

CONGREGANT. Okay
PASTOR. Thank you, Jenny.
CONGREGANT. just

        one other thing I don't understand
            (*She won't look* PASTOR *in the eyes.*)
another thing the guy I was seeing said to me.
And I didn't like that he said it
but it stuck with me
and it left me wondering why
you preached that sermon when you did.
He said he just wondered why,
you did this after,
            just after
the church paid off its debt.
It just seems that—he said, he thought—the timing
seemed too convenient.
That if you had done this before the church was paid off
and people had left, then you'd be in a bad spot.

And he said he feels taken advantage of

PASTOR. I never

CONGREGANT. and he, he feels like you took our money.

PASTOR. no

CONGREGANT. he wanted to know—I'm going back to reading here—

> (*She reads.*)

why you did what you did when you did it,
because he thinks that what you said about Hell
couldn't have been something that just occurred to you,
that you must have known for a long time
that Hell is Greek for trash dump,
that you didn't just figure that out,
which means you had this thought,
but had been preaching something different—
which seems to me kinda like lying sorry to say that—
and then you suddenly decided
that once the church was paid off,
you could risk losing money,
and tell us what you really thought.

Is that it?

PASTOR. ...

CONGREGANT. ...

PASTOR. I don't think I ever really talked much about Hell in my sermons

CONGREGANT. because you never believed in it to begin with?

PASTOR. ...

CONGREGANT. ...

PASTOR. I had questions, I had doubts about it.

CONGREGANT. So why didn't you tell us that earlier

PASTOR. what would I have said?

CONGREGANT. that you're not certain about certain things we believe

PASTOR. would that have made you feel better, to hear me get up here and say that I don't know?

CONGREGANT. I just can't help but feel used, Pastor Paul, I don't have much money, I give 20% every week, I live on food stamps and out of clothing bins, and it's a big deal, I don't do the minimum 10%, I go over that, because this church is really important to me and giving to God is important, and there's so much that me and my son have had to do without because of it.

PASTOR. ...

CONGREGANT. ...

PASTOR. I'm sorry

CONGREGANT. for what?

PASTOR. that you feel the way you feel.

I'm sorry.

CONGREGANT. ...

PASTOR. can we

can the church help you in some way

CONGREGANT. how? I don't—

PASTOR. give you some money, some assistance

CONGREGANT. why?

PASTOR. you seem to be under the impression that I'm preoccupied with money, and I'd like you to understand that I don't care about the money, that I don't—

CONGREGANT. are you trying to pay me off?

PASTOR. No, no, not at all the idea is to

CONGREGANT. why—is it guilt?

PASTOR. to show appreciation for what you've given, the idea is to give back a blessing

CONGREGANT. What I want is for you to tell me the truth

PASTOR. I am.

CONGREGANT. no lying—not in this church, not at this pulpit

PASTOR. I don't.

CONGREGANT. this business about Hell, would you have brought it up, before the church was paid for?

PASTOR. God had—

CONGREGANT. ...

PASTOR. ...

God had not yet told me to deliver that message

CONGREGANT. so you're saying you never thought about how that sermon could maybe make it so the church wasn't paid off, you're telling me that you never worried about it, never crossed your mind.

PASTOR. ...

CONGREGANT. ...

PASTOR. no, I'm not saying that.

CONGREGANT. ...

PASTOR. I do make decisions based on what's best for the church. I try to make decisions based on—I think about what the congregation is ready for, and when they're ready for it

CONGREGANT. how do you know what I'm ready for and what I'm not ready for, what gives you that—

PASTOR. in my heart—I felt that we needed to overcome one hurdle before we took on another—and I do think about—it's not just about me—we have a board of directors—they handle the business of the church—I don't—and it's an enormous burden, right Elder Jay?

ELDER. ...

CONGREGANT. I just want a good answer is all,
because that guy I was dating,
he made a lot of good points,
and I don't know what to say back to him.

PASTOR. ...

CONGREGANT. ...

PASTOR. ...

CONGREGANT. (*Off mic.*)
you gonna say anything?

PASTOR. ...

CONGREGANT. ...

PASTOR. (*Maybe half off mic.*)
I I I see how you um—

CONGREGANT. ...

PASTOR. ...

> (*And the* SILENCE *goes on for a bit.*
> PASTOR *is awkward.*
> *Maybe there's hemming and hawing here.*
> *And it goes on a bit.*
> *And maybe the Choir leaves, or portions of the Choir leave.*
> *But* JENNY *stays.*
> *But then she lowers her head, she nods.*)

CONGREGANT. okay, I guess I'm gonna go.

PASTOR. ...

CONGREGANT. ...

PASTOR. ...

> (*And she goes...*
> ELDER JAY *stands and exits.*
> *And then the Choir Director goes, too.*

And then the Choir.
PASTOR *turns back and looks at his* WIFE, *regards her.*
Long pause.)

PASTOR. and I look at my wife and I say

hey

    (*Pause.*
    WIFE *takes a microphone.*)

WIFE. hey

    (*Pause.*)

PASTOR. I say

how're you holdin' up there?

WIFE. I'm not sure

PASTOR. she says

WIFE. I think more people just left our church

PASTOR. and she says

WIFE. maybe

PASTOR. she says

WIFE. maybe it's not such a good idea to talk about Hitler.

PASTOR. And we lie in bed
and I think, and she asks

WIFE. what are you thinking

PASTOR. and I say

I'm thinking
about that woman

WIFE. what woman

PASTOR. that woman Jenny, the woman who

WIFE. thinking what about her?

PASTOR. ...Did she go to your Women's Bible Study group?

WIFE. she did

PASTOR. and she had all those questions

and it sorta made me wonder if she ever asked you
any of the questions she asked me,
and made me wonder if you ever tried to answer those questions,
and if you did, I found myself wondering what you said
to try to answer those questions.

I'm not suggesting you did anything wrong, or any of what happened was
your fault

WIFE. oh no, I know

PASTOR. I'm just curious.

WIFE. No.
She never asked me any of those questions.

PASTOR. and have others—?

WIFE. have others what—?

PASTOR. asked those questions or similar questions
to the questions Jenny asked—
have other women in your Women's Bible Study group,
ya know, since I delivered that sermon,
have others come to you with
similar questions
and concerns?

WIFE. Yes.

PASTOR. And what do you tell them?

WIFE. I tell them that if they have questions about something you've said,
then they should ask you,
not me.

PASTOR. oh, okay

WIFE. Because I don't want to put words in your mouth

PASTOR. oh sure,
thank you, I, no, yeah, that's—I appreciate that,

but I was also thinking,

maybe you could—

I wouldn't mind if you

fielded some of those questions, I wouldn't take it as you putting words in my
mouth, I think it helps to hear answers coming from you,
not just from me, it shows
that we're in this together.

WIFE. right

PASTOR. and you're such a gifted communicator

WIFE. thank you

PASTOR. because

what Jenny said, kinda got me thinking about the role women play in our
church, and really, in a larger sense, in the family.

WIFE. okay(?)

PASTOR. because ya know, they're the ones who actually keep the family on track in all things spiritual: How they get the family to church, and guide the husbands and the children, telling the family when they sense something is wrong. The family does what the wives say.

WIFE. oh is that necessarily true—?

PASTOR. I think so

And I think
if you were to speak
to the women in your group,
it could do a lot to help,
to help them see the value
in what I'm talking about.
I think it could help keep
more people from leaving the church—
it's startin' to feel sorta like our church has sprung a leak

WIFE. you want me to help plug up the leak

PASTOR. I could help you, prepare a message for you,

show you the verses that will help them understand

what I'm saying.

WIFE. ...but what if it's better that the people who are leaving just go ahead and leave

if they're not inclined to go along with the change

PASTOR. I think they just don't understand the change

WIFE. what is there to understand?

PASTOR. I don't want people to leave

WIFE. there were some you wanted to see go

PASTOR. of course not

WIFE. you were happy to see Joshua go

PASTOR. okay well

WIFE. you've been wanting him to leave for a long time,
you and Joshua had been preaching different things.

PASTOR. it was a problem that needed fixing

WIFE. and those 50 who sided with him,
those 50 who sided with Joshua,
you were also happy to see them go.

Come on now, admit it.

PASTOR. in order for a tree to grow
some pruning is necessary.

WIFE. an amputation so that the rest of the body doesn't get infected.

PASTOR. yeah, it's sorta like that.

WIFE. you're saying that absolute tolerance requires intolerance of the intolerant

PASTOR. in some cases yes.

WIFE. So—

... what if I were to tell you,
that when the offering plates went around,
the little piece of paper I put into the plate
said Joshua,
and not Paul

PASTOR. ...

WIFE. ...

PASTOR. ...

WIFE. ...

PASTOR. is this a hypothetical question?

WIFE. no.

PASTOR. oh

WIFE. ...

PASTOR. ...

WIFE. Should I be amputated as well?

PASTOR. uh, no

WIFE. are you sure about that

PASTOR. yes

WIFE. Because I believe in Hell.
I believe in the Devil.
I believe that believing in Jesus,
believing that He's the son of God,
and believing that He died for your sins
is the *only*
the only thing that can earn you a place in Heaven.

PASTOR. Why didn't you tell me earlier that you disagreed with my sermon?

WIFE. Why didn't you tell me earlier that you were going to deliver that sermon?
Why didn't you tell me that you were going to forcibly
change

what our church
believes?

PASTOR. ...

WIFE. In your sermon you talked like you had been struggling with this
message,
tormented,
but you never told me any of that.

PASTOR. I don't normally check my sermons with you

WIFE. And I think it's kind of too bad that you don't.

I think what you did
was actually
incredibly selfish

PASTOR. selfish?

WIFE. yeah

PASTOR. how???

WIFE. You haven't thought about
how what you're doing affects other people

PASTOR. Everything I'm doing is about other people.

WIFE. What about me? What about our daughter?

PASTOR. what about her

WIFE. you know that most of her classmates go to this church

PASTOR. okay

WIFE. and some of the parents of some of those classmates
talk about you in front of their kids.
And the kids come to school,
tell her that her daddy is going to Hell.
Did you know that?

PASTOR. no

WIFE. and she doesn't know what to do,
she wants to stand up for you,
but doesn't know how.

PASTOR. How would I have known about that?

WIFE. if you just opened up your eyes and paid attention to the people
around you

PASTOR. you hide things from me. All the time you—

WIFE. you never consulted with me,
never told me that you were struggling with something.
that tells me, I'm not on the same level as you.

You don't see me as someone you would talk to about the things you're thinking,
that I'm just the preacher's wife,
that I just sit in the background,
just nod my head,
and support you in every decision you make.

I'm not that kind of preacher's wife

PASTOR. no, I know you're not.

WIFE. I think you figured that if I experienced your amazing sermon
with the rest of the church, I'd be all swept up with all the rest of them,
and just buy into it on account of your own magnificence.

PASTOR. I don't think I'm magnificent

WIFE. But Paul, it didn't work on me,
and for those for whom it did work,
your magnificence is starting to wear off.

PASTOR. and she says

WIFE. It feels so
strange, that
almost overnight,
you don't have the same beliefs as me.

PASTOR. Our beliefs are mostly the same

WIFE. no, no they're not

PASTOR. and she says

WIFE. and I wonder what else you believe,
that I don't believe,
that I don't know about yet,
that would scare me to know you believe.

And when will I find out about that.

And then I wonder if someday you'll convince me of what you believe.
And then I sit here and I think about me,
a version of me, say, two years from now.

And she believes what you believe,
and she believes what I don't believe, not right now.
I think about that future "me,"
and I think about that future "me" thinking about the "me" I am right now.
That version of me thinks I'm stupid for thinking what I think now,
but also,
I'm here thinking that she's so wrong,

and I don't want to think something so different from what I think now…

…because there's a slipping that happens.

PASTOR. and she says

WIFE. I feel so alone right now,
because where you are is so different from where I am

PASTOR. I'm sorry
I'm sorry
You're right
I should have told you
I think I…

WIFE. Here's the deal:

The way I see it, I have one of two options.
My sister said I could stay with her
indefinitely, I figured I could go there
our daughter would come with me, we'll go for a visit,
and then figure out from there where to go,
what to do.

Or,

I stay

PASTOR. well I think that's the option I'd prefer

WIFE. and I continue the Women's Bible Study

and preach what you're not preaching.
Use my ministry as a, I dunno, a platform
a pulpit, not sure what to call it—
for correcting what you're saying,

PASTOR. correcting?

WIFE. balancing things out, I guess.

　　　　(*Pause.*)

PASTOR. seems like that would tear apart the church even worse than it already is.

WIFE. …

PASTOR. What do I do—? what do you want me to do—?

WIFE. what I want you to do
I don't want you to do because I want you to do it.
I want you to do something
because you want to do it,
because you believe it,

and I think that *is* what you're doing now,
and that's the problem.
PASTOR. I'm doing what I think God has told me to do.
WIFE. me too.
PASTOR. Do you still like me?
WIFE. ...I do still like you.
PASTOR. Do you still...find me attractive?
WIFE. I do.
...Do you still find me—?
PASTOR. Of course
WIFE. you
PASTOR. yes
WIFE. well that's nice—
PASTOR. you're very attractive—
WIFE. good to know.

But

But I wish I didn't
I wish I didn't like you
I wish I didn't find you so attractive
I wish I didn't want you here in bed beside me
I wish I didn't think that you're so smart
and kind
and good
And I wish I didn't find you so magnificent
Because if I didn't feel all those ways
It would be so easy to—

I'm worried that we won't be together forever,
and I'm worried that it'll be my fault,
and God will say—when it comes time to say the things He'll say—
"Why did you fail him?"
"Why did you let him fall away?"
"Why did you not do everything you could to keep him from falling away?"

And so this is me, doing everything I can do,
but really, I'm afraid to do everything that I could do,
but I know I have to do everything I can do,
because I want to be with you forever.

By staying with you, I am making it easier.

Aren't I?
It would be harder if I weren't here.
PASTOR. ...

> (*She takes her seat on the stage.*
> *Enter the* ASSOCIATE)

ASSOCIATE. They say

they say that people don't attend the church anymore
PASTOR. attendance went down
ASSOCIATE. They say your wife is leaving you.
PASTOR. where did people hear that?
ASSOCIATE. they say your daughter is having a rough time at school
PASTOR. she's doing better
ASSOCIATE. They say the church has gone back into debt
PASTOR. we've hit a rough patch
ASSOCIATE. unable to pay for its staff
PASTOR. I've been paying folks out of my own savings
ASSOCIATE. unable to pay for the lights
PASTOR. okay well—
ASSOCIATE. They say—

The church's Board of Elders—they said to me "will you come back"
I said I don't want to come back
they said "please think of coming back"
I said no way
they said "no,
no, we're not asking you to come back as Associate Pastor
we're asking you to come back
as Head Pastor."
PASTOR. ...When did this happen—?
ASSOCIATE. A couple of days ago.
They said don't tell Paul,
I said, "so you haven't said to him what you said to me?"
They said, "No."

I said that's not right.

I said, "I don't feel comfortable discussing this
if he doesn't know what I know."
I said it feels like I'm going behind his back.

I said, "I'm gonna tell him."
They said, "Don't."
I said nothing.

I thought you should know.
          (*Pause.*)
PASTOR. Are you going to accept?
ASSOCIATE. What would I be accepting?

The people who stayed here wouldn't have me.

You have characterized me
as being hateful ·
as being judgmental
as being

a bad Christian.
PASTOR. no, I don't think I have
ASSOCIATE. many people have told me
PASTOR. I...never speak specifically about you
ASSOCIATE. I walk down the aisle here,
and the people who stayed
look at me with a look that says I am not welcome here.
PASTOR. I think that's all in your head
ASSOCIATE. You've made it out to sound like
what I believe is a cartoon Hell
with cartoon Devils,
pitchforks and

well when you make it look like that,
it's hard to take what I say seriously.

You make it sound like what I want is to see people punished.
PASTOR. well do you?
ASSOCIATE. You make it sound like I *want* to believe there is a Hell.
PASTOR. I think you're choosing to believe in it
ASSOCIATE. choosing
PASTOR. yes
ASSOCIATE. It's not easy for me to believe in Hell.
PASTOR. Are you sure about that?
ASSOCIATE. I think for you, being a Christian is easy.
PASTOR. no, it's hard, it's really—

ASSOCIATE. Your parents were Christians,
your parents' parents—
your grandmother took you to church,
          everyone wanted to see you saved,
          and for you, you had nothing to lose
          by believing what you believed.

     But ya know, I lost everything.
     My parents—they didn't believe
         in what I believe.

     I tried. Again and again, I tried
     to bring them to Jesus,
     wanted nothing more,
     right up until the end,
         I tried.

     So that my mother, when she died,
     I was there in the hospital,
     standing by her side,
     telling her about Jesus,
     telling her what Jesus did for me.
     I asked her, please please
     hear what I have to say,
     open your heart, just a little.

     And she said, "Baby, I don't like how you sound when you preach at me,"
     she said, "When you talk Jesus talk, you don't sound like you."
     And I said, "That's cuz I'm filled with the spirit."
     And she said, "No it's just creepy is all."

     And there at her side,
     while she's all hooked up to machines,
     I prayed for her,
     And she said to stop,
     and if I didn't she'd have the nurse take me away.

     I said this is your last chance.
     I said, "Mama, listen:
     any moment now, you're gonna go,
     and when you do,
     I will never get to see you again."
     I said, "In the coming age, after I have also left this earth,
         if you die a believer

we will be reunited,
and we will live together in eternity."
I said, "Mama, don't you want to see me again?"
And she said, "Yes, baby, yes, baby,
of course, I want nothing more."

And I said,
"Then just say you believe, say it with me
I believe in Jesus, and I believe He died for my sins, say it with
me."
and she said

"I would like to say I believe,
but if I did it would be a lie"

I said,

"But maybe that's enough—
Say you believe in the hope that as you say you believe
you will believe
and maybe you'll truly believe."
And she said,
"Honey, I am going, I am leaving this earth,
and I will not spend my final breath,
sayin' a damn lie."

and she said, "When I close my eyes,
my eyes won't open again.
And when I close these eyes,
I'll see black,
and there will never again be
anything but."

And I said please please please.
And she said nothing.
And in a couple of seconds her eyes would close...

But before her eyes closed and closed for good,
there was a moment,
a moment that was terror,
dread,
pain—
our eyes connected, and she saw me seeing her
fall,
and at that moment, her hand reached out
and grabbed my wrist, like she was grabbing for help.

It's not easy for me to believe there is a Hell.
It doesn't make me feel good to believe there is a Hell.
In fact, it hurts, because I know,
          every day,
that I will never see my mother again,
and if I do, it will be me, high above her,
          looking down,
          seeing her suffer,

                    for the rest of eternity.

An' I wonder sometimes—Pastor Paul—if my Heaven will be a
kind of Hell.

PASTOR. ...
ASSOCIATE. so just

show me.
PASTOR. ...
ASSOCIATE. Show me.

Show me.

Show me that there is no Hell, show me, don't play word games with
the Bible, show me and and

and I'll come back to this church, not as a head pastor but as your
associate and I'll support you and your message, just show me that
what I saw I didn't see
because when my mother died, I did—I saw it—

I saw it, I felt it, I saw first hand
what Hell looks like
And nothing can take that away from me
so that when I look at the Word of God,
all I can see
is the truth that, yes, Hell is there
waiting for us.

So what business do I have
preaching the *possibility* that it doesn't exist.
I'd be leading hundreds,
          thousands,
                    into Hell
while setting aside for myself something even worse

for bein some kinda
     false shepherd.
...

PASTOR. I can't show you the absence of something.

ASSOCIATE. well then,
there we have it.

PASTOR. he says

ASSOCIATE. I'm not accepting the offer

PASTOR. he says

ASSOCIATE. the Elders will have to find someone else to take your job

PASTOR. he says

ASSOCIATE. I've got my own church now

PASTOR. I hear it's doing really well

ASSOCIATE. we hold services in a
YMCA

PASTOR. the one on on

ASSOCIATE. Maple Drive

PASTOR. not a bad spot

ASSOCIATE. the bathroom situation could be better,
and the microphones they've got there
tend to give a lot of feedback.
But I make it work

PASTOR. I bet you do

ASSOCIATE. I tend to just use my own voice instead.
It carries.

I'm praying for you, brother.
          (*Exit* ASSOCIATE
          And then...)

PASTOR. fewer people in church this week than the last.
     this year fewer
          and next year even fewer.

I wonder

     I wonder

          might be a time,
                    when

          there are no more Christians.

And will people believe what we believe
    100
        1,000
            10,000 years from now?

Many religions have died.

                        now—why do I believe what
                        I believe

I believe what I believe because I know it is true—but why do I know it's true?—it's a feeling. And where did that feeling come from?—God. God put it there—but how do I know it's God that put it there?—I know it's God because I believe God is there—but how do I know God is there? because there's a feeling He put inside of me—but

What if I were different?
What if I had a different family
and were raised differently,
not taken to church…?
       But I was taken to church, and
I had the family that I had
and they raised me to believe that the feeling I feel is from God,
       but what if this—?
       and what if that—?
       but no—what didn't happen didn't happen
           because God made it that way.

WIFE. …

PASTOR. I have a powerful urge to communicate

       but I find the distance between us

              insurmountable.

WIFE. I think back to me
    and my younger self
    on an airplane flight from California to Florida.
I think back to the handwritten note
    handed to me by the stewardess.
I think back to me
    looking back
    up the aisle,
    and seeing a handsome man waving at me.
And I think back to me
    in that moment

    hearing a voice that sounded like God
    saying that's the man
    you'll spend the rest of your life with.
But sometimes,
    sometimes it's really hard
    to really know
    which voice is God
    and which one is your own wishful self.

PASTOR. Be patient with me,
and stay a little longer.

WIFE. My bags are packed.

PASTOR. They can stay packed.

WIFE. We're losing the church

PASTOR. which means you're all I have.

WIFE. We might not be together forever.

PASTOR. Then shouldn't we spend together what time we know we have

WIFE. ...

PASTOR. Don't worry about trying to figure it out now.
It will make more sense later.

WIFE. ...

    (*Lights out.*)

End of Play

brownsville song
(b-side for tray)
by Kimber Lee

ABOUT *brownsville song (b-side for tray)*

This article first ran in the January/February 2014 issue of Inside Actors, *Actors Theatre of Louisville's subscriber newsletter, and is based on conversations with the playwright before rehearsals for the Humana Festival production began.*

"He was not." These are the words that echo through the beginning of *brownsville song*, Kimber Lee's poignant and lyrical new play. They come from Lena—an African-American woman near sixty who lives in the Brownsville neighborhood of Brooklyn, who works two jobs without enough hours in her day, who raises her grandchildren as if it's the most important thing she could do in this life. Because it *is* the most important thing in her life. And as this play begins, Lena is in pain. One of those grandchildren, Tray, has just died, shot in a senseless altercation. Lena knows how his death will be reduced to a footnote, and she refuses to allow it. Because he was not a statistic, just another eighteen-year-old claimed by the streets. Tray was the glue that held their family together; he was the rising amateur boxer, the promise of a better future. So over the course of a sorrowful and bristling speech, Lena honors her grandson as best she can, with a three-word refrain that defies all easy narratives: *"He was not."*

This monologue's jarring, insistent assertion—that a young man's life matters, that people should feel something about this loss—was precisely Kimber Lee's impetus to create *brownsville song*. "I was supposed to be writing something else," she recalls. But after she read a blog post written by a female boxing coach at a Brooklyn gym, Lee found herself circling this idea. "She had written about this kid that they lost at the gym," the playwright recalls. "He was visiting his grandmother in Brownsville, and it was one of those things where he was caught in the middle of a fight that had nothing to do with him, and he died. It wasn't a super-long post, but the way she described him so gently, it stuck with me."

As she looked into this story further, Lee grew increasingly disconcerted by how little attention the media paid to this tragedy. In fact, aside from a few brief mentions in the local news, his death seemed barely to have registered. "There was no outcry, there were no marches," the writer continues. "So when I sat down to start writing, that first speech that Lena has just kind of came out. It was a feeling of pressing against this massive wall of silence, that this young man's death didn't matter, that it had disappeared from anyone's consciousness except for his family and loved ones. And it's part of a bigger thing, too, that there are certain neighborhoods, in our cities and our communities, where if a young black male gets shot, everybody thinks,

'Well, that's what happens there.' As if the loss of a life is somehow just the norm if you look a certain way and live in a particular kind of place."

Yet while *brownsville song* may begin with a grief-stricken call to honor a young man's passing, this is not a play built around absence. Indeed, what makes Lee's elegy extraordinary is how *alive* it is. It glides back and forth between now and memory, moving through kitchens and bedrooms still pulsing with Tray's presence. It shows us Tray's love for his little sister Devine, his forgiveness for those who have hurt him, and his ambition to continue his education in college. Through dozens of gracefully observed, delicately rendered moments, this play celebrates a young man at the center of a loving family. Because Lee so skillfully animates both before and after, always keeping us in an emotional present tense, Tray remains this story's beating heart. He doesn't haunt this play; he *inhabits* it.

Though a tragedy launches this tale, what may be so unusual about the world of *brownsville song* is that it's not unusual at all. Lee describes the neighborhood that her characters occupy with refreshing simplicity: "It's families living there, trying to get by with what could seem like insurmountable obstacles. But they're just people trying to put the food on the table, get the kid out of bed, get him dressed, get him to school, doing all the things that all of us do." Lee takes these small, everyday gestures—attending a child's dance concert, or asking for help with a difficult essay—and mines them for great meaning. "This is a place where violence can enter at any moment," Lee notes, "but it's also a vibrant place."

Lee even reflects that sense of vitality in how she titles her drama—as a *song*, not a story. "There's such a musicality and a hum and rhythm to life in Brooklyn," the writer remarks. "So it felt right to have the title be some kind of musical thing." And the play's subtitle takes this idea one step further. "The b-side is always the song that nobody's heard," she continues. "It's the one that people aren't talking about." Yet while some songs may be forgotten, Lee crafts a memorable composition that implores us to remember. This play begins by telling us what Tray was not. But it proceeds to make a more powerful statement: This young man *was*, and beautifully so.

—Steve Moulds

BIOGRAPHY

Kimber Lee's plays include *fight, tokyo fish story,* and *brownsville song (b-side for tray),* which premiered at the 2014 Humana Festival and will also receive 2014-2015 productions at LCT3, Long Wharf Theatre, and Philadelphia Theatre Company. In May 2014, Center Theatre Group presented the world premiere of her play *different words for the same thing* directed by Neel Keller, and *tokyo fish story* will premiere at South Coast Repertory in March 2015. Her work has also been presented by Lark Play Development Center, Page 73, Hedgebrook, Seven Devils, Bay Area Playwrights Festival, TheatreWorks (Palo Alto), the Old Globe, Magic Theatre, Great Plains Theatre Conference, and Dramatists Guild Fellows Program. Lee is a Lark Playwrights Workshop Fellow (2014-2015), member of Ma-Yi Writers Lab, and is currently under commission at Lincoln Center Theater/LCT3, South Coast Repertory, Denver Center Theatre Company, Long Wharf, Hartford Stage, and the Bush Theatre (London). She is the recipient of the 2014 Ruby Prize, the 2013-2014 PoNY Fellowship, the 2014-2015 Aetna New Voices Fellowship, and the inaugural 2015 PoNY/Bush Theatre Playwright residency in London. She holds an M.F.A. from the University of Texas at Austin.

ACKNOWLEDGMENTS

brownsville song (b-side for tray) premiered at the Humana Festival of New American Plays in March 2014. It was directed by Meredith McDonough with the following cast:

LENA	Cherene Snow
DEVINE	Sally Diallo
TRAY	John Clarence Stewart
MERRELL	Jackie Chung
JUNIOR/ BROOKLYN COLLEGE STUDENT	Joshua Boone

and the following production staff:

Scenic Designer	Dane Laffrey
Costume Designer	Connie Furr Soloman
Lighting Designer	Ben Stanton
Sound Designer	Jake Rodriguez
Stage Manager	Stephen Horton
Dramaturg	Jacqueline E. Lawton
Casting	Nora Brennan Casting, Zan Sawyer-Dailey, Meg Fister
Movement Director	Hattie Mae Williams
Properties Master	Jay Tollefsen

Associate Scenic Designer	Scott Tedmon Jones
Production Assistant	Suzanne Spicer
Directing Assistant	Betsy Anne Huggins
Assistant Dramaturg	Sam Weiner

brownsville song (b-side for tray) was developed with support from the Lark Play Development Center, the 2013 Seven Devils Playwrights Conference, and the 2013 Bay Area Playwrights Festival (a program of the Playwrights Foundation, Amy L. Mueller, Artistic Director).

CHARACTERS

LENA. Black. Late 50s – early 60s.

TRAY. Black. 18 years old.

DEVINE. Black and Korean American. 9 years old.

MERRELL. Korean American. 36 years old.

JUNIOR. Black. 18 years old.

BROOKLYN COLLEGE STUDENT. Black. Early 20s. Played by JUNIOR actor.

SETTING

late spring, mid-summer, and late summer of the same year.

various locations in and around the Brownsville and East Flatbush neighborhoods in Brooklyn, NY.

note: the fluidity of time in the play should be embodied in the fluidity of the staging; in whatever way the transitions are accomplished, they will be most effective for the story if they are actor-driven and in rhythm.

A FEW ITEMS

things in parentheses are not meant to be spoken, just thought

line breaks *usually* mean a new thought, an interrupted thought, or a turn in the same thought but do not *always* require a pause

"pause" means a brief silence

"silence" means a slightly longer pause

pauses or silences in this play are not negative space, they are held moments where the internal activity of the character arcs into the external world – they hold the space of a thought just as a rest in a musical score holds the space of a note

A NOTE FROM THE PLAYWRIGHT

The aliveness of the play lives in the rhythm and flow of the language, which includes the syncopation of the pauses and silences. Those spaces should be just as full and driving forward with the need of the characters as the words, and if the pauses are honored, they will do good work for you.

Because the story pivots around a deep loss, there may be a tendency to sink into that emotion, but this should be resisted. The scenes, even the ones after Tray's death, must drive forward, as we all must do in life even in the midst of heartbreak. Especially for Merrell, a healthy measure of trust that the depth of feeling is present, and simply saying the words to get the job done will be most effective. Merrell presents a dual challenge: to stay present and purposeful and strong, without sinking into regret and pain or playing her angry or defensive – dry humor is a useful tool.

*

Although the reality of loss is currently an unfortunately frequent part of life in the neighborhood, it is important to know and remember that Brownsville is a vibrant, hopeful community filled with people fighting for change.

It is my hope that any production of this play would express the light, humor and resilient humanity of the Brownsville community, and not add weight to their struggle by presenting the neighborhood as only a dark, dangerous place where violent things happen – they are sadly accustomed to being stereotyped in this way in the media. But as we have seen in recent years, our collective failure to stem the tide of gun violence has spread beyond the borders of any particular neighborhood, and so the challenges and pain of the Brownsville community belong to all of us, no matter our zip code, and with every loss, we are all diminished.

This play is dedicated to the Brownsville community in gratitude for their tremendous heart, courage, humor, and relentless hope in the face of sometimes overwhelming circumstances.

"Before I go back to the Heavenly Father
Pray for me if it ain't too much bother
Whatever don't break me a-make me stronger
I feel like I can't take too much longer
It's too much lyin, and too much fightin
I'm all cried out 'cause I grew up cryin
They all got a sales pitch I ain't buyin
They tryna convince me that I ain't tryin
We uninspired, we unadmired
And tired and sick of being sick and tired
of livin in the hood where the shots are fired
We dyin to live, so to live, we dyin
You just like I am…"

—The Roots, 2010, "How I Got Over"

"The sea rises, the light fails, lovers cling to each other, and children cling to us. The moment we cease to hold each other, the moment we break faith with one another, the sea engulfs us and the light goes out."

—James Baldwin, 1964, "Nothing Personal"

Sally Diallo and John Clarence Stewart
in *brownsville song (b-side for tray)*

38th Humana Festival of New American Plays
Actors Theatre of Louisville, 2014
Photo by Bill Brymer

brownsville song
(b-side for tray)

[LENA]

> *Twilight darkness.*
> *Periodically, headlights slide onto the walls, stretch sideways, and swoop away.*
> *Dim lamplight around* LENA, *sitting in a chair, and a dim rectangle of light*
> *through a doorway behind her.*
> *She leans slightly forward, chin out, listening to see if she really heard what she*
> *just heard.*
> *Which she did.*
> *She leans back.*
> *Her lips curl slightly – not a smile, but like one.*

LENA. No

> *(She shakes her head slowly.*
> *As she speaks, her rage mounts, but she keeps it in check with deliberate and*
> *measured speech.)*

Do not begin with me
Do not start your telling with me
Trust me
It ain't the way you want this story to begin
Not here
Not with me
Nah
Y'all ain't want my

I got words crowdin up from my belly
through my neck
shovin my mouth into the same shape
formin the same out loud thought over and over
HE WAS NOT
HE WAS NOT
HE WAS NOT
I just
I been scooped out like a jack o lantern
Carved up and
emptied of every thought but one

He   was   not
> (*Beat.*
> *She breathes.*)

Nah now
Listen
This ain't what you wanna put in fronta people right from the jump
they ain't tryna hear all this shit
all this all this
all THIS comin at em
It's too much it's it's
ain't *comfortable* and what they gon do
what should they do
stop eatin dinner turn off they TV call somebody
why
what
who the fuck they gon call and for what
what is there they gon do about this shit
They don't know me
They don't know Tray
It's too much
You ain't say these kinda things at the beginning
I'm not the beginning
I'm the end

> (*Her throat closes around her words.*
> *She presses her lips together again.*
> *She breathes.*
> DEVINE *enters, a small skinny silhouette in the doorway behind* LENA.
> DEVINE *clutches a small, worn New York Jets football-shaped pillow, and*
> *we may not be able to see her clearly, but her focus is fixed on* LENA *like a*
> *laser sight.*)

LENA. I am so
You know I got a like a
On my back a
thing
There's some
thing
Got a
a uh weight to it
Dig into my ribcage every step I take every hour of the day
Drippin scratchin on my skin with its red saliva
Writin his name over and over
Those letters just be burnin through to my bones

burning me with *why*
and *he knew better*
and *didn't I say to him*

     (*She presses her lips together, glares.*)

And what is this
Huh
What is this to you
Same Old Story huh
A few damn lines in the paper
A split second a some poor old woman
Wringin her hands and cryin on your evening news
And then
Nothing
and the truth
Aftermath is damn boring and grief be a tedious muthafucker
And you gon go on to the next one or whatever you gon do
walk-a-thon
cookie push
pour ice water on your damn head
Same Old Story so you gon feel bad and move on
Cuz he just another
Ain't he
To you

he was not

Whatever rest my words been havin before
Whatever home they made of this world
They be wanderin the wilderness now
Repeatin that hollowed out refrain
why   why   why
He ain't been in a gang
He ain't run with no crew
He ain't beef with nobody
He was not

And what he is

     (*Pause.*
     A jagged breath.)

What he was

     (*The rage begins to breach her control — she struggles, gets it in check.*
     Her telling about TRAY *starts quietly, her love and joy in him insistently*
     showing through, but the heartbreak overtakes her by the end.)

He was goin to college this fall
He was a Golden Gloves Champion
He was savin up for a car
My cousin Ronda's old Mazda Protege
He was workin nights and weekends and he just got his one year raise
He was goin to the dentist next week and get his first filling
Eighteen years old and never hadda cavity
You ever met a boy that age got that kinda dental hygiene No you ain't
He was a back talker
He was a terrible liar and semi-reliable bout everything but his baby sister
and boxing
He was a mule when he dug in
I tried to break him a drinkin out the milk carton for all eighteen of his years
and for eighteen years that boy snuck round me and drank all my damn milk
and for eighteen years
He was not the same old story
he was mine
he was mine
he was mine

> (*Rage and grief choke her.*
> *She clamps her mouth shut, glaring through tears but not crying.*
> *She breathes.*
> DEVINE *slides silently into a sitting position, huddled against the doorframe,*
> *still holding tight to the pillow.*)

LENA. So don't begin your telling with me
It don't begin here where I sit shook stupid
Start with him please
Start with Tray

> (*Beat.*
> LENA's *jagged breathing.*
> *Sound of cars whooshing by, headlights sweep the wall to:*
>
> *Blackout.*
> *Sounds of a school hallway, bells ringing, noise of kids going to class.*)

[DEVINE]

> *Fourth grade classroom.*
> DEVINE *enters, carrying a paper.*
> *She reads softly, overwhelmed with nervousness.*

DEVINE. My Friday Feature Family Member Be My Brother Tray
by Devine
My brother Tray like many sports
Some sports he like be football and boxing and such
This be his New York Jets souvner football

> (DEVINE *looks up and out, listening to the teacher.*
> *She gives a little nod, says it again.*)

This *is* be his New York Jets soovenner football

> (*She looks for the football, can't find it.*
> *She panics a little, freezes up.*
>
> TRAY *appears, upstage in shadow.*
> *He pops a deuce and poses.*
> DEVINE *turns and sees him, relief and joy flood her little body.*)

Tray

> (*Light shift.*
> *Sharp, angular, blue-white light shafts in from the sides, sculpting the stage into*
> *a dream space:*
>
> *This is* DEVINE*'s World.*
> *It doesn't exist entirely inside her head, it corresponds in sound and shape and*
> *boundaries to the "real world," but light and weight and time run on a different,*
> *parallel track here.*
>
> *Some kinda Brother Sister Dance:*
>
> TRAY *moves rapidly, in a fluid, arcing line around* DEVINE, *surrounding*
> *her, sketching in the lines of her world.*
>
> *He takes out the New York Jets football pillow.*
> DEVINE *smiles.*
> *He teaches her the proper way to throw a football.*
> *They play catch.*
> *He makes her hold it for him to kick.*
> *She shies away when he runs toward her, drops the football.*
> *They argue.*
> *She tries to hold it again, but cringes away at the last second.*
> *He turns his back, walks away.*
> *She goes absolutely still, the way you would if a wild animal jumped in your path.*
> *A loaded beat.*
> *He places a gentle hand on her shoulder.*
> *Something passes between them, silently.*
> *They breathe together.*

He moves back and they resume their game of catch.
He moves back.
He moves back.
He is swallowed by the shadows.
She throws the ball.
It falls to the ground where TRAY *was standing.*
She walks over and picks it up, looking for TRAY, *confused.*

Lights shift.
LENA *crosses left to right downstage,* DEVINE *watches her, clutching the football.*
Like a movie screen wipe, LENA *brings the light/scene shift with her to:)*

[SUTTER & RALPH AVES]

LENA's *kitchen.*
TRAY *sits at a table in a chair that seems too small for him.*
A beat-up outdated laptop is open on the table, but TRAY *is focused on his cellphone.*
In the other room, LENA *works out to a reggaeton Zumba DVD playing at low volume.*

LENA. Tray

TRAY. (*Still looking at phone.*) Yo

LENA. I ain't hearin no damn typin out there

TRAY. I'm thinkin

LENA. How bout you put your think on the damn computer keys

TRAY. Aight

LENA. *Tray*

TRAY. Aight yo calm down

LENA. Boy I know you did not just tell me to *calm down*

TRAY. Sorry sorry
Ima get it done

LENA. You better

ZUMBA DVD VOICE. "You're warmed up now
And Talisha is ready to blast your quads
Let's
Get
BUMPIN"

(TRAY *clicks on the laptop, cell still in the other hand.*
He scrolls through a document, lips moving slightly as he reads silently.
He types with two fingers.
He types, deletes, types, deletes.)

TRAY. (*Mutters.*) Awww man
fuckin fuck muthafuckin
fuuuuuuuuuuuck

(*He looks at his cell.*
He gets up and shadowboxes for a few seconds.
He looks at the screen, sighs heavily.
He types again.
He reads it, he groans in frustration and runs a hand over his face.
He looks up at the clock.
His cell beeps, he looks at it.)

TRAY. Shit

(*He texts rapidly.*
The Zumba DVD shuts off abruptly.
LENA *enters, wearing a fuschia and orange track suit, wiping her face with*
a towel.

TRAY *hurriedly flips his phone shut and pockets it.*
LENA *glances at him, gets herself a glass of water.*
TRAY *closes the laptop and starts to exit.*)

TRAY. Welp
Ima get on

LENA. Not so fast my boy
Let's see it

TRAY. I ain't done yet

LENA. Then where you goin

TRAY. I got boxing

LENA. Not til you finish that shit you ain't

TRAY. Come on Grams
I do it when I get home
For real
I only got the last part left to do and I gotta
I gotta think on how to end it right

LENA. Sit your ass down

TRAY. Man

LENA. Read me what you got

TRAY. Aw shit Grams come on

LENA. Now just who you think you talkin to
Watch your damn mouth

TRAY. Psshhh

LENA. Go ahead now

TRAY. FINE THEN

> (TRAY *goes to the laptop, brings up the document.*
> *He glances at* LENA.)

Now
Keep in mind
This a rough draft yo

LENA. Uh huh

TRAY. I ain't done yet

LENA. I heard

TRAY. So you gotta
you know
Withhold and shit

LENA. withhold

TRAY. Judgment

LENA. Psshh

TRAY. And that includes blowin ya nose air at me like you do

LENA. Blowin what now

> (TRAY *makes a disdainful, airy nose snort at her.*
> *She throws her towel at his head.*)

Oh go on

TRAY. Now later on
when I got time I

LENA. Boy what you talkin bout
"When you got time"
It's time right now

TRAY. No I gotta go
I told you

LENA. Oh you *told me*

TRAY. I mean
I just now explained to you that I gotta be at boxing
Remember
We got Metros coming up right

LENA. Metros

TRAY. Yeah Metros
Boxing tournament

Grams come on
You signed the dang release forms for me two months ago

      (LENA *struggles to remember, he watches her closely.*)

TRAY. Alla coach's schedules and permission slips
You ain't remember alla that
We sat right here and

      (LENA *waves her hand at him.*)

LENA. Aright aright aright

TRAY. (*Are you okay.*) You remember

LENA. (*Shutup.*) Look here
Ima tell you again and believe me when I say
You miss another one a those scholarship deadlines
Ima mess you up good boy

TRAY. I know I know
Dang
Grams comin up all thug life right here in the kitchen

LENA. Oh lord child
Sometimes you ain't make no kinda sense

TRAY. Yo all I'm sayin is
Hugs Not Thugs

LENA. Boy

TRAY. Just Say No Grams

LENA. Back up now

TRAY. Only You Can Stop The Cycle Of Violence

LENA. I'll cycle you

      (*She playfully bats him on the head, he laughs.*)

Quit your stallin

      (TRAY *sighs.*)

TRAY. Okay

LENA. Okay

      (TRAY *clears his throat.*
      He reads.)

TRAY. My name is Tramaine Berry Thompson

      (*She blows her nose air at him.*
      He looks at her.)

LENA. (*Covering her blunder.*) Well now
That's a good start Tray
And a true fact

      (TRAY's *cell rings.*)

Boy don't you (dare)
>   (TRAY *flips his phone open.*
>   LENA *glares at him.*)

TRAY. (*Into the phone.*) Yo

Yeah I'm here I

Nah nah
Hold up
>   (*He glances at* LENA *who makes a point of not giving him any privacy.*
>   *He turns away, lowers voice.*
>   LENA *watches him like a hawk.*)

TRAY. I told you
Ima be there

No I

Yeah

Yeah

Aight then
>   (*He flips his phone shut.*
>   LENA *stares at him, he won't meet her eye.*)

LENA. (*Tell me that wasn't who I think it was.*) Tray
>   (*Silence.*
>   LENA *shakes her head.*)

Uh Uh
Mm Mm
Do NOT

TRAY. Okayokayokay
Come on it ain't what you thinkin
I just got a uh
a
I made a promise

LENA. To who
>   (*Beat.*)

To WHO
>   (*Silence.*
>   LENA *presses her lips together, stands, and begins making dinner loudly.*)

TRAY. I can't uh

Grams come on

LENA. We ain't havin this again my boy
Not again
And you know I mean what I say

TRAY. (*I know your worries and Ima be fine, I promise.*) I know
I do
I know

>   (*Silence.*)

Grams
It ain't what you thinkin
I swear it ain't

Grams
Hey come on Grams

>   (*She looks up at him fiercely.*
>   *She reaches out suddenly, he slips to the side (boxing reflexes), she waits for him*
>   *to come back up (grandma reflexes), grabs his face, holds it firmly, looking into*
>   *his eyes.*)

LENA. *Not you*
Okay

TRAY. Okay

>   (*She hugs him, sudden and tight.*
>   *She shoves him toward the door.*)

LENA. Now get outta my kitchen
I ain't tryna make dinner with your overgrowed hulk ass in the way

>   (*He kisses the top of her head, goes into the front room, gathers his boxing gear*
>   *quickly.*)

Don't forget
Devine gon be down the hall at Miss Coles' classroom
cuz today creative dance day
aright Tray

Tray

TRAY. I got it
I'm gone

>   (*He grins and exits.*
>
>   *As the lights shift, street sounds from the block fade up:*
>   *Cars whooshing by, distant subway rattle and hum, car horns, baby crying,*
>   *shouting and laughing, cell phones ring, car alarms, slap of plastic sandals as*
>   *kids run past, shop doors open and close, boom of subwoofers in passing cars, and*
>   *at least three different languages can be heard.*

LENA *goes to the window and watches him walk down Ralph Avenue toward the subway.*

We hear TRAY *walking down the block, passing a group of dudes on the corner, hear* JUNIOR *calling out to him.*
TRAY *enters with* JUNIOR.
They stop and talk, and though we can't hear them, there's an exchange that ends with TRAY *shaking his head.*
Laughing, good-natured shoving back and forth between JUNIOR *and* TRAY.
TRAY *says his goodbyes, smiles and continues down the block.*
JUNIOR *calls after him.)*

JUNIOR. YO
WHAT I SAY
YOU GOTTA GET PAID T

(TRAY *keeps walking, flashes a deuce behind him without turning or breaking pace.*
Subway sounds get closer, overtake and drown out the other sounds as the train passes in a rush of clacking air and squealing brakes that take the lights with it to:

Blackout.)

[DEVINE]

In the darkness, a solitary oboe plays the first phrases of "Flight of the Swans" from Swan Lake.

DEVINE's *World – lights up on a fourth grade classroom.*

DEVINE *enters, crosses a few feet, and stands holding her arms out at angles – she's a tree by the lake of swan tears.*

Shadows flap past behind her – her classmates, the swans.
They dance in the lake of tears.

DEVINE *watches the teacher carefully, bobbing her head slightly with the beat, then on cue, moves her arms in a small, vaguely tree-like way in time with the music.*

At first, she is nervous and stiff, eyes latched onto the teacher.
The shadows of her swan classmates flap around her.

After a few repetitions, she starts to move more freely with the music.
DEVINE *sees the teacher gesture for her to move less so she pulls back, but the music gets into her and slowly, her body pulls her into a dance.*

Lights up on TRAY, *in the boxing gym.*
He jumps rope, light feet.
The beat of the rope on the ground is in perfect time with the music.

A hip-hop beat surfaces through the music, threading through the Tchaikovsky, a duet of rhythms flowing back and forth.

TRAY*'s feet dance with the rope as he jumps.*
DEVINE *dances her tree dance, throwing a little more flavor on it.*

Music builds.

DEVINE*'s dance expands, becomes more urgent.*
Thunder over the lake of swan tears.
She dances away from the classroom, out of the school building.
Rain of swan tears starts to fall.

TRAY *stops roping, breathing hard.*
He goes to his gym bag, takes out his cell phone and checks it.
Lights down on TRAY.

DEVINE *keeps dancing, her feet splashing through puddles.*
The music builds to a BOOM – *subwoofers vibrate in a passing car.*
At the boom, *the shadows of her classmates flap loudly up and away, like a disturbed flock of pigeons, leaving* DEVINE *alone and confused on the school playground.*
Rain falls.
DEVINE *notices she is soaked, she shivers.*
She walks to a bench and sits.
She waits.
It grows later, sky turns from grey to navy blue.
Rain falls.
Another car passes, subwoofers booming.
Neon signs from the neighborhood flicker on.
Sounds flare up suddenly, filling the air: arguing voices approach, horn honks, the hiss of car tires on wet pavement.
The arguing voices get closer, louder.
DEVINE *gets under the bench.*
The voices pass.

A car swooshes past and lights shift from playground to:

[FLATBUSH GARDENS BOXING GYM]

> *A small neighborhood boxing gym.*
> *A floor ring, heavy bags, speed bags, slip ball, gym clock.*
> *It's early in the afternoon, the gym is quiet.*
>
> TRAY *sits on a folding chair, clicking on his cell phone, gym bag at his feet.*
> MERRELL *enters, sees him, hesitates, then crosses to him.*

MERRELL. Tray

> (TRAY *looks up.*
> *Loaded beat, they take each other in slowly.*)

Been a long time
You look
God you got so ah

tall

> (*Silence.*)

How's the boxing going
Does the

TRAY. You late

MERRELL. I know
I

TRAY. Coach told me you was straight with all your shit
Wasn't gon be none a this or that
We set a time
Boom
You gon be there

MERRELL. I just
Had a
Thing
with my Metro Card I

TRAY. Yeah
Always somethin ain't it

> (*She looks at him.*
> *He raises his eyebrows and looks away.*)

MERRELL. Yeah

> (*Pause.*)

I am really
so grateful to Ray for
and to you
for letting me come in here and I

If you don't wanna do this with me
I get it

> (*Slight pause.*)

TRAY. Still here ain't I

MERRELL. Okay
Real sorry about being late
It won't happen again

> (TRAY *nods, but doesn't look at her.*
>
> *Pause.*
> MERRELL *takes a deep breath.*)

Tray
Before we um
I wanted to tell you

TRAY. Nah
I ain't need to hear all that

MERRELL. But I do want to
um
I owe you an apol

I owe you so much and

TRAY. Ayo
what I say
I ain't tryna go into alla that
That's your trip lady

MERRELL. I know but I

TRAY. Are you gon help me

MERRELL. Just
I'm really

TRAY. You supposed to be helpin me
So we gon put in work or what
Cuz if not I got me some places to be yo

MERRELL. Okay
yes
okay

TRAY. And yo
I don't know what you thinkin bout what we doin here but
Don't get it twisted
You gon slide back up in here this way
We keepin it all business
You my Flatbush Gardens volunteer tutor

That's it
Anything else you got in mind
You gon have to go through Grams and you know it

MERRELL. I do
I know
I know

> (*Pause.*)

I wasn't trying to to

> (*Pause.*)

Yes
Yes I was trying
I didn't mean
Not anything bad I just
It seemed like a
The best way

TRAY. Nah I get it
You scared a Grams when she fired up
You and everybody else on the eastern seaboard but look yo
I can't give you none on this
You know I can't
and you know why

> (*Pause.*
> MERRELL *takes a couple of deep breaths, nodding.*)

MERRELL. Yeah
Sorry

> (TRAY *shrugs.*)

No really
I am
I was wrong

> (*Pause.*
> MERRELL *tries to keep herself from going to pieces.*
> TRAY *watches her through narrowed eyes.*)

TRAY. Yo
Ain't the only one ever been that

> (*Pause.*)

D is fine
Doin good

> (MERRELL's *head snaps up, she looks at him gratefully, reaches a hand toward his arm.*
> *He does not return the warm look, leans away from her hand.*)

TRAY. (*Without malice, business-like.*) She ain't none a your concern neither

And Ima take your help cuz coach told me
But you best adjust your
If you gotta idea bout some kinda vibe be ready to jump off
You think you still get to be Devine's mama or
Some "good ol' days when we was a family" shit gon come back and
fill up space between Then and Now
Nah
That be burned up dead space
Ain't nothing breathin there and
truth
She ain't thought a you any more than I thought about my mama after she left
So
We gon be like strangers Merrell
or even
Less than strangers cuz I ain't know what a stranger do
But you
I seen in action

     (*Pause.*)

So if we understandin the situation here
We can get on with it
If not
I go ask coach to get me another tutor

     (*Pause.*
     She nods.)

Aight then

     (*Silence.*
     MERRELL *gets a folder out of her bag.*
     She sits next to TRAY, *opens the folder and takes out a printed copy of his*
     rough draft essay, a single page.)

MERRELL. Okay
Let's take a look
I printed out what you sent me and

TRAY. Whoa whoa whoa
Hold up
I thought you was just gonna do it

MERRELL. You
what

TRAY. Yeah I mean
You said on the phone

you was like
MERRELL. I said I was gonna help you
TRAY. Yeah but
MERRELL. What do you think that means
TRAY. I dunno
I tell you some shit and
You gon put the
you know
Lay down the actual words
MERRELL. Uh yeah
No
TRAY. Come on
Still gon be my words right
MERRELL. Tray
TRAY. So what it gon matter bout
exactly who did the exact
putting of the words
MERRELL. Because it does
TRAY. Psshh
MERRELL. The scholarship committee
They wanna hear you
Your voice
TRAY. my what
MERRELL. They wanna know who you are
TRAY. What
No
School counselor said
Just talk about goals and accomplishments and shit
Make it sound
you know
Slick
MERRELL. Phony
TRAY. Yeah
MERRELL. No
TRAY. Man
MERRELL. That's not
TRAY. what
MERRELL. Look
They go through stacks of these essays

They don't wanna read a resume
you know what I mean

TRAY. psssh

MERRELL. They wanna know who you are
What your dreams are
How this scholarship is going to help you achieve your uh
you know
Do what you wanna do

TRAY. That shit ain't none a they business

MERRELL. If you want their money it is

(*Silence.*)

Look this doesn't have to be a
There's a way to use this essay to show them
what sets you apart from other people
Why you need this scholarship
you know
You gotta

TRAY. beg

MERRELL. What

TRAY. Get down on my knees like a good boy
Make sure they feelin good bout
helpin a poor negro chile from the ghetto

MERRELL. Well
not
I mean not exactly
but
It's not going to hurt for them to understand where you come from
The challenges that you've

TRAY. I ain't feelin that yo

MERRELL. I don't mean uh
I just think you can

TRAY. Nah I know what you sayin
And I ain't tryna play up some bullshit
talkin bout
"oh Ima poor black boy from the violent ghetto"
That ain't my life
Ain't gon be my life you understand

MERRELL. Good and
This is a chance to tell them that

(*Slight pause.*)

TRAY. Aight then
>   (TRAY *looks at his cell phone.*)

MERRELL. So
How do you think you might start

TRAY. (*Distracted, looking at his phone.*) Start

MERRELL. What's the first thing you'd like them to know
>   (*Pause.*
>   TRAY *shrugs, looks at his cell.*)

Tray
>   (*Pause.*
>   *She hands him the copy of his essay.*)

I am not going to write this for you

TRAY. man
whatever
>   (*Silence.*
>   TRAY *looks down at the paper.*
>   MERRELL *rubs her face, sighs.*)

MERRELL. Okay
Forget all that for a sec
>   (*She takes a deep breath, resets.*)

MERRELL. So um
How's boxing
You're getting ready for Metros coming up right

TRAY. Yeah

MERRELL. And Ray says you did real well in the Gloves last year
even though you lost in the finals
>   (*Pause.*)

TRAY. I guess
>   (*Pause.*)

MERRELL. So
What happened
Ray said you had some trouble in the first round
>   (*Pause.*)

TRAY. I got injured

MERRELL. oh shit

TRAY. Yeah uh
you know it was
that summer I was ten and we went to Zadie Miller's birthday party at Underhill
remember I tweaked out my right knee playin basketball

Well in my first fight
Dude was real short and thick
just walkin straight into me every time and
mostly I caught him with short hooks and straight rights when he came in
but one time
we got in a clinch and
muhfucka stepped on my foot and just
leaned alla his weight onto me
and pop
I felt that old knee go
and the rest a the bout
Every time I stepped left it was like a knife

MERRELL. Ray said he could see the pain on your face in the corner
Then at the bell
You walked right back out there like it was nothing

TRAY. Yeah
I guess

MERRELL. How'd you keep yourself goin

TRAY. I dunno

MERRELL. Tray
Come on

TRAY. Nah serious
I ain't even know
I just

I ain't wanna quit
Ain't wanna go out like that

MERRELL. I remember that about you

       (*Slight pause.*)

First time I came home with your pop
First time I met you
You were just a little kid but you had this uh
Weird inner strength

TRAY. what you talkin bout
weird

MERRELL. Well yeah
For a kid that age to have that kind of
If you fell and hurt yourself you didn't cry and wail
And once you started something
A puzzle   A coloring book   A Lego house
you never gave up on it

And you didn't throw tantrums you
You did this thing where you uh
You'd go find a place
Like behind that big green chair we had
and you'd just sit
Silent
until you got over it
You never complained
You were a little man

>(*Silence.*
>MERRELL *watches him, he looks away.*)

TRAY. nah

>(*Pause.*)

I mean I guess I

Yo I just put it some place else
I don't dwell on it cuz
you know
If they a job to get done
I gotta get it done yo
Ain't no use be always thinkin on pain cuz
Truth
It ain't gon go away
and it ain't gon stop me

>(*Silence.*
>MERRELL *watches him, pained and proud.*)

MERRELL. I think that's a good thing to put in your essay

TRAY. What
boxing

MERRELL. Not just boxing
About how you keep going
I mean
For someone your age
There's a lot of really
difficult things you've had to deal with

>(*Pause.*)

TRAY. Nah
I told you
I ain't gon cry bout things can't be changed
Ain't gon let that shit fade me neither

My life is good
I got Grams and D

MERRELL. I'm not saying complain
It's more about
Dealing with obstacles

> (*Pause.*
> TRAY *checks his cell phone, sees the time.*)

TRAY. oh shit
I gotta get on

> (*He zips up his gym bag.*)

MERRELL. But

TRAY. I call you later

MERRELL. Okay but just
Here's your homework okay

TRAY. What
Nah man
I ain't tryna have no homework on this shit

MERRELL. Hey
You want this thing or not

TRAY. psshh

MERRELL. Look just
Don't think about it like you're doin it for them
You understand
Do it for you
What do you want people to know about you
Not words someone put in your mouth
Me or
your school counselor or Lena
But what you want to say
Not for them or for anyone else
For you
Tell them who you are

TRAY. yeah yeah okay

> (*He turns to go.*
> MERRELL *puts a hand on his arm.*)

MERRELL. I know I fucked everything up
I know I can never make it right
but

I wish

ah

No

All I want to say ah
I'm so proud to have known you Tray

> (*They lock eyes for a beat.*
> TRAY *nods at her and exits.*
> MERRELL *sits again.*
> *She takes a deep breath, and on her big exhale:*
>
> *Lights shift to school playground.*)

[DEVINE]

> DEVINE *crouches under the bench.*
> *Heavy footsteps approach – pounding, urgent.*
> TRAY *runs onto the playground.*
> *She watches him from under the bench.*

TRAY. D
aw dammit
Yo D
you out here baby

D

> (TRAY *scans the playground desperately.*
> *He spots her.*)

TRAY. (*Under his breath.*) shit

> (*He crosses to the bench, gets down on his knees.*
> *He looks at her face, which is perfectly blank.*)

Oh god D
I

> (*She doesn't move.*
> *He swears at himself again, quickly under his breath.*
> *He speaks to her as if calming a frightened horse.*)

It's okay mami I'm here
You okay now
It's me
come on baby

> (*He holds out a hand.*)

Come on D
please
I straight fucked up today boo
I know it
But we gotta go home now
and
We gon make us some grill cheese and tomato soup
and you gon do your Dora worksheets for school and and
you gon get your bath and your fuzzy orange jammers and
we gon go find that dang Waldo on page 12 and then
oh yo
When Grams come home from work tonight
she said y'all gon talk about your swan dance outfit
get your swan dance on
and
come on baby girl
I'm here now
You okay now
please

> *(She nods.*
> *She takes his hand and crawls out.)*

TRAY. Shit
you just soakin mami
hold up

> *(He takes a clean t-shirt from his gym bag and towels her off with it, then takes*
> *off his jacket and wraps her in it.)*

Sorry bout bein late
I ain't mean to I
shit
I just
am so sorry
for real D

> *(He looks at her.*
> *She looks back, the blankness almost gone.*
> *They breathe together.*
> *She nods, he nods back.*
> *He puts his bag over his shoulder and holds out his hand.*
> *She takes it.*
> *The world around them shifts slightly: softer, muted, the light warmer even*
> *through the drizzle.*
> *They walk home.)*

TRAY. So how was your day kid

DEVINE. I ain't a swan

TRAY. You
what now

DEVINE. Ain't a swan

TRAY. Right

DEVINE. Ima tree

TRAY. (*What are we talking about.*) A tree

DEVINE. Yeah
Ima be a weeping willow

TRAY. (*No idea what we're talking about.*) Oh word

DEVINE. Yeah
Ima stand over the Lake of Swan Tears

TRAY. You gon
Oh yeah yeah okay I got you
This for your afterschool dance thing

DEVINE. Ima be a weeping willow
by the Lake of Swan Tears
Get it

> (*Slight pause.*
> TRAY *does not get it.*)

DEVINE. *weep*ing
*will*ow
lake of
tears

TRAY. Got it
You gon be a
Wait
Hold up
You gotta be a *tree*

DEVINE. Yeah

TRAY. What the other kids

DEVINE. They the swans

TRAY. (*That's fucked up.*) And you a *tree*

DEVINE. Yeah
I do like

> (*They stop walking.*
> *She does her tree pose – she throws a little swagger on it.*)

And the swans

they be doin like

> (*She waves her arms, sketching in the swans flapping around and past her tree, excited to be showing him the dance.*)

TRAY. Nah nah

That's fucked up man

DEVINE. (*Confused about what he means.*) Well

but cuz

TRAY. Why you gotta be the tree

> (DEVINE'*s face falls.*)

DEVINE. I

dunno

> (*Pause.*
> DEVINE *pulls nervously at the loose hem of her t-shirt.*
> TRAY *realizes what he's done, kicks himself silently.*
> *They keep walking.*)

TRAY. Yo

Tree's da bomb sister

> (DEVINE *shrugs.*)

For real

A tree's like

Trees is whassup

They be all

makin oxygen and shit

> (DEVINE *ignores him.*)

You gon be the flyest tree anybody ever did see

> (DEVINE *ignores him.*)

Come on girl

Show me that tree move again

> (DEVINE *keeps walking.*
> TRAY *stops.*)

Aight then

I do it

> (*He strikes a silly tree pose.*)

Whassup

> (DEVINE *looks at him, sniffs disdainfully, looks away.*
> *He strikes another pose.*)

Whassup yo

kumbayah you swans

check me out

(DEVINE *looks, can't help herself.*)

DEVINE. Trees ain't be talkin fool

    (TRAY *moves through a series of tree poses as she watches.*)

Tray

You ain't doin the

No like THIS

    (*She shows him the pose.*)

TRAY. Ohhh

I got you

    (*They do it together.*
    TRAY *adds a little dance.*)

Unh unh

I be

A dang tree

Is you lookin at me

unh unh

and when you lookin at me

yo what you think you gon see

not a bee or a flea

unh unh

just a dope ass tree

And nah I don't ski

Cuz Ima damn tree

    (*She laughs.*)

Oh you gon laugh at me

Now you got laughs huh

Aight that's it

    (*He makes a play swipe at her.*
    Her hands come up, she goes into a boxing stance.
    He swipes again, she slips to the side.)

TRAY. That's real good mami

You remembered good

Now slip both ways

and come up with your hook and right hand like we did before

    (TRAY *throws a soft one-two at her, she slips right, then left, then comes up*
    with a left hook and straight right hand, punching into TRAY's *open palm.*)

Pretty slick girl

Now show me that shuffle

    (*They do the Ali shuffle, circling each other.*
    She yells and rushes in, pummeling him with body shots, laughing.)

oh no
oh no
he's in trouble
she backs him up to the ropes with a flurry
aaaaaaa
he ties up

> (*He grabs her and lifts her over his shoulder.*
> *She laughs.*
> *He tickles her.*
> *A car passes, slows.*
> TRAY*'s eyes follow the car.*
> *He sets her down.*)

TRAY. Yo D
You wait here
Ima be right back

> (*She steps toward him, he stops her.*)

I ain't goin out your sight mami
Just a few steps over there aight
Stay here

> (*He exits.*
> DEVINE *watches him.*
> *A frown grows over her face as she watches.*
> TRAY *comes back, distracted.*
> DEVINE *stares at the car.*
> *He takes her hand.*)

TRAY. Let's go

> (*He pulls her, she walks slowly, her eyes still fixed on the car.*)

D
Come on
Come with me

> (DEVINE *still looks back toward the car.*
> TRAY *pulls her around, not rough but firm.*)

Hey
Look at me
D
Look at me

> (*She looks at him, the blankness is back.*)

TRAY. (*Don't stare at them, D, please don't stare.*) Everything aight D
hey listen

> (*He holds out his fist, looks straight in her eyes.*

She looks back.)

You know me

DEVINE. Yeah I know you

TRAY. Aight then fam

Gimme some love

> (*They do an obviously familiar tap/bump routine with their fists.*)

Come on

We goin home now

> (*He takes her hand, they keep walking.*
> *They make it to the corner of Sutter and Ralph Aves, right in front of* LENA'*s*
> *building.*
>
> DEVINE *slowly turns to look back at the car, and as she watches—*
> *The car pulls away, swooshes past, its headlights sweeping over* TRAY *like a*
> *searchlight.*
> *He lets go of her hand as the light sweeps over him, carrying him offstage like a*
> *tidal wave, his hand still reaching for hers and—*
>
> *Lights shift out of* DEVINE'*s World.*
>
> *Car sounds fade into the distance.*
> *Dim neon twilight.*
> DEVINE *stands by herself, still wrapped in* TRAY'*s jacket, still staring*
> *after the car.*
>
> *Distant sounds of car tires hissing on pavement, sounds of the block.*
>
> *Lights shift.*)

[SUTTER & RALPH AVES]

> LENA'*s kitchen.*
> *Two coffee mugs on the table.*
> LENA *sits across from* MERRELL.
> *Charged silence.*
> LENA *sips from her mug.*
> MERRELL *shifts in her seat, uncomfortable.*
> *Throughout the following,* MERRELL *has a hard time making eye contact*
> *with* LENA.
> LENA *does not have this problem and seems to get something (satisfaction?)*
> *from drilling* MERRELL *with her gaze.*

MERRELL. Do you uh
mind if I smoke

LENA. What you think

>   (MERRELL *raises a wry eyebrow, nods, and looks away.*
>   *Silence.*)

MERRELL. If this is a bad time I
I could come back

LENA. No need

>   (*Silence.*)

MERRELL. You sure

LENA. What I say

MERRELL. Yeah but
Seems like maybe it's
Not a good
you know
time

>   (LENA *just looks at her.*
>   MERRELL *lets out a breath, trying to alleviate her nerves.*)

So ah
Subway stop got that summertime smell
you know

LENA. Mmhm

>   (LENA *sips her coffee.*)

MERRELL. Was on the job hunt for months and
man
Pretty rough out there so it's uh
It's a relief to be working again even though it's ah

You
You still working at that insurance office

LENA. Asked me that already
Answer same as it was five minutes ago

MERRELL. Sorry I
sorry

>   (*Silence.*)

This wallpaper new or

>   (LENA *just gives her a look: "For real Now you gon talk to me bout*
>   *wallpaper"*)

not

>   (*Pause.*)

Lena
I wanted to tell you
ah
I am so sorry about Tray

LENA. (*Quiet, firm.*) No

MERRELL. what

LENA. You in my house
You can keep his name out your mouth

MERRELL. Lena

>   (LENA *sips her coffee.*
>   MERRELL *looks down, picks at her sleeve.*)

I know
What right do I have
but
At one time
he was like my

LENA. Don't you (dare)

MERRELL. You think I'm not sick about it
Blamin myself

LENA. What

MERRELL. what

LENA. What you say
You *blamin* yourself

MERRELL. I should have (been here)

LENA. You don't get the privilege of *blamin yourself*
You don't get to feel that his life had anything to do with you at all

>   (*Pause.*)

MERRELL. (*Quietly.*) I'm always gonna be grateful to him
Everything he did for
for me and
for D

LENA. Aright I heard
You said it
Now you can leave it alone

MERRELL. I'm truly sorry for your trouble

LENA. I said you leave it alone

MERRELL. Can't stop me grieving or
Or bein grateful to him
Just cuz you hate me

LENA. Ain't tryna stop you
But I ain't tryna hear you sayin his name
Like you a part of something to do with him
Like you been here for it
MERRELL. Yeah okay
I get it

> (*Pause.*)

Look
I know you don't want me here and
You probably wish I went ahead and died in that place but

> (LENA *leans across the table toward her.*)

LENA. Ohhhh
No no no now
You mistakin me grievous if you thinkin this somehow
personal or or
To do with you
I ain't got no quarrel with you missy
You gon handle your business how you do and I say
Go with god
Glad you found a new road and you gon have a new start and alla that
but hear me now
You takin a new road ain't change nothin that been
Ain't change nothin for her
Or Tray
Or me
Ain't no use for your turned over leafs in this house
And Ima tell you straight up same as I did before
The day you take that girl from me gon be the same day they lay me in the dirt
Ya heard

> (*Pause.*
> MERRELL *is very still.*
> LENA *sits back in her chair, sips her coffee.*)

Now
You got any other business with me
MERRELL. Lena please I just
LENA. Then I ain't gon keep you

> (LENA *takes both of the coffee mugs to the sink.*
> MERRELL *is very still again.*
> LENA *leans against the counter, watching her.*
> *Deeply awkward silence.*
> LENA *finally turns and starts washing dishes.*)

MERRELL *takes a deep breath, looks around the kitchen.*)

MERRELL. I used to have dreams about this kitchen
all those months in that pale green room at rehab
uh

So much happened and
So many years flew past but
in my dreams
Always right back here
            (MERRELL's *breathing becomes a little jagged.*)
I'm sorry I came here today
I didn't come cuz I thought I had a right
I didn't mean that
but
You get to a point where
You don't got a sense of
the direction maybe
You sit and stare and think
Where is the beginning of my wrongdoing
Are there footprints I left somewhere
a trail I can follow
back to the start and try to
Not fix anything
but stand
Stand and reckon with what I have done
            (LENA *turns and looks at* MERRELL.
            MERRELL *shakily meets her eye.*)
But I'm
This is not about me
or you
LENA. You damn right it ain't
MERRELL. I am not here to take anything from you
LENA. Oh don't you worry
You won't
MERRELL. I just want to see her
LENA. I'm sure you do
MERRELL. And
I can get other people involved
LENA. You gon do what you must
And that ain't change a thing my girl

MERRELL. Fact is
She is *my daughter*
LENA. Biologically
You are correct
But you are not her mother
MERRELL. *Lena*
LENA. *No*

> (*Pause.*)

You gave that away the day you left Merrell
The day you left her
The day you walked off and left her waiting for you
She said you told her Wait right here
So she waited
outside the goddamn Key Foods
She waited
Three years old she waited
all night
hiding behind a dumpster
waiting for you
and I ain't find her til the next morning
And do you know
when I hold out my hand to take her home she say
No
No Grams
My mama gon be right back
She say she gon be right back

I told her then
and I mean it now
That woman ain't your mama

> (*Silence.*
> MERRELL's *face is ashen, she can barely breathe.*
> *She nods, gets up, and exits.*
> *Sound of the front door closing.*
>
> *Cars, a bus whooshing past outside.*
> *Distant honking, dog barking.*
> LENA *leans against the counter, sunk in deep thought.*
> *She glances at the clock, her brow furrows.*
> *She crosses to her handbag, takes out a dog-eared day planner, flips a few pages,*
> *looks at the clock again.*)

LENA. oh lord

oh shit

Friday

> *(She grabs her jacket and handbag, looking inside for her keys, but she can't find them.*
>
> *She rifles through the handbag, finally emptying it onto the kitchen table.*
>
> *No keys.)*

Dammit

Ain't I just

have them I

no no no

They was right here

> *(She looks on the counters, she goes into the other room and we hear drawers opening and shutting, things being moved.*
>
> LENA *comes back into the kitchen, searches again, becoming more frantic.)*

I ain't take em to the

laundry room

did I

no

> *(She searches her own pockets again, her movements becoming more and more frantic.*
>
> DEVINE *enters quietly, still wearing* TRAY's *jacket.*
>
> *She watches* LENA, *who is rifling through a drawer.*
>
> LENA *turns and sees* DEVINE.
>
> LENA's *hand goes up and covers her mouth.*
>
> *She goes to* DEVINE, *kneels in front of her, putting a gentle hand on* DEVINE's *cheek.)*

LENA. Oh baby girl

you

Grams just lookin for her keys

I just had em I was

I

> *(DEVINE *runs into the other room, where she pulls the keys from the front door knob.*
>
> *She takes the keys to* LENA.
>
> LENA *sits in a chair heavily.)*

LENA. oh now

well I

Thank you Devine baby I

don't know why I ain't
find em my own damn self
I just ah

> (LENA *stares at the keys, confused, struggling.*
> DEVINE *watches her.*)

How did you get home baby

DEVINE. Tray walked me

LENA. Tray

> (*Silence.*
> LENA *struggles to maintain her calm.*)

Oh

> (DEVINE *sits at the table, starts taking things out of her pockets, stuff she
> picked up on the way home: a rock, a leaf, an empty toilet paper tube.*
> LENA *watches her.*)

Aright then okay
You home now
You home and that's

> (*Loud honking and shouting from the street outside.*
> LENA *places a gentle hand on* DEVINE's *head, kisses her head, breathes
> "I'm sorry" into her hair.*
> DEVINE *stills for a beat: something passes between them.*)

Aright
Ima just get alla this shit out the way
and we gon have some dinner right quick

> (*Pause.*)

You ain't walk home the back way

> (DEVINE *shakes her head.*
> LENA *drops a kiss on her cheek.*)

Good girl

> (*Clinking and clacking as* LENA *swiftly clears up the mess, then dumps some
> kinda pale casserole from a Tupperware into a pan to reheat on the stove.*)

How was your day

> (*Silence.*)

Everything go all right

> (DEVINE *shrugs, focused on the rock.*)

Well now
Startin off the school year ain't always so smooth
but things get better right
I saw your teacher from last year

What's her
Miss Miller right
She say she miss you kids from last year
You was a good class

Okay baby
You wanna set the table for us
>   (*Pause.*
>   DEVINE *doesn't respond.*)

LENA. Devine honey
>   (DEVINE *scoots down from her chair, and goes to the silverware drawer.*
>   *She sets the table throughout the following.*)

Oh
You know that Marcus and Bebe right
from the second floor
They mama be that young lady wears that big red hat
Ain't they in your class this year
>   (*Pause.*)

Yeah
I spoke with they mama in the laundry room and
What's her name
Shondra Mondra
whatever
She say it's a nice classroom
Y'all got big windows and
everybody get they own desk this year
You got a desk
>   (*Pause.*)

That ShondraLondra gal had her a bunch a stickers
She say the kids be decoratin they desk with
all kinda stickers
You want Grams to get you some
We go down the block to Family Dollar tomorrow
Gon get you some stickers and and
Gotta get that headband for finishin up your dance costume right
>   (LENA *turns and stops abruptly.*
>   DEVINE *has set three places at the table.*
>   LENA *steadies herself.*
>   DEVINE *looks between the table and* LENA, *stricken, unsure what to do.*
>   LENA *dishes up the casserole on two plates, puts the pan back on the stovetop.*
>   *She places a gentle hand on* DEVINE's *head, then she takes her seat.*)

LENA *eats slowly,* DEVINE *pokes at her food, sniffs it.*

DEVINE *stares at the third empty chair.*
A car swooshes by outside, headlights sweep the wall.

A dull thump, *sounds like it comes from the walls or the ceiling.*
DEVINE *looks up.*

Another thump.
DEVINE *looks at* LENA, *she doesn't seem to hear it.*

Another thump: *the front door opens and closes.*

Lights shift abruptly: the room feels suddenly warmer, somehow more cozy or full.
TRAY *enters, carrying his gym bag and clicking on his cell phone.)*

LENA. Hey
Shoes

> (TRAY *goes back to the door and kicks off his wet shoes.*
> *He comes back through the kitchen, distracted, avoiding* LENA's *eyes.)*

TRAY. Welp
Ima get a jump on my work yo
Later

LENA. Hold up

TRAY. what
I dropped her home
I just hadda go um
I had me some shit to do

LENA. You ain't gon have no dinner

> (LENA *gets the pan from the stove.*
> TRAY *glances at the pasty casserole, makes a face at* DEVINE *while*
> LENA's *back is turned.)*

TRAY. (*Oh man that shit looks scary.*) Ooooo uh
yeaaaah uh

> (DEVINE *giggles.*
> LENA *turns,* TRAY *grins sweetly at her.*)

Nah Grams I ain't really uh
I'm all good
Naveen gave me a samosa from the deli just now

> (*He swoops in and gives her a smothery, mooshy hug.*)

But thank you for makin this this
Whatever this is you be makin
And thanks for bein *you* Grams

For real
You just soooo

(*He mooshes her.*
She slaps his arm, laughs.)

LENA. Get off

(TRAY *exits.*
LENA *watches him go, suspicious.*
A rhythmic thump thump of music comes from his room.
LENA *sighs and starts to exit.*
DEVINE *gets up.*)

No Devine
You stay and finish your dinner baby
Ima be right back

(DEVINE *watches* LENA *leave the kitchen, taking the scene shift with her.*)

[LENA]

LENA *pounds on* TRAY*'s bedroom door.*
TRAY *opens the door and music tumbles out at a very high volume – maybe*
Nas, or Biggie, or Wise Intelligent.
A warm glow from a desk lamp.

TRAY. Whatup G
what you want

(LENA *barges past him and turns off the music.*)

Damn son
Slow down that heavy heavy roll

LENA. what you say to me

TRAY. I mean
I be listenin to that my good woman

LENA. You and the rest a the block
What's a matter with you

TRAY. What you mean
It ain't nothin but my school writin groove yo

LENA. And you know I ain't talkin bout no damn music neither

TRAY. I just doin my work like you said

LENA. The hell

(TRAY *grabs a notebook.*)

TRAY. Peep this woman
Workin on my damn scholarship essay is all

LENA. Good
Okay that's
Good

> *(She looks closer at the page.)*

What you
Hey
You talkin bout me in here

> (TRAY *grabs it away from her.*)

TRAY. Aight
that's enough a that

LENA. Lemme see what you sayin bout me

TRAY. I ain't done yet

LENA. Aw come on

TRAY. Grams
For real just
Leave off

LENA. I wanna see

TRAY. I told you
Ima show you when I get done

LENA. MmHm

TRAY. MmHm

LENA. Aright then
how bout you tell me

TRAY. What

LENA. I seen the way you slink in the door tonight
What you got goin on Tray

> *(Slight pause.)*

TRAY. Nothin

LENA. (*Amused.*) Boy you a terrible liar
you know that

TRAY. Yeah
So

LENA. (*Nah I ain't complainin.*) Oh it's been a blessin for real
On more than one occasion
Now
You gon tell me

> *(Pause.)*

Why you ain't eat no dinner
          (*Pause.*)
Ain't got nothin to do with alla them phone calls you gettin lately
Huh
Nothin to do with that huh
          (TRAY *shrugs.*
          LENA *watches him like a hawk.*)
Junior be draggin your ass into alla his bullshit again
Is that it
Told that boy Ima smack his ass to kingdom come
I ever catch him messin with you again

TRAY. Nah it ain't

LENA. He gon strut round the neighborhood
Actin a fool
Runnin his big fat toothy mouth

TRAY. Grams

LENA. Boy think he such a hard little rock now
Shit
He ain't *seen* hard til he gon see the backside a my good right hand
I go hunt down his ass this very minute
Wear him *out*

TRAY. It ain't Junior

LENA. Then what
Spill it my boy
          (*Pause.*
          TRAY *sighs.*)

TRAY. Okay but yo
You gotta promise you ain't gon go all
"Backside a your hand" on nobody
aight
          (LENA *mutters something.*)

Grams
Aight

LENA. FINE THEN
          (*Pause.*)

TRAY. Merrell's back
          (LENA's *face goes dangerously quiet and she sits on* TRAY's *bed.*
          Unseen by both of them, DEVINE *appears in the shadows outside the room,*
          listening.)

Came to see me at the gym
> (*Pause.*)

I guess
Coach Ray been talkin to her
and she tryna
She been outta rehab for
bout maybe eight nine months already
> (*Pause.*
> LENA's *jaw is very tight.*)

She ain't just walk in
she uh
Talked to Ray and cleared her shit with him
He makin sure she ain't
you know
Off on one a her things
but uh
She wanna help out so

LENA. MmHm

TRAY. Grams

LENA. So

TRAY. listen

LENA. She gon try work her way around Ray huh
What Ray know bout that woman

TRAY. I dunno
They old high school friends or some shit

LENA. Ray ain't know bout what happened

TRAY. Nah he does
I think
I dunno
> (*Pause.*)

She gon be my tutor I guess

LENA. Your what

TRAY. Yeah
Remember
Coach been tryna find someone
like a tutor or some shit can help with my college applications and

LENA. Oh and so he just *find* her then huh

TRAY. Well
She a teacher right

LENA. *Was*

TRAY. Was

LENA. Uh huh

And what you say bout alla that

>   (*Pause.*)

Tray

>   (*Pause.*)

TRAY. Coach say she all straightened out

LENA. Uh huh

And

>   (*Pause.*
>   TRAY *makes a noncommittal shrug.*)

So help me

TRAY. Come on Grams

LENA. Oh

So

You feel *sorry* for her and

Now you gon just let her back in the damn door

Is that right

What you think

You think she gon

>   (LENA *clamps her mouth shut over the words about to come out.*)

A leopard ain't change spots just by puttin on a sheep jacket my boy

It still be a *leopard*

TRAY. (*I have no idea what you talkin bout.*) yo that's

what

LENA. So you seen her then

TRAY. Yeah

LENA. What you tell her

TRAY. Nothin

LENA. You ain't say nothin bout D

TRAY. Grams

Come on

It's me

LENA. Nah but I know her

I know how she gon try and get round

Get what she want

TRAY. Yeah I heard

I been knowin her fore you did

LENA. So you ain't say nothin bout D

TRAY. I ain't tell her nothin
Except she gon have to come to you
she want anything to do with D

LENA. Aright

Aright then

> (*Beat.*)

TRAY. OH
yo I got you
"A leopard don't change its spots"
That's what you was sayin

> (LENA *gives him a look.*)

Aight nevermind

> (LENA *starts to exit.*)

Yo Grams
listen
I ain't tryna say nothin bout nothin

LENA. Then don't

> (*She turns to leave again.*)

TRAY. I know
what she been

> (LENA *stops with her back to* TRAY.)

I ain't ignorant a nothin that woman done
I been there for it

LENA. MmHm

TRAY. But I gotta
I dunno
I got a like a
I hadda thought

> (LENA *blows her nose air derisively.*)

Serious
I

> (*He takes a deep breath.*)

She tryna handle her business
That's all
And I
You know
I see her tryin
And I ain't sayin nothing to her

And I ain't sayin nothin bout what you gotta do
or nothin bout what gotta be done by nobody
but just

She ain't the only one ever
ever uh

LENA. Ever what

        (*Pause.*)

Ever what Tray

TRAY. Fucked up

LENA. Uh huh

TRAY. You know it
Around that time
We was all messed up for real
All of us
You me her Devine
I mean yo
The things I did then

LENA. You was a child
You was nine years old

TRAY. But I had you
I always had you
Who she got
And I know you ain't forgettin alla my
When I been runnin with Junior three years ago
I ain't makin excuses for none a that shit I come up on
That was me Grams
Old enough to know better by then right but I

And then you hadda come down

LENA. Boy

TRAY. Bail out my sorry ass
Right in the middle a your second job
You gotta be takin two buses and the subway
get my sorry ass home
And not just one time

LENA. Ain't the same

TRAY. Time after time after time
A whole year you done that mess for me Grams

LENA. One thing ain't got nothin to do with t'other
You my blood

TRAY. She your blood too

LENA. The hell she is

TRAY. She Devine's blood and
We Devine's blood
How you gon sort out blood yo
Cell by cell
Pick the ones you gon care for
Nah
We all mixed in Grams
No matter what we thinkin bout it
We all gon sink or swim together just the same

> (*Pause.*
> *She glares at him.*)

TRAY. Just sayin

LENA. Yeah well shut up 'cuz I'm
uh

Look here
Ain't nobody ask you
be *sayin* this or *sayin* that

> (*Silence.*
> *She takes a few steps, looks out the window, sighs.*)

sheeeiiiiit

> (TRAY *swoops in and hugs her tight.*)

TRAY. (*Teasing.*) I know I know
You proud a me huh
You raised me right

LENA. Boy did you fall on your head

TRAY. Awwwww

LENA. Leave off

TRAY. Nah nah don't speak
Ya ain't gotta say it Grams
For real
I can feel the love yo

LENA. Ridiculous child

> (*He doesn't let go.*
> *She wiggles around.*)

If you ain't gon eat your damn dinner
They some
pudding pops

in the freezer
for dessert

TRAY. Now how'd you get to be such a sweet old woman

LENA. That's some thin ice you treadin on my boy
Now get off fore I put you on the damn floor

> (TRAY *laughs, picks her up, gives her a big smooch on the cheek, sets her back down, ducks under her hand flapping at him, and exits.*
> *She chuckles, sighs, and shakes her head.*)

Oh my lord that child
Blessed thorn in my side
Blessed pain in my ass

> (*A car passes outside – the headlights sweep the wall:*
>
> *Lights shift, emptying out* TRAY's *room – it's colder, the warm glow from* TRAY's *desk lamp fades away, replaced by a cold bluish circle of light on the wall from a streetlight outside the window.* LENA *sits on his bed in the dark, lost in remembering.*)

LENA. Nah
I raised you right as I knew how
But I ain't give you that
You just a

You just a better person than me
that's all

> (*A sob rises from her belly, almost a thing separate from weeping or sorrow, guttural but not crying – a physical reaction to missing him.* LENA *swallows the sob, and lies down on* TRAY's *bed, breathing in the scent of him left on the pillows and blanket.*
>
> DEVINE *comes into the room softly.*
> *She looks around, sees* LENA, *hesitates.*)

LENA. It's okay baby

> (LENA *holds out a hand.*
> DEVINE *goes to* LENA, *nestling in next to her on the bed.*
> *They hold each other in the dark.*
> LENA's *ragged breathing.*
>
> *Another car passes, headlights stretching, sliding to:*
>
> *Lights shift.*)

[STARBUCKS—EAST FLATBUSH]

> MERRELL *sits at a table in the faux coziness of a small Starbucks.*
> *It's early in the day on a Sunday, quiet.*

> TRAY *enters, wearing a barista uniform with a green apron and visor, carrying*
> *a large box of 16 oz. hot cups and a clipboard.*
> *He sets down the box, puts the clipboard on a table, sees* MERRELL, *who*
> *sees him at the same time.*

TRAY. (*What are you doing here.*) Yo
uh

MERRELL. (*Oh man you work here.*) Oh
hey
Tray

> (*Uncomfortable pause.*)

TRAY. What's uh

We got a tutor thing I forgot about
or

MERRELL. Oh
No no I
I don't think so

TRAY. You don't think so

MERRELL. I mean
No
No we don't I
No

TRAY. Aight then
uh

> (*Pause.*)

What you doin here

MERRELL. Um I'm

TRAY. How'd you know I work here

> (*Pause.*)

MERRELL. I have an interview

TRAY. You
For this

MERRELL. I didn't know

TRAY. what

MERRELL. That you worked here I
I'm a little early for my
TRAY. Back up yo
You applyin for
This job
MERRELL. yeah
TRAY. For real
MERRELL. yeah
TRAY. You ain't on the list
Yo
Hold up

>   (TRAY *gets the clipboard, looks over the first page.*)

Your name supposed to be on the

>   (*He flips to the second page on the clipboard, sees her name.*)

oh
MERRELL. yeah
TRAY. shit
MERRELL. yeah

>   (*Pause.*)

You know
When that uh
what's her name
the person comes in to do my interview
I'll just tell her that I'm
TRAY. Yo
I be the person today
MERRELL. You
what
TRAY. Ima do these interviews
Gilda's kid got the flu so
She said just
Go 'head
Ask people the questions on the list and
write a note bout
they lookin like good workers or not
and she call up the good ones when she back
MERRELL. oh
TRAY. yeah
MERRELL. that's

TRAY. yeah

> (*Beat.*)

Aight

Let's get to it then

MERRELL. What

you mean you're

TRAY. You on the list

MERRELL. But

You don't want me here

TRAY. True I ain't

You wanna do this or what

I got six more comin in after you done

MERRELL. Really

okay ah

well

> (*Pause.*
> MERRELL *sits.*)

TRAY. You got a resume

MERRELL. Um

> (*She takes it out of a folder and hands it to him.*
> *He glances over it, then looks over the clipboard, clears his throat.*)

TRAY. So Ms. Merrell Kim

Tell me

Why you wanna work for Starbucks

MERRELL. Oh uh

Mostly

because I really

need a job

> (*Pause.*)

TRAY. That's it

That's your whole answer

MERRELL. well

TRAY. Okay

> (*He writes something on the clipboard.*)

MERRELL. And I am uh just

Passionate

About coffee

Starbucks coffee of course

TRAY. Uh huh

(He writes on the clipboard, reads the next question.)

What are your strengths and weaknesses

MERRELL. Oh uh

I am

willing to work very hard and I

Although I sometimes make mistakes ah

while I am learning ah

I

always try to take um

responsibility

TRAY. You do

MERRELL. I mean

I try

TRAY. MmHm

I'm sure you do

(He writes on the clipboard, reads the next question.)

Where was your most recent place of employment

MERRELL. Um

I was a

I was a 9th grade English teacher

TRAY. That was *most* recent

MERRELL. Well

Official employment

yes

TRAY. And how far back was that

MERRELL. *(You know how far back.)* Tray

TRAY. Nevermind

I'll just check your resume

(Pause.)

Oh

Hm

I see

So this teaching job ended and uh

And what was your reason for leaving

MERRELL. You want to hear this

TRAY. *(Sorry didn't catch that.)* what

MERRELL. When I saw you at the gym

before

you said you didn't want me to uh

(Pause.
TRAY *stares her down.)*

I didn't leave
I was
let go

TRAY. You were

MERRELL. Fired
Yes

TRAY. Really

(He writes on the clipboard.)

Ain't you got kids to support

MERRELL. What

TRAY. Answer the question

MERRELL. Yes
I did
I had two kids

TRAY. *Had*

MERRELL. They
They went to live with their grandma
right before I lost my job

TRAY. Because

(Slight pause.)

MERRELL. Because I was
Not able to ah
I

TRAY. *(Say it.)* Yes

(Pause.)

Because you abandoned them

MERRELL. I
That's not completely ah

TRAY. Aight then
So this teaching job was uh
almost four years ago
You ain't work since then

MERRELL. Tray
you already know what I

(Pause.
They lock eyes.)

There were
Odd jobs
TRAY. MmHm
You wanna describe the
MERRELL. Okay I get it
TRAY. Excuse me
MERRELL. You wanna hear me say it
Perfectly understandable
TRAY. Yo I'm just followin the
MERRELL. I was fired because of my drinking and my habit
and then no one would hire me
TRAY. So
you ain't work in four years
MERRELL. Well not
No
At first I found some ah
odd jobs
TRAY. Meaning
MERRELL. Whatever I could hustle my way into
Temp work
Chinese food delivery
yeah I know
ah
Raking leaves
TRAY. I ain't see that on your resume
MERRELL. Because I
never stayed more than a couple weeks at any of the
They'd either find out I lied to get the job
or
TRAY. Or
MERRELL. Well
Addiction is really
Its own full time job so
TRAY. So
Fired
From raking leaves
MERRELL. And then it ah
Got to a point where
I'd go in to a like a
bodega for example and ask

beg really
beg to sweep someone's floor if they'd just
give me a dollar
fifty cents
anything
TRAY. And this was all
where
Down Philly with your mom's people
MERRELL. No

        (TRAY *looks up at her.*)

TRAY. what
MERRELL. I

I never left Brooklyn

        (*Pause.*)

TRAY. You mean
you was still here
that whole time
MERRELL. yes

        (TRAY *stares at her.*)

I hid
Whenever I caught sight of you or your Gramma or
or
or Devine
I hid from you
And then one day I was
I don't know what I was
doing or
But
I saw her
I saw Devine crossing the street with you and
She turned
before I could find a hiding place
She turned and   and
I don't know if she saw me
I don't know if she actually saw me or
Maybe I imagined it
But
I thought
She looked at me
And she knew me

and her face just
shattered
and
ah

        (MERRELL *breathes, struggling, then gets her emotions in check.*)
I don't remember how long it was until I um
or exactly how
but I
Got myself to a rehab center and then
for a while
I was in rehab
Not Lindsay Lohan style
It was more like uh
Work study rehab for people with no money
So I did
Basic uh basic uh
Clerical work to pay for my treatment
I got out and
Seven and a half months
I was out for seven and a half months and
I had a relapse
Went back in and
They had someone else on clerical so I
Cleaned
the bathrooms and common areas
in the west wing of the building
Toilets
I cleaned a lot of toilets

TRAY. MmHm
        (*Slight pause.*)
And was that hard for you
Cleanin up other folks' shit
        (*Slight pause.*)
Cuz I got some experience doin that myself
and I know
It ain't easy
        (*Slight pause.*)
MERRELL. No
It's not

Anything else

(*Pause.*
TRAY *frowns, looking down, away from her.*
MERRELL *leans in.*)

Go on kid
I know I got it comin
What else

(*Silence.*
MERRELL *watches him.*
TRAY *focuses on the clipboard, doodles with the pen.*)

TRAY. You know uh
Grams won a prize
At her work
She ain't miss a day a work for a whole year so
They give her two movie tickets to the AMC in Times Square
And you know Grams
whatever she got she gon give to me or Devine
So we goin to the movie but
Devine she got a
a uh like a phobia
She scared a crowds you know
Which I think
maybe it be somethin about that dang Waldo make her scared
She got those damn books from the library
and that Waldo dude
He always lost in a crowd ain't he
All alone
waitin to be found and
yo we got this one Waldo page where we ain't find him
and Devine she
Take that real personal you know
She uh
She worry a lot for a kid
I told her
Yo when we walkin on 42nd Street
They gon be some crazy pushy ass crowds a people
And I said
So how we gon do mami
And she said
We gon hold hands
We gon hold tight
We ain't gon let go
And that's how we do

(*Pause.*
TRAY *pins* MERRELL *with an earnestly pained, troubled gaze.*)

TRAY. Yo
You thinkin I'm tryna
I dunno
Make you pay or some shit
You dead wrong
I just

I ain't understand you

I know you loved my pop
I saw it
I ain't never doubt it
And when he brought you home the first time
Me and Grams was so glad cuz
we saw how it was with y'all
It was real
And when he got killed
when alla that shit go down outta the blue like that
I saw you
I was watchin you and
I knew you was ah

Cuz we was all ah

We
was all
lost

But even when alla that shit come pushin in on us
On me and D and Grams
We hold tight
We ain't let go
And I ain't understand
For real Merrell
If you could just tell me maybe I

We ain't let go
Why did you
Why did you

(TRAY *gets up and exits.*
MERRELL *stays in her chair, silent, wiping away tears that keep rolling
down her face.*

Music comes on — some kinda Starbucks Jazz compilation.
MERRELL *stands and exits.*

TRAY *comes out of the back room.*
He looks at MERRELL's *empty chair.*
He goes to the window and looks down the street, watching MERRELL's
progress as she walks away.
He stands a moment, having some kind of internal debate.
He exits into the back room again.

Lights shift.
The music morphs into the sounds of LENA's *block.*)

[SUTTER & RALPH AVES]

LENA *walks down the block toward home.*
She carries some stickers and a package of gummy bears from the Family Dollar.
Her crisp footsteps keep time with the symphony of sounds on the block.
*She stops in front of her building, about to go in, then keeps walking farther
down the block.*
*She stops at a particular patch of sidewalk, in front of a stoop on the corner of
Sutter and Ralph Avenues, a couple doors down from her building.*
She stares at the sidewalk.
The sounds of the block surround her.

We hear JUNIOR's *voice, laughing and talking shit.*
LENA *watches him approach.*

JUNIOR. (*Offstage.*) Aight then
Holla when you back yo
Later

(JUNIOR *enters, walks toward* LENA *looking at his cell phone.*
LENA's *eyes follow him like laser sights.*
She steps into his path.
He bumps into her.)

Ayo heads up muthafuckah

(*He recognizes her.*)

oh
yo

(*Loaded pause.*)

How you feelin Ms. Lena

What you doin off work inna middle a the mornin

LENA. How come you ain't been to see me

JUNIOR. Yeah uh

I been havin all kinda shit goin on

you know how it is

gotta stay on the grind

tryna take care a business

LENA. What you find out

JUNIOR. Uh

LENA. Hey

You know what's good for ya

better look me in the eye when we talkin boy

(JUNIOR's *eyes snap up to* LENA's.)

Now go on

What you got

JUNIOR. (*Eyes sliding away again.*) well

You know I tried like I told you but

I ain't uh

It ain't uh

LENA. Look here son

Worst thing could ever happen to me

Already happen twice

JUNIOR. twice

LENA. Losin him

Losin his daddy

(JUNIOR *can't look at her, but he nods.*)

What you think

You think anything you got gon bring me to my knees

You think you capable a hurtin me now or

You feel *sorry*

Nah

Folks bein sorry ain't shit to me you hear

You got feelins

You handle it son

Now

You said you gon find out why

You promised me

Is you a liar

JUNIOR. No ma'am

LENA. Then what you know
> (*Pause.*
> JUNIOR *nods again, speaks reluctantly.*)

JUNIOR. Yo uh
I just
I want you to consider
Ain't none a this gon make you feel no better Ms. Lena

LENA. You gon let me be the judge a that
Talk

JUNIOR. Aight
So first
I gotta explain how things be workin on the street
> (LENA *glares at him.*)

LENA. Boy
Who the hell you think you talkin to
I been livin on this street longer'n you been breathin air through yo big
mouth

JUNIOR. I heard I heard
But things be changed since back in your day

LENA. Oh "back in my day"
I show you the back a my day right quick

JUNIOR. Nah listen see
Way it be workin
If you comin up in a crew
You gotta be lookin for ways to show you about it
So out here now
Body count be like trophies or
Like a score
You get points for every one you put down

LENA. Points

JUNIOR. Yeah like uh
Be like a game score but
bodies
You get points for the shot
You get points if they die cuz
You know
That gon uh
Bodies gon build up your reputation and then
ain't nobody wanna mess with you

LENA. (*To herself.*) points

(Pause.)

JUNIOR. But this
Wasn't nothin tryna go down that night Ms. Lena
I swear to you
We just out on the corner cuz
Just tryna
tryna get away from the heat you know
Damn air conditioner ain't never work right so
It wasn't nothin big tryna go down just
Women with kids and Ziploc bags a ice cubes
Music playin
Brothers shootin dice
We all just chill out there for real when Tray come by

(Pause.)

He walkin home from work and
I call out to him
He borrowed my Call of Duty
so he come over to give it back and just
say whassup
Talkin bout that car he gon buy so he ain't gon ride no stinkass subway no
more
That's all he doin and uh

*(Pause.
         JUNIOR's face and voice take on a hard edge.)*

And then bout that time
Kingsborough crew roll up
Dude named SJ comin up with em now
He saw me and Tray talkin and

(Pause.)

Tray just
Caught in the mess a some Kingsborough bullshit from last April
One a they crew's old lady got shot inna arm on some child custody shit and
Now they think they got a beef with us
Shit ain't got nothin to do with Tray
except

LENA. except

JUNIOR. Except he knowin me
Except he stoppin to talk to me and

(Pause.)

LENA. say it

JUNIOR. Tray seen the trouble comin
He peaced out
and ah

      (Slight pause.)

SJ step to him
and Tray
ah
He put his hand up
you know
like this
to get past
not tryna start nothin
he just keep on walkin
but SJ be like
"Yo bitch you gon put your hands on me"
Tray turned back
And SJ put four in his chest

      (LENA *makes a sound like someone punched her in the gut — not a sob or*
      crying, but like all the air is squeezed from her body by a giant hand with one
      short hard squeeze.)

JUNIOR. Folks round here know Tray
They know he ain't run with nobody
They know he a working kid
Got his school and his boxing
Even guys I know on the inside sayin it's a bitch move killin a guy like Tray
for
well

You ain't get no points for that bullshit
And SJ ain't even know what he do til after
Just run away laughin and when he hearin that Tray ain't in no crew
He talkin bout
"Oh well charge it to the game"

      (LENA *puts a hand over her mouth, her knees unsteady.*
      JUNIOR *reaches out, gently takes her arm, supporting her, his face pained.*
      LENA's *body shakes with muffled sobs that wrack her from deep within.*
      Tears roll down JUNIOR's *face.*

      They hold each other for a moment.

      LENA *struggles to get her emotions in check.*
      JUNIOR *speaks through his tears.)*

JUNIOR. Tray was my dude Ms. Lena
I would never uh
I been knowin him longer than anyone
He ain't deserve it
I know he ain't
Not like (me)

LENA. No
No
Look at me
Hey
Look at me

    (JUNIOR *reluctantly raises his eyes to hers.*)

Ain't nobody deserve it my boy

JUNIOR. But

LENA. No
You listen to me
You ain't nothin but a dumbass kid
But you ain't deserve it

    (JUNIOR *shakes his head, looks away.*)

JUNIOR. I swear to you on my life
This ain't gon go unanswered
Ima even this shit up
Ima bring it to SJ
same as he brought to Tray

LENA. (*Softly.*) Did you know

Did Tray ever tell you how his daddy died
    (*Pause.*)
Four in his chest
    (*Pause.*
    LENA *places a gentle hand on* JUNIOR*'s arm.*)
I remember the day you were born Anthony
Please
Please let me
ah
    (*She breathes, she smiles at him.*)
Let me run into you
someday
on some sidewalk
twenty years from now

Let me see you grown
strong and happy
and hear you sayin
"You was right Ms. Lena"

> (JUNIOR *shakes his head, pauses.*
> LENA *watches him.*
> *He breathes, wipes away his tears angrily.*
> *He shakes his head again, his face hardens.*
> LENA *is overwhelmed with wanting to save him and knowing she can't.*)

LENA. Thank you Anthony
Thank you for tellin me the truth

> (JUNIOR *looks at the ground.*)

Y'all come see me sometimes
Aright
You don't Ima come check up on you
Ya heard

> (JUNIOR *nods slightly.*
> *Sounds of the block, cars passing, subway clacking in the distance.*
> *She turns to go, pauses, looks back at* JUNIOR *again.*
> JUNIOR *walks off down the block.*
>
> LENA *watches til he's out of sight, then turns toward home, walking slowly and heavily – maybe the first time we have ever seen her move like an old woman.*
>
> *Subway sounds rush up, clacking and whining, bringing the light shift to:*)

[STARBUCKS—EAST FLATBUSH]

> *Afternoon lull in the café.*
> *A Starbucks roots music compilation plays softly.*
> MERRELL *stands in front of the POS register, wearing the Starbucks uniform.*
> TRAY *stands next to her.*

TRAY. Enter

> (MERRELL *hits the wrong button, the POS beeps.*
> TRAY *looks at it, clears her last mistake.*)

Aight
Now hit enter and

> (MERRELL *hits enter.*)

Subtotal

MERRELL. (*Where is it where is it.*) sub
totale

>   (*She pushes a button, the POS beeps at her.*)

oh
crap
crap
crap

>   (*She pushes another button, the POS beeps again.*
>   TRAY *reaches over and pushes a few buttons in rapid succession, resets the
>   system.*)

MERRELL. (*God I suck ass at this.*) Sorry
I

TRAY. Yo
Just don't forget the steps gotta go in order
You gotta subtotal first

MERRELL. Right

TRAY. Cuz if they got some kinda gift card or coupon
The POS gon ask for that *before* y'all total out
aight

MERRELL. Okay

TRAY. Also if you got a customer gon change they mind bout somethin
If you got it at subtotal it ain't no thang
And then you ain't gotta do a whole void transaction
aight

>   (*Pause.*)

You want me write it down for you

MERRELL. That's okay I uh
I think I got it

>   (*She stares at the buttons, earnestly trying to remember what he's just told her,
>   lips moving slightly as she repeats his instructions silently to herself.
>   He watches her, then gets out some polish and starts cleaning the stainless steel
>   machines behind the counter.*)

MERRELL. Oh
Here
I can do that

TRAY. Nah
Why ain't you uh
You can Windex the pastry case and front door if you want
and if they still time after that

Maybe do some sweepin
we know you good at that right

MERRELL. (*Okay, go ahead, get in your little digs.*) uh yeah

> (*She looks at him, but he keeps his eyes on his work.*)

okay
soooo
Windex

> (*She pauses a beat, trying to remember where the cleaning supplies are.*
> TRAY *watches her out of the corner of his eye.*
> *She tentatively opens a few cupboards.*
> *No dice.*
> *She glances at him, not wanting to bother him.*
> *She opens a few more cupboards.*
> *She tries to remember what he told her.*)

OH
yeah

> (*She exits into the back, returns a beat later with some Windex and cleaning
> towels.*
> TRAY *dismantles one of the espresso machines, cleaning parts.*
> *Squeaking of towel against glass as* MERRELL *works.*
> TRAY *glances her way, watching her surreptitiously.*
> *She Windexes as though her life depends on it.*)

TRAY. How come you ain't go down to Philly

MERRELL. Hm what

TRAY. Before

MERRELL. Oh
you mean
Before

TRAY. Ain't you got family down that way
Your mom's people
how come you ain't go to them

> (MERRELL *keeps her eyes on her work.*)

MERRELL. (*Matter of fact.*) I tried
They didn't want me

> (TRAY *looks at her.*)

TRAY. For real

MERRELL. Nope
They for real did not

> (*Slight pause.*)

TRAY. You think uh

Why you think they been that

> *(She looks at him, he keeps his eyes on his work.)*

MERRELL. I think

I don't know
but
the real answer is Two

TRAY. Two

MERRELL. How many shits I *don't* give
for what they think about me
and for what they thought about me and James

> *(She Windexes extra vigorously.*
> TRAY *keeps working, watching her with side-eye, assessing.*
> *She stops suddenly, and looks at him – he looks back at his work quickly.)*

Do you
uh

> *(Beat.)*

You don't remember that trip do you
Before Devine was born
when James borrowed Hector's van
and we drove to Philly

TRAY. yeah
I remember

MERRELL. *(Her face falls.)* oh

god I was
you were so little then I was

Hoping you didn't
but

> *(She goes back to work.*
> TRAY *pauses and looks at her, open and softer than we have seen him look*
> *at her before.)*

TRAY. why

MERRELL. oh
what my mom said to us
it was

you know

TRAY. yeah

(*Pause.*)

But what I also remember
Pops
eatin all them sunflower seeds
leavin his shells all on the floor a that stank ass old van
And the freeway
I ain't never see no freeway fore that
Be like a giant river or some shit
ain't be like no drag ass East River neither
Be all shiny and slick
and on the freeway that air come in the window
be all hot and fast on my arm

>   (MERRELL *has stopped Windexing, stands looking at him, pained, but in*
>   *control.*)

And I remember
we gettin to stay one night in a for real muthafuckin motel by the freeway exit
that shit was off the hook
They got tiny soap each in they own little wrappin paper
and white towels
and they got a strip across the toilet
that gotta fancy flourish sayin
"Fresh For Your Enjoyment"
ya heard that
For *my* enjoyment yo

>   (MERRELL *laughs.*)

TRAY. I remember we stayin in that motel 'cuz a you

And truth
what I remember mostly a that whole mess
was you

You onna front porch a you daddy's house
You standin in fronta your mama
Hands on your hips
Leanin forward
like you tryna make your words
fly out yo mouth like a fist and punch her dead in the face
sayin
"*This be my family*
And you ain't havin them
You ain't havin me
You hear me woman"

And Pops be puttin his big hand on your shoulder
tryna calm you down
You look at him
He look at you and say
"It's all right baby"
You breathe together
Then you whip round
look in my eyes
kiss my cheek and pick me up
And Pop take your hand real tight
and we get right back in that stank ass van
and drive
And you been so mad
And Pops been so mad
then alla sudden
Pops laughin
"Thought you gon put a hurtin on her right there baby
I ain't tryna pay no hospital bill on this shit
Ya heard"
And you both laughin til the water come out your eyes
We all three laughin
Laughin all the way to the for real muthafuckin motel
　　　　(TRAY *looks at her, she looks back.*)
Ain't never forget that shit
　　　　(MERRELL *nods.*)
yeah
MERRELL. (*Simply.*) yeah
James
he

saved me
　　　　(*Slight pause.*
　　　　TRAY *looks at her, she looks back.*
　　　　TRAY *nods, she nods.*
　　　　They go back to work.

　　　　Starbucks music plays softly.
　　　　A customer, a BROOKLYN COLLEGE STUDENT, *enters.*

　　　　MERRELL *looks at* TRAY, *he nods at her to take the customer.*
　　　　MERRELL *nervously darts behind the counter.*)

MERRELL. Welcome to Starbucks

What can I get for you today

BC STUDENT. Ummmm

Can I have a grande soy triple shot vanilla latte

One regular two decaf

Not too hot

MERRELL. Whoa wow

Oooookay

Could you please repeat that

> (MERRELL *stares at the POS keys, slowly hunting and pecking as they go through it.*
> TRAY *starts making the drink, keeping an eye on* MERRELL *as well.*)

So it's a

BC STUDENT. Grande

MERRELL. gran

de

BC STUDENT. Soy

MERRELL. soy

BC STUDENT. Triple

MERRELL. triple

latte

Remembered latte at least heh

> (MERRELL *smiles nervously.*
> *The* BC STUDENT *isn't particularly amused.*)

BC STUDENT. Yeah

and

Vanilla

MERRELL. oh oh

right

vanilla

BC STUDENT. One regular shot

Two decaf

Not too hot

> (MERRELL'*s lips move as she repeats this last bit while punching buttons slowly.*
> *She makes it through entering the order, then pushes the wrong button and the POS beeps loudly.*
> *She tries another button.*)

It beeps.
The BC STUDENT *is getting restless.*)

MERRELL. Um
Sorry
sorry
Um
Oh oh oh okay
there

      (She punches a button and total comes up.)

Sorry about the wait
That will be
Twelve ninety-five

BC STUDENT. Uh that
For real
Twelve ninety-five

MERRELL. Oh shit no
No no no no no
Of course not that's
That would be crazy
So sorry about that
uh

      (She tries to void the sale, but the POS keeps beeping and adding to the total. Her face gets more and more red, the BC STUDENT *goes from restless to impatient.)*

I am so sorry
Let me just

BC STUDENT. *(Checks his watch.)* Yeah um
I gotta get to class so uh

MERRELL. I'm so sorry
uh
can I

      (TRAY brings the drink over, along with a paper bag, gives both to the BC STUDENT, *flashing a charming smile.)*

TRAY. Yo
Here's your grande soy triple shot one regular two decaf vanilla not too hot latte
And
A madeleine on the house for you sir
Just give us a moment
We gon get you on your way right quick

(MERRELL *steps back from the register, but* TRAY *gently pushes her back, resets the POS.*
He stands next to her and talks her through the transaction, firmly and patiently – like a good coach or teacher.)

Aight

Go ahead and put in the drink order again

(*She looks at him, panicked – she can't remember it.*)

A grande latte

soy

triple shot

No

Just add one shot because a grande size come with two already remember

Right

And vanilla

(MERRELL *punches buttons, a little quicker.*)

Good

then

Wait

(*He points to a button.*)

Remember

MERRELL. oh

right

Sorry

TRAY. It's aight ma

You doin fine

And then

Subtotal

Hit enter

MERRELL. Oh

(*The correct total comes up,* MERRELL *takes the* BC STUDENT'*s money and hands back change.*)

TRAY. Sorry bout the wait

BC STUDENT. No worries man

Thanks for the cookie

(*The* BC STUDENT *hurries out.*)

MERRELL. (*Faintly.*) Thank you

Come again

(*She looks at* TRAY *sheepishly.*)

Who knew coffee work would give me so much

you know
performance anxiety

TRAY. Don't worry about it
you get it

> (*She goes around the counter, picks up the Windex and rag.*)

Aight well
That's it
You done for today

MERRELL. Oh
is it six already

TRAY. Yep
Good work

MERRELL. (*Wryly.*) Uh yeah

TRAY. Nah for real
I know it's a lot to take in all at once
You shoulda seen me on my first day

MERRELL. Thanks Tray

> (TRAY *shrugs.*
> *Awkward pause.*)

All right
well
I'll just uh

> (MERRELL *exits into the back room, taking off her apron and visor as she goes.*
> TRAY *pauses, then gets a folder from his backpack, takes out a piece of paper.*
> MERRELL *enters, carrying a handbag.*)

So I guess
I'll see you tomorrow

TRAY. yo
you got a sec

MERRELL. Sure

> (TRAY *hands her the paper.*)

TRAY. What you think a that

MERRELL. A whole new draft
wow

TRAY. I did like you said
Or I tried to
I mean
I think

(She reads quickly, he watches her.)

MERRELL. Nope

TRAY. What

MERRELL. Not buyin it

TRAY. what you talkin bout
"buyin"

MERRELL. This isn't you Tray

TRAY. Woman
What you mean
I just tryna do what you told me

MERRELL. *(Reads.)* "Ever since I was a very small child
I have always dreamed of going to college"

TRAY. Ayo
that be some quality shit right there

MERRELL. Well
It's definitely shit

TRAY. man

MERRELL. This is the same generic crap that every other essay is gonna
start with

TRAY. So
Maybe that's what I got

> (MERRELL *gives him a look.*
> *He looks away.*)

You on my ass with all this shit bout
Tell em who you are
Be yourself
well
Maybe my self ain't nothing special yo

MERRELL. Bullshit

> (TRAY *shrugs, looks away.*)

You're not trying

TRAY. I am

MERRELL. You're not

TRAY. I *am*
I don't know what you want me to

MERRELL. Don't try playin me on some
"oh I don't know how to do this"
You do

TRAY. whatever

MERRELL. Come on Tray

You gotta stop fucking around and take this shit seriously

What's the problem

> (TRAY *looks at the espresso machine parts.*)

Listen

It's not about trying to be

the most impressive writer of essays in the world

You hear me

It's about having the balls to

to put yourself on the line personally

to show them

who you are and what you love

Show them your heart

TRAY. man

whatever

> (*Pause.*
>
> MERRELL *looks over the essay again, crumples up the paper and tosses it at him.*)

MERRELL. Sack up

Throw this shit out

and do it again

TRAY. pssshh

MERRELL. We got our regular tutor meeting coming up on Friday

Look over those notes from the other day

That list you made

> (TRAY *looks away, nods slightly.*)

Just bring me one good paragraph kid

Just one

And we'll go from there

okay

> (TRAY *nods without looking at her, annoyed.*
> *She smiles at him anyway, and exits.*
> *Starbucks music plays.*
> TRAY *uncrumples the paper and reads through it.*
> *He sighs: she's right.*
> *He crumples the paper and tosses it in the garbage, goes back to cleaning the machines, thinking hard about his essay.*
>
> *Hip-hop Swan Lake fades in over the Starbucks music, bringing the lights shift to:)*

[DEVINE]

> *Elementary school auditorium.*
> *The hip-hop Swan Lake plays over crummy speakers.*
>
> DEVINE *is onstage in her full tree costume under a crummy follow spot and a couple of scoop lights.*
> *Her costume is quite sparkly and elaborate, and is worn over* TRAY's *sweatshirt, which she refuses to take off.*
>
> DEVINE *does her tree dance as the swan shadows of her classmates flutter in and around her.*
> *She alternates between concentrating on her tree dance and scanning the crowd for* LENA, *who is not there.*
>
> *She becomes increasingly distracted, starts forgetting her part, keeps looking for* LENA.
>
> *The spotlight moves from her area of the stage, following the Swan Princess.*
> DEVINE *takes advantage and runs to the edge of the stage, peering into the audience, looking for* LENA.
> *She sees the shadow of someone standing in the back wearing that bright green Starbucks apron.*
> *Is it* TRAY?
> *She raises her hand in greeting.*
> *No response.*

DEVINE. Tray
> (DEVINE *waves.*
> *A murmur of disturbance among her swan classmates.*
> *The swan dance begins to go off the rails a bit.*
> DEVINE *stays where she is.*
>
> *Lights shift into* DEVINE's *World.*
>
> *Bluish-white light shafts in from the sides on the Starbucks apron person: it is* TRAY, *and he raises a hand to wave back, then moves in an arc toward and around her.*
>
> DEVINE *and* TRAY *do a Tree/Brother/Sister Dance.*
>
> *Music builds to the conclusion.*
>
> DEVINE *tree dances her heart out, holding her pose at the end.*
> *Applause, shadows of swan classmates hopping around excitedly.*

TRAY *hugs* DEVINE, *sets her down amid the flapping shadows of her classmates.*

Lights shift, come up brighter, <u>shifting out of</u> DEVINE's World – also, the sounds of a crowd come up – parents and teachers and kids murmuring, laughing, folding chair feet scraping gym floor.

DEVINE *pauses, a bit overwhelmed at the shift.*
She looks around the sea of parents and kids, trying to get her bearings, looking for TRAY.

DEVINE *glimpses the back of the Starbucks apron leaving the auditorium.)*

DEVINE. Ayo Tray
Wait up

(DEVINE *runs out of the auditorium.*

Crowd murmur bumps up, faintly in the background we hear a song starting, car passing sound swooshes into:

Lights/scene shift – the song comes up, bringing us to:)

[STARBUCKS—EAST FLATBUSH]

(MERRELL *comes out of the back room, wearing her Starbucks uniform, with the green apron, green visor.*
The song is Lena Horne's 1941 recording of "Where Or When."
MERRELL *hums and sings along as she cleans the counters, restocks cups, etc.)*

MERRELL. The clothes you're nuh nuhhh
are the nuhh you nuhhh
The smuh you are smiling you were smuh nuh nuh
But I can't remember where or when

(DEVINE *enters the Starbucks, unnoticed.*
She still wears TRAY's *sweatshirt and her tree costume.*
She sits on the floor in a corner, out of the way, almost hidden, watching the counter.)

Luh things that happened for the fuh muuuh
Nuh nuh muh happening again
And so it seems that luh luh nuh before
And muuuh before and loved before
But who knows where or

(*She turns and sees* DEVINE, *stops cold.*
MERRELL *crosses to* DEVINE, *slowly, carefully.*)

MERRELL. (*Softly.*) Oh

(DEVINE *does not look at her fully, or recognize her.*
She stands, back against the wall, nervous, looking at her feet.)

Hello there

(*Pause.*
DEVINE *fidgets.*)

Devine

(*Pause.*
DEVINE'*s eyes flash up to* MERRELL'*s face briefly.*
No recognition.)

What are

DEVINE. Can I talk to Tray

(*Slight pause.*)

MERRELL. Tray

DEVINE. He's my brother
Ain't he in here

(*Pause.*)

MERRELL. No honey
he isn't

(DEVINE *looks confused.*)

DEVINE. Well but
Cuz
I seen him just now

MERRELL. you

DEVINE. He was at the swan dance
and then I saw him come go in here

MERRELL. You followed

DEVINE. Yeah
I saw him he
At my school
I saw his green apron standin in the back

MERRELL. Oh
baby girl

that was me

(MERRELL *steps toward* DEVINE – *again, carefully.*)

Tray told me about the

About your tree dance a while ago and I
I wanted to see it ah

>(DEVINE *examines* MERRELL *closely, more confused.*)

DEVINE. you
nah
It be that green apron he always wearin for his work
I saw his green apron

>(DEVINE *sees* MERRELL's *green apron.*)

oh

>(DEVINE *reaches out and touches the apron, puzzled.*
>*She looks up, recognizes* MERRELL's *face.*
>DEVINE *takes in a sharp breath, her face goes blank, and she involuntarily*
>*takes a step back.*
>MERRELL's *head droops, she breathes.*
>*She looks at* DEVINE *sadly, keeps her distance.*)

MERRELL. It's okay

>(MERRELL *nods.*)

I know (I'm sorry)
I know (I'm sorry)

>(MERRELL *takes careful breaths.*
>*She smiles wanly at* DEVINE.)

It's okay D
I'm gonna go tell Gilda I gotta step out
And then I'm gonna take you home

>(DEVINE's *forehead furrows anxiously, she steps back again.*)

oh not with me baby
To Lena's
To your gramma's
Okay

>(DEVINE *nods.*)

Okay
Just give me a sec
I'll be right back

>(MERRELL *pauses, remembering the times she said that to* DEVINE *years*
>*before, and never came back.*
>DEVINE's *eyes dart around, looking for something to get under.*
>MERRELL *turns back and holds out her hand.*)

MERRELL. Or why don't you just come with me
We'll go together

(DEVINE *hesitates.*

She does not take MERRELL's *hand, but follows her into the back room.*

Music comes up, Lena Horne sings the last lines of the song.

Lights shift.)

[SUTTER & RALPH AVES]

LENA's *kitchen.*
Celery sticks and string cheese sit on a plate on the table.
Keys in the door.
LENA *enters, wearing her receptionist clothes — nice slacks, nice blouse.*
She carries a laundry basket which contains stacks of clean folded clothes and a bundle of mail.
She sets the laundry basket on a chair in the kitchen, takes out a Duane Reade cashier smock, puts it on, puts on a nametag.
Her cell phone beeps.
She digs it out of her purse, looks at it, and dials her voicemail.
She listens.
Her face widens in shock and she grabs her purse and runs for the door.
She opens it.
DEVINE *and* MERRELL *stand there, about to knock.*
LENA *covers her mouth.*
She nods, steps aside to let them in.

DEVINE *goes into the kitchen, sits at the table, and begins taking things out of her pockets: a yoyo with no string, a metal tab from a soda can, an eraser shaped like a bee, a Starbucks hot cup sleeve.*

LENA *and* MERRELL *stand awkwardly by the door.*

MERRELL. She came to the café
she
Lena
She was lookin for Tray
    (*Pause.*)
Does she think he's
LENA. No
She knows
MERRELL. But she

LENA. I
I ain't always knowin
Where the uh
lines be drawn for her
specially when it come to Tray
Two a them been so close
you know
MERRELL. Ah

> *(Pause.)*

Well
She's home now
I'll just

> *(MERRELL turns to go.)*

LENA. thank you
MERRELL. what
LENA. for being
for bringing her home to me

> *(Pause.)*

MERRELL. You're welcome

> *(Pause.)*

LENA. I don't know how I could have ah
I mean

> *(LENA takes a breath.)*

No
No excuse for it
I wasn't there

my

> *(LENA suddenly seems very small and old.*
> *She rubs her forehead, troubled.)*

My memory ain't been good lately so
I been tryna write everything in a
you know I got me one a them day planner books so I
So I ain't forget but I

> *(Pause.)*

I promised her
MERRELL. Lena
LENA. No I did
I promised her
That I would never

> (*Pause.*
> *They lock eyes.*)

MERRELL. Well I

> (MERRELL *nods.*
> *Awkward silence.*
> MERRELL *starts to go again.*)

LENA. Merrell

> (MERRELL *pauses.*
> *Silence.*)

Would
You wanna stay for snack

MERRELL. I
snack

LENA. This be our ah
Afterschool snack time right now and
You can stay

MERRELL. oh I
I'm actually still on the clock at
no
Sure
I can stay for a minute

LENA. Aright

MERRELL. Aright

> (*They start into the kitchen.*
> LENA *stops, puts a hand on* MERRELL's *arm, looks into her face urgently.*)

LENA. Before Tray passed
Not long fore he passed
He said to me
He said you changed

> (*Pause.*
> MERRELL *goes very still.*)

When you first come back
He real quiet on it
He ain't wanna mess up Devine's head
And he
Well he know I gon hit the ceiling with both hands and feet once I heard
But that boy
He always makin up his own mind bout things
And some kinda time go by
and

He seen how you had so much ah

He said it's like you was runnin a marathon with a broken leg
But you kept runnin
And he start in at me sayin
She ain't the only one ever fucked up
She changed

>   (LENA *looks into* MERRELL's *eyes.*)

That true

>   (*Pause.*)

MERRELL. I don't know
I am trying
But I don't know

>   (*Pause.*)

LENA. Well
If that a lie it ain't a very good one

>   (*Pause.*)

MERRELL. I don't know Lena
I
Most days I find that I ah
Anyway you were right
All the the uh
Fuss I made about seeing D
Tray was telling me
To wait
To have patience
That it was about what's best for her and

Because I am still
Tray was right
Every day is
A long steep hill
but

I am
trying

>   (MERRELL *swallows hard, nods, breathes.*
>   LENA *watches her.*)

LENA. Aright then
How bout
You wanna have snack

>   (MERRELL *nods.*)

Let's go have snack

MERRELL. Lena

LENA. Nah

We ain't gon worry bout alla every last thing

Just this

just right now

just snack

So come on if you comin on

> (*They go into the kitchen.*
> MERRELL *sits tentatively at the table across from* DEVINE, *who doesn't look up.*)

Devine

Your mama gon have some snack with us

What you think about that

> (DEVINE *keeps doing what she's doing for a beat.*
> *Then she looks up briefly, pushes the dish of celery and cheese to* MERRELL.
> MERRELL *blinks back the tears that spring up when* LENA *calls her* DEVINE'*s "mama," takes celery.*
> LENA *picks up the mail and starts looking through it.*)

LENA. Well now

That right there was rare as frog's hair

Girl be mindin her manners

sharin her snack

without I even ask her

Mm mm

> (LENA'*s hand pauses over an envelope.*
> *She opens it, takes out the letter, sits heavily in a chair.*
> MERRELL *and* DEVINE *watch her.*
> *She reads and looks up.*)

LENA. It's

from the Flatbush Gardens Community Fund

> (*Pause.*)

Tray

He won

> (*Pause.*
> LENA *reads:*)

"Dear Mr. Thompson

Congratulations

You have been selected as one of five recipients

of the $5,000 Flatbush Gardens Community Scholarship

The committee was impressed with your
academic record and athletic accomplishments
But they especially responded to the way you expressed yourself
in your personal essay"

>   (LENA *pauses*.

>   TRAY *bursts out of his room down the hall.*
>   *As* TRAY *enters the kitchen:*
>   *Lights shift – warmer, full.*)

TRAY. Ayo
Grams
I'm done
you wanna hear

LENA. Lord
You gon give me a heart attack with your damn shoutin

TRAY. Yo
I'm done with my essay
You wanna hear

LENA. I do indeed

TRAY. Aight then
Ima lay it on ya now
Bout to drop this sweetass joint up in here

LENA. You go on and drop it like it's hot baby

TRAY. You ready

LENA. I am ready

TRAY. You best get ready

LENA. Born ready

TRAY. Aight then
here it go

>   (TRAY *reads from the paper he's been working on.*
>   LENA *listens, face aching with love and pride.*)

My name is Tramaine Berry Thompson
and I am more than meets the eye
For this scholarship
I must be presenting to you a lot of facts and figures
But cold facts and figures will only tell you
the way my life is seen by people who mostly
don't know me at all
A quick look at the surface of my life and you might see
A black male

An amateur boxer
A high school graduate
But that quick glance cannot show you the whole story
and will not reveal what is the true foundation of my life
The real heroes who inspire me to be what I am and do what I do
The real heroes are my family
I am held up every day by the strength of my grandmother Lena
who works without stopping to make a home for me and my little sister
who will never stand for excuses or sass in the place of hard work
and who cannot cook to save anyone's life but

> (LENA *gives him a look.*)

TRAY. (*Laughing.*) but even this was a gift she gave me because
I learned how to cook myself and saved us all
I am blessed every day by the heart of my little sister Devine
who has held my hand through every dark day in my life and never let go
whose love comes to me pure and without demands
whose constant faith in me is my compass and my true north
And I am challenged by the legacy of my father James whose life
more than his death
showed me that there is a different path
You can decide to write your own story
Instead of buying the one other people may bring to you
You can refuse that story
You can work to bring change
for yourself
for those around you
And to do this
more than anything else
to do this is what it means to be a man in this life

> (*Lights fade on* LENA, *until all is in shadow except* TRAY.)

One day I hope to be a man my father would have been proud of
This scholarship will help me to achieve that goal
I plan to graduate from college with a teaching degree
I want to pass along the gifts I was given
The strength of my grandmother
The heart of my little sister
And the challenge to change left by my father
Because I am living proof that
No matter what anyone else says to you
or thinks about you
or does to you
You define your life

By living it
Day by day
Every moment a chance to rise
To fulfill the gifts of your life
To write hope into your story

My name is Tramaine Berry Thompson
I am eighteen years old
I am writing my own story
And this is not the end
This is the beginning

> (TRAY's *desk lamp gives off a warm glow.*
> *Silhouettes of* LENA, DEVINE, *and* MERRELL *in the kitchen in the*
> *shadows.*
> TRAY *looks up from the paper, super pleased with how it turned out, very*
> *excited to be done with it at last.*)

TRAY. whassuuuuuup

> (*He grins at us, does a little dance move, and throws a deuce — full of life and*
> *hope.*
>
> *Blackout.*)

End of Play

SOME PREPARED REMARKS
(A HISTORY IN SPEECH)
by Jason Gray Platt

BIOGRAPHY

Jason Gray Platt's work has been produced and developed around the country by the American Repertory Theater, Actors Theatre of Louisville, The Flea, Round House Theatre, The Institute of Contemporary Art/Boston, The Playwrights Realm, Prelude NYC, Page 73, Red Bull Theater, Source Festival, Ensemble Studio Theatre, Clubbed Thumb, Abingdon Theatre Company, and through residencies at The MacDowell Colony and the Djerassi Resident Artists Program. He received a Helen Hayes Nomination for The Charles MacArthur Award for Outstanding New Play in 2013 and was the 2007 runner-up for the Princess Grace Award in playwriting. Originally from Arizona, Platt now lives in New York. He is a member of Woodshed Collective, and holds a B.A. from Vassar College and an M.F.A. from Columbia University.

ACKNOWLEDGMENTS

Some Prepared Remarks (A History in Speech) premiered at the Humana Festival of New American Plays in April 2014. It was directed by Les Waters with the following cast:

THE SPEAKER..Bruce McKenzie

and the following production staff:

Scenic Designer...Dane Laffrey
Costume Designer .... Kristopher Castle
Lighting Designer...Seth Reiser
Sound Designer....................................Christian Frederickson
Stage Manager ....Stephen Horton
Dramaturg..Jessica Reese
Directing Assistants.........................Cara Phipps, Jacob Sexton
Production Assistant ....Suzanne Spicer

CHARACTERS

THE SPEAKER. Male? Female? Trans? Human, probably? Let's definitely say human.

Age: All of them.

[Feel free to shift pronouns to adjust for The Speaker's gender and/or sexuality as you see it. Caitlin can easily become Colin.]

TRANSITIONS

Transitions between sections should be indicated only by shifts in voice and body language. No costume changes except for the one noted.

TEXT MARKINGS

A dash (—) means the speaker has stopped him or herself.

A backslash (/) denotes a point of overlapping or interruption by the following dialogue.

Text in parentheses (text) is spoken sotto voce.

Bruce McKenzie
in *Some Prepared Remarks (A History in Speech)*

38th Humana Festival of New American Plays
Actors Theatre of Louisville, 2014
Photo by Bill Brymer

286

SOME PREPARED REMARKS
(A HISTORY IN SPEECH)

THE SPEAKER *enters carrying a few sheets of colored construction paper.*

THE SPEAKER. So um.

I told my dad? That Mrs. Barnes had said we had to prepare some brief remarks for the, for my presentation.

And he said. Um. "I can't give you brief remarks 'cause-a I wear boxers?"

And then he said you should always do, always start with a joke.

And then my mom said, "So when does the joke start?"

And then she laughed. So maybe that was the joke.

My presentation about my parents is that, I chose my dad.

He's a heart doctor. And my mom said that was ironic.

(I don't know what that is.)

K the heart is the most important thing in your body 'cause-a it makes all your blood go everywhere and if it didn't you would get super sick and die. Caitlin said that's not true 'cause-a her dad's a brain doctor and she said the brain is more, is better than the heart and I said so how come there's no special day where everyone gives pictures of brains like they do hearts on Valentine's Day and she said 'cause that's stupid anyway but I know it's just that she knows brains aren't as good.

Sometimes my dad will open up people's stomachs and, like, he'll take someone's whole heart out, and give them a whole new one, if theirs was broken. Like last year? My grandma had died and got hit by a car, and then, like, two weeks later my grandpa died? And they said he died just 'cause he had, uh, his heart broke, and so I said how come you didn't give him a different one, and my dad said that when you're really old your heart's been inside you so long it got glued to everything else, so if it breaks then all the stuff inside you breaks too. Like a Jenga.

(THE SPEAKER *pulls some index cards from a pocket. Transition of eight seconds.*)

THE SPEAKER. I want to say thank you first of all, Principal Fisher, and Mrs. Thompson, for giving me the opportunity to speak tonight. It's truly an honor to represent my class.

I want to talk about a topic that's been on my mind lately for. Many reasons. Having to fill these five minutes, being in the trough of a four-year cycle, turning eighteen.

That topic is time.

It's not an easy thing to discuss, so I've come up with some guidelines.

(Yes, Caitlin, I made a LIST.)

Here they are:

A clock is the least effective way to measure time. Using a star or a planet is far better.

When speaking, avoid the phrases "time passing" or "passing time." Once you believe that IT has a direction, you'll think you need to have one as well. It doesn't, and you don't.

None of us "have" any time. We can't sell it, we can't eat it, we can't jump up and down on it and crush it into tiny bits. Don't idolize it the way you do everything else in the world you wish you could "have." Don't disrespect it as much as some of the things you already "have," either.

>	(Beat.)

When my father was in the hospital.

He would joke that his bucket list wasn't things he needed to do, but things he wanted to be sure he told me.

And.

One of the things was that, when you're young, you notice that every year seems to go by a little faster.

He said that never stops.

And that.

By the time you hit fifty, you'll try to think back over the last five years, and realize it's actually been ten.

I've heard so often over the last few months: "I can't wait to get to college. I can't wait to get out of college."

But you can wait. You can wait here, for a bit.

Life has its own gravity, its own acceleration.

You don't need to make yourself more aerodynamic.

Be grateful to fall slowly.

>	(THE SPEAKER *takes a few folded pieces of worn-out yellow notepad paper from a pocket. Transition of six seconds.*)

THE SPEAKER. Everyone can see how prepared I was.

All right.

As most of you know, my wife—"wife," I like saying that—she and I have been in each other's lives for a very long time. It's difficult to find a way to put so many years into a toast; god knows we all want to get to the drinking.

So I came up with a little story.

You'll understand in a minute why the only things I'm usually allowed to write are prescriptions.

There once was a table and chair.

Ever since Table was purchased from the store and taken to his new patio home, his favorite thing in the whole world was when someone would come to sit and spend time with him.

Someone would put their hands on his iron top, or fold their legs into his sturdy stand, and he and his new friend would watch the sunset, or share a meal.

But soon Table noticed that these people would never stay with him for very long. Only for fifteen minutes, maybe an hour, then they would leave again.

Table began wondering if there was something wrong with him. If his corners were too sharp, or maybe he wobbled when you put your weight on him.

(*Beat.*)

He started to get very sad, and when nobody was looking, from time to time, he would rust silently in the dark.

One day, he realized that the people who lived on the other side of his patio door had been gone for months. No one ever came out in the morning, the afternoon, or even to watch the stars at night.

During this lonely time, keeping each other company, Table and Chair became very close. They had more in common than you would expect, coming from very different sides of the mine, and some would even say they looked like a perfect match.

Table thought back over all the time that he and Chair had been in each other's lives, and realized that even when no one had visited him, Chair had been around. And in the times when people had visited, Chair was there to support that too. In fact, Chair was the only one who had never let Table down.

(*Beat.*)

Even though they had been together for so many years, it had taken this long for Table to appreciate just how desperately he loved Chair.

Then, during a storm one spring afternoon, as they sat in shelter underneath Umbrella, the wind blew Chair over next to Table, and Chair's arm touched his side for the first time.

And at that moment, Table finally realized he never wanted anyone else to visit the patio ever again.

(THE SPEAKER *puts away the paper and pulls a Post-it note out of a pocket. Transition of four seconds.*)

THE SPEAKER. Okay got your, okay, and your special shoes? Good, okay, and, great.

(THE SPEAKER *consults the Post-it.*)

Daddy knows you want to go, honey, but I just had a couple things I wanted to tell you and I want to do it now because when I drop you off we'll be in front of all your new friends and then I'd embarrass you, wouldn't I? Yes, I would.

Okay.

You know I love you SO much, and I'm going to be thinking about you all day. And the teacher has my phone number which I'm always going to have with me just in case.

If ANYONE is mean to you, tell me, okay? ANYONE!

Even if it's the teacher. Especially if it's the teacher.

Don't worry about being popular. Are you old enough to worry about that yet? If you are, don't.

Don't take food if any of the other boys or girls offers it because I don't know their parents and god only knows what they're sending kids to school with these days. Razors, knives, poison; kindergarten's like a Tarantino film.

But most of all HAVE FUN! FIRST DAY OF SCHOOL! YAY!

(*Beat.*)

You look so cute with your backpack on.

I'm so sorry Mommy's not here. But you'll tell her all about it this weekend, okay?

And if, maybe you shouldn't tell any of your new friends about Mommy not being at home for a while, because she, also, we don't know if she's moving back soon, but. She probably will, and we don't want to confuse people, so we just won't say anything, okay?

Okay.

Sometimes. Things change and it's very hard to understand them.

(THE SPEAKER *pulls out two crisp sheets of white paper folded in half and a pair of reading glasses to wear. Transition of two seconds.*)

THE SPEAKER. If there's one thing we should remind ourselves of tonight, it is: what brought us here?

And hopefully the answer is not that you'd already paid the $5,000 and you wanted to make sure you at least got the abalone dinner.

I'm here today because my daughter shamed me into it.

(I see by your faces that some of you can sympathize.)

But humor aside, I think, in a way, that is true for all of us here. The struggle to instill in this country a more humane spirit is about creating a worthwhile future for our daughters, our sons, for any future to be possible at all.

It's an attempt to prevent us all from waking one morning, looking at the world around us and asking ourselves: when did this happen? After we worked so hard, and spent so long—

So many years simply doing what we believed was the right thing.

(*Beat.*)

I think that, at its heart, is why we are all deeply afraid of change. Afraid that the things we love will slip out of bed in the middle of the night without leaving a note.

Or even that the sadnesses we know so intimately, the anguish whose body we have traced with every fingertip, will be replaced by some other sadness whose language we don't even speak.

But we also know change is inevitable, and so we seclude ourselves deep in our cages, wild animals afraid of what we know must come.

What makes this fear even greater? The knowledge that the only power we have to shield ourselves against the future is our capacity to love and to fight for those very things we know we will lose someday.

(*Without stopping,* THE SPEAKER *puts away those papers and removes a napkin from a pocket. Speech continuous.*)

THE SPEAKER. And yet there comes a time when we all have to say our goodbyes. For some reason it still comes as a surprise, even when you're my age. Sometimes you look back, and you think your whole life was just a search for a better way to say goodbye.

(*Of the card.*)

A doctor knows it's time to retire when you can actually read what you've written.

Parkinson's just steadies our script.

I truly never imagined my practice would have lasted this long.

I also never imagined it would take so much effort to get out of bed in the morning.

It seems the only things you remember in life are the ones you never imagined until the moment they became real.

I certainly never presumed. I'd have the chance to be with the love of my life again.

You know we, we, she and I first became close, well we'd known each other for a number of years but then we both lost parents. Much too young. My father when I was seventeen and her mother a few months earlier.

So when our daughter was ill last year— Well, adversity always seemed to be our matchmaker. We're hoping for an earthquake or nuclear war so we can renew our vows.

All I really want to say to everyone is that I am grateful. Very grateful, for everything.

I have been. So blessed. And I want to say, I want to say, that, uh—

> (THE SPEAKER *looks at the napkin for a moment, then puts it back in a pocket.*)

THE SPEAKER. I just wanted to say a few words.

I had something prepared, but now, mm—

Doesn't seem right putting a life into only a few sentences when death is the last word.

> (*Beat.*)

She hated— The only other, mm, speech I ever gave. About Caitlin, was at our wedding. A story I wrote about this table and a chair, that she thought was awful. "That's your wedding toast?" she said. "Furniture?"

In the story, mm. A Table and Chair, they grow old together, and, I recall— I recall wondering how to end it. When they're young? Old? When they die?

So here's, mm. Here's what I would have said, if I'd kept going.

There's this old iron table and chair, match set. They're ancient now, paint faded, metal not so strong. And they know that, their, uh, time, is approaching.

Finally, mm, a truck pulls up into the yard where they are, middle of the day. And they're put in the truck.

And as they make the drive, mm, they know where they're going, Table and Chair, that they're no use anymore.

But they're just happy to be on that truck together, because. What else is there?

After a few miles, the truck stops. The back opens, and they see a sign that says, mm: "Recycled Metals."

> (*Beat.*)

Mm. That's the last moment they spend together. They get. Separated, after that.

But even as they say goodbye, they know in their heart of hearts, that as they're both melted back down, they will meet each other in the fire. Elemental once more.

And that maybe, mm. Maybe parts of each one of them will end up in a new table, or new chair, or a magnet.

And they'll be together again.

They know this.

Because, mm. Because they measure lifetimes by the stars.

End of Play

STEEL HAMMER
directed by Anne Bogart
music and lyrics by Julia Wolfe
original text by
Kia Corthron, Will Power,
Carl Hancock Rux, and Regina Taylor
recorded music performed by
Bang on a Can All-Stars
and Trio Mediaeval
performed and created by SITI Company

All inquiries concerning *Steel Hammer* in its entirety—directed by Anne Bogart, music and lyrics by Julia Wolfe, original text by Kia Corthron, Will Power, Carl Hancock Rux, and Regina Taylor, performed and created by SITI Company—should be addressed to: SITI Company, 520 8th Avenue, Suite 310, New York, NY 10018. ATTN: Michelle Preston, 212-868-0860, ext. 101.

All inquiries concerning rights to perform individual playwrights' pieces, including amateur rights, should be addressed to:

For Kia Corthron: The Gersh Agency, 41 Madison Avenue, 33rd Floor, New York, NY 10010. ATTN: Seth Glewen, 212-634-8124.

For Will Power: William Morris Endeavor Entertainment, 1325 Avenue of the Americas, New York, NY 10019. ATTN: Susan Weaving, 212-903-1170.

For Carl Hancock Rux: Victoria Sanders & Associates, LLC, 241 Avenue of the Americas, Suite 11H, New York, NY 10014. 212-633-8811.

For Regina Taylor: Bret Adams Ltd., 448 West 44th Street, New York, NY 10036. ATTN: Bruce Ostler, 212-765-5630.

ABOUT *STEEL HAMMER*

This article first ran in the January/February 2014 issue of Inside Actors, *Actors Theatre of Louisville's subscriber newsletter, and is based on conversations with the artists before rehearsals for the Humana Festival production began.*

Well, John Henry said to the captain,
"Oh a man ain't nothin' but a man.
'Fore I'd let your steam drill beat me down,
Well, I'll die with the hammer in my hand, Lord, Lord,
I'll die with the hammer in my hand."

You may have heard the legend of John Henry. It's the account of an epically strong, steel drivin' railroad worker who out-hammered a steam engine and lost his life in the process. It's a fable pitting the work of human hands against technological efficiency in a battle of man versus machine. It's a paean to the virtues of our everyday toil. Or it's a cautionary tale about killing yourself with work. And it's based on a real man from the 19th century, or several men...unless, of course, it's all a myth. In all of its shifting meanings, this most American of folktales captures something about our national character. Just what it captures—and the story we tell about it—comprises the central inquiry of *Steel Hammer*, Anne Bogart and SITI Company's latest project to premiere in the Humana Festival.

Though the tale of John Henry has taken a winding road from its Appalachian origins to today, *Steel Hammer*'s lineage is easier to trace. Before it became a piece for the theatre, *Steel Hammer* began its life as an experimental score of the same name, composed by Julia Wolfe. (The piece was a finalist for the Pulitzer Prize in 2010.) With her company, the international experimental music collective Bang on a Can, Wolfe approached Bogart with this proposal—to turn an art ballad examining the complicated history of the folk song "John Henry" into a work of music theatre. Bogart jumped at the chance to collaborate on this project. "I was intrigued by the John Henry story traveling over the years and being appropriated in so many different ways," she relates. Indeed, the durable folktale has proven fertile ground for multiple interpretations, including one in particular that fascinated the director. "The song was used on railroad crews to set the rhythm of the stinting, when they hoisted the steel hammers," Bogart notes, "and it was a reminder to slow down or you'd die. It was actually more a tool than an entertainment."

That notion, of a story told not merely to please but for a specific purpose, inspired the theatrical conceit around which *Steel Hammer* is built: a storytelling contest. And to generate an array of approaches to John Henry's tale that could fuel this contest, SITI Company commissioned four playwrights—Kia Corthron, Will Power, Carl Hancock Rux and Regina Taylor—to author their unique takes on this American legend. Bogart's prompt for the writers was liberatingly simple: What is the story of John Henry in the way *you'd* like to tell it? From there, each was free to explore those aspects of the folktale that attracted them. "The John Henry story is just about the closest thing we have in America to Greek mythology," Will Power explains. "And folktales, like the Greek myths, have all kinds of entry points." Power believes this multiplicity of narratives is actually how traditional lore is designed—and how it speaks for the culture that produced it. "I think mythology is a collection of stories that tells the truth of a people," the playwright continues. "There are all these different perspectives. And they're all true."

As *Steel Hammer* unfolds, the members of a diverse six-person ensemble step onto a platform and take turns telling their versions of the story of John Henry, using every means at their disposal to connect with the audience. Music merges with the spoken word, woven together by movement, dance, and percussion on multiple surfaces (including the human body). Humana Festival audiences who witnessed past SITI Company collaborations such as *Cabin Pressure*, *bobrauschenbergamerica* and *Hotel Cassiopeia* will be familiar with the ensemble's protean and richly textured style of theatre. But for Bogart, their multidisciplinary approach to *Steel Hammer* also reflects how individuals use any available medium to connect with each other, regardless of how difficult or impoverished their circumstances might be. "Storytelling is an attempt to signal in the dark to one another, to communicate through whatever it is you have," she proposes. "Even with nothing, you still have something to say; with nothing, you are making bridges between yourself and others."

Ultimately, the legend of John Henry does much more than provide this play with its source material; it also serves as a visceral example of how storytellers shape narratives to their own ends, be they political, cultural, or practical. "For me, this project is not about getting to the absolute truth of this tale," Bogart offers. "It's about how we mold stories for the times we live in." *Steel Hammer* investigates our human need to explain the world through the tales we tell, making sense of our lives in conversation with each other. "People have this impulse to get up in front of each other and send out a signal," the director concludes. "I guess you could say that's what theatre is."

—Steve Moulds

PLAYWRIGHT BIOGRAPHIES

Kia Corthron's previous Humana Festival productions include *Moot the Messenger, Slide Glide the Slippery Slope* and *The Open Road Anthology*. Other productions include *A Cool Dip in the Barren Saharan Crick* (Playwrights Horizons/The Play Company/Culture Project), *Light Raise the Roof* (New York Theatre Workshop), *Snapshot Silhouette* (Children's Theatre Company), *Slide Glide the Slippery Slope* (Mark Taper Forum), *The Venus de Milo is Armed* (Alabama Shakespeare Festival), *Breath, Boom* (The Royal Court Theatre, Playwrights Horizons, Huntington Theatre Company, Yale Repertory Theatre), *Splash Hatch on the E Going Down* (Yale Repertory Theatre, Center Stage, New York Stage and Film, Donmar Warehouse), *Digging Eleven* (Hartford Stage), *Seeking the Genesis* (Goodman Theatre, Manhattan Theatre Club), *Trickle* (Ensemble Studio Theatre), and *Force Continuum* (Atlantic Theater Company). Awards include a McKnight National Residency, the Callaway and Fadiman Awards, and NEA/TCG, and in 2014 she was awarded a Windham Campbell Prize, the USArtists Jane Addams Fellowship, and was the Honored Playwright at the Great Plains Theatre Conference. She has also received Writers Guild and Edgar Allan Poe awards for *The Wire*. She is an alumna of New Dramatists and serves on the Dramatists Guild Council.

Will Power is an award-winning playwright and performer. Plays include *Stagger Lee* (Dallas Theater Center), *Fetch Clay, Make Man* (New York Theatre Workshop, Marin Theatre Company), *Steel Hammer* with SITI Company (Humana Festival), *The Seven* (Lucille Lortel Award for Best Musical, New York Theatre Workshop, La Jolla Playhouse), *Five Fingers of Funk!* (Children's Theatre Company), *Honey Bo and The Goldmine* (La Jolla Playhouse) and two acclaimed solo shows, *The Gathering* and *Flow* (his solo shows toured to over 70 cities nationwide, as well as Europe and Australia). Power's numerous awards include a United States Artist Prudential Fellowship, the TCG Peter Zeisler Memorial Award, the Jury Award for Best Theatre Performance at the HBO U.S. Comedy Arts Festival, and the Trailblazer Award from The National Black Theater Network. Power's numerous film and television appearances include *The Colbert Report* (Comedy Central) and *Bill Moyers on Faith & Reason* (PBS).

Mr. Power was a guest of the U.S. State Department on five separate occasions, traveling to South Africa, Botswana, Lesotho, Turkmenistan, and Kyrgyzstan. On these trips and others, Mr. Power taught community workshops in shantytowns, worked with poets in former regimes of the Soviet Union, and lectured at various libraries, grammar schools, and colleges. Power is currently on the faculty at The Meadows School of the Arts/Southern Methodist University, and is the Andrew W. Mellon Foundation Playwright in Residence with the Dallas Theater Center.

Carl Hancock Rux's work has been presented at McCarter Theatre Center, the Walker Art Center, Penumbra Theatre, and Off-Broadway at Lincoln Center Theater, The Public Theater, Playwrights Horizons, 651 Arts and BAM's Next Wave Festival. Rux's work has also been produced at Maison des arts de Créteil, Montclair State College, Hong Kong Arts Festival, Esplanade Theatre of Singapore, Scuola di Danza Mimma Testa in Trastevere, and Teatro de natal infantil Raffaelly Beligni. Rux has received an Obie Award, an Alpert Award in the Arts, and a New York Press Club Journalism Award for Entertainment News. He is a New York Foundation for the Arts Gregory Millard Fellow, as well as the recipient of a NYFA Prize and a CINE Golden Eagle Film and Video Award. Published works include *Pagan Operetta* (SemioText), *Talk* (TCG) and *Asphalt* (Simon & Schuster).

With an impressive body of work that encompasses film, television, theatre and writing, **Regina Taylor** is best known to television audiences as Lilly Harper in the series *I'll Fly Away* and as Molly Blane in CBS's hit drama *The Unit*. Her credits as a playwright include *Oo-Bla-Dee* (Recipient of the American Theatre Critics Association New Play Award), *Drowning Crow* (Manhattan Theatre Club), *The Trinity River Plays* (Dallas Theater Center and the Goodman Theatre; Recipient of the 2010 Edgerton Foundation New American Play Award), *Magnolia*, *The Dreams of Sarah Breedlove*, *A Night in Tunisia*, *Escape from Paradise*, *Watermelon Rinds*, and *Inside the Belly of the Beast*. Taylor's critically acclaimed *Crowns* continues to be one of the most-performed musicals in the country, and is the winner of four Washington, D.C. Helen Hayes awards. Taylor also wrote and directed *Post Black* for New York's Ensemble Studio Theatre. Taylor is a member and Artistic Associate of the Goodman Theatre and a resident playwright at New York's Signature Theatre Company. She received the Hope Abelson Artist-in-Residence Award from Northwestern in 2010. She has received honorary doctorates from Columbia College, DePaul University and Lake Forest College. Most recently, Taylor both wrote and directed *stop. reset.* at Signature Theatre Company. She will direct *stop. reset.* again at the Goodman Theatre in 2015. Taylor has also received a Golden Globe, an NAACP Image Award, two Emmy Award nominations, and the Oscar Micheaux Award from the Chicago Film Critics Association. Visit ReginaTaylor.com for more information.

ACKNOWLEDGMENTS

Steel Hammer premiered at the Humana Festival of New American Plays in March 2014. It was directed by Anne Bogart, with music and lyrics by Julia Wolfe and recorded music performed by Bang on a Can All-Stars and Trio Mediaeval. *Steel Hammer* was performed and created by SITI Company, with the following cast:

> Akiko Aizawa
> Eric Berryman
> Patrice Johnson Chevannes
> Gian-Murray Gianino
> Barney O'Hanlon
> Stephen Duff Webber

and the following production staff:

> Scenic and Costume Designer............................James Schuette
> Lighting Designer...Brian H Scott
> Sound Designer......................................Christian Frederickson
> Stage Manager .... Ellen Mezzera
> Dramaturg...Steve Moulds
> Special Project Producer.....................................Megan Wanlass
> Choreographer...Barney O'Hanlon
> Assistant Director ....Laura Sheedy
> Properties Master..Mark Walston
> Directing Assistant ....Jacob Sexton
> Assistant Dramaturg...Eric Werner

The original musical score of *Steel Hammer* was commissioned by Bang on a Can with generous support from Maria and Robert A. Skirnick and Carnegie Hall.

Steel Hammer was funded in part by the National Endowment for the Arts.

NOTE

The components of *Steel Hammer* published here are the work of the four playwrights commissioned by SITI Company to write original text for this project. More information about Julia Wolfe's music may be found at juliawolfemusic.com. For additional information about SITI Company and *Steel Hammer*, visit www.siti.org.

Eric Berryman (foreground), Akiko Aizawa, Barney O'Hanlon,
Stephen Duff Webber, Gian-Murray Gianino,
and Patrice Johnson Chevannes
in *Steel Hammer*

38th Humana Festival of New American Plays
Actors Theatre of Louisville, 2014
Photo by Michael Brosilow

TUNNEL TALE
by Kia Corthron

CHARACTERS

(*in order of speaking*)
Cliff SANDERS, a man
Chloe GRAHAM, a woman
Aisha COX, a black woman
JOHN HENRY, a black man

> *Carnival music.* JOHN HENRY, *large man of inordinate strength, driving*
> HIS *large steel hammer. As it is* <u>very</u> *heavy, every swing will require excessive*
> *effort, the clangs well-spaced between each other, and loud.*
> *A few feet away, on either side and slightly downstage of* JOHN HENRY, *are*
> SANDERS *and* GRAHAM. *On the other side of* SANDERS *is* COX.
> *The illusion of a tent-show audience observing* THEM. *Unless otherwise*
> *indicated,* SANDERS *and* GRAHAM *address the audience.*

SANDERS. (*Grinning at* JOHN HENRY, *admiring:*) Steel driver!

GRAHAM. "John Henry," 19th Century folksong. To give you an idea of the
popularity, go to iTunes: five hundred recordings.

SANDERS. Then they got tired and wrote "Less relevant items are not
displayed."

GRAHAM. Countless versions.

COX. Almost all referencing death off the bat: first stanza.

GRAHAM. In American folklore we have our fictional Paul Bunyan, Pecos
Bill, and the tall tales surrounding real figures: Johnny Appleseed, Calamity
Jane. All white. John Henry stands alone as a black legend. For us *all*.

SANDERS. We consider this a very important tribute to African American
culture.

GRAHAM. (*Sings:*) *This old hammer*
Killed John Henry
Killed my brother
Can't kill me.

SANDERS. Another version of the song:

GRAHAM. (*Sings:*) *John Henry was a little bitty baby*
Sittin on his mama's knee

He picked up a hammer and a little piece of steel
Said,

> (JOHN HENRY *joins in here without looking at* GRAHAM *or inter-*
> *rupting* HIS *work.* SHE *turns to* HIM, *surprised by* HIS *participation,*
> *delighted.*)

GRAHAM and JOHN HENRY. *Hammer's gonna be the death of me*
LawdLawd
Hammer's gonna be the death of me.

COX. Or (*Chants:*) This ole hammer, mos too heavy

COX and JOHN HENRY. *Huh.* (*Should coincide with* JOHN HENRY's
hammer coming down.)

COX. Killed John Henry, killed him dead.

COX and JOHN HENRY. *Huh.*

SANDERS. The way to start is to start at the start. John Henry put his
mama to conniptions bein born, he pop out lookin like a toddler, lookin
ready to walk. John Henry, black as coal, born in the heat a the heart a Dixie.

GRAHAM. (*Sings:*) *Some say he's from Georgia*
Some say he's from Alabam

> (*Suddenly music out, lights out except for the light on* JOHN HENRY, *who*
> *has stopped working, has turned to the audience.*)

JOHN HENRY. Elizabeth City, New Jersey born. But come down Virginia
I'm a prisoner. Convict, what I'm guilty of? Stealin from Wiseman's Grocery
they claim, but they got a math problem: If the law say twenty dollars the
minimum for gran larceny, and *everything* in Wiseman's store 'cludin the two
big ole hogs out back sum up to *fifty* dollars, how the hell I carry out half
the merchandise on my back, broad daylight with the proprietor settin right
there? So they make up some'un, rename it all "housebreakin," *now* I'm a
felon.

GRAHAM. (*Sings:*) *But it's wrote on the rock at the Big Ben Tunnel*
That he's an East Virginia Man,

JOHN HENRY. Ten years.

> (*Back to carnival music, general light,* JOHN HENRY *swinging* HIS
> *hammer.*)

SANDERS. So big little John Henry grows up to be a giant of a man. And
while he's growing so's somethin else: the railroad.

GRAHAM. Track was being laid for the Chesapeake and Ohio, tie by tie,
rail by rail.

SANDERS. Originating in Richmond with nothin between it and the Ohio
River – cept a few mountains.

GRAHAM. Hilly land had to be flattened, mountains tunneled through.

SANDERS. The men hammered.

>   (JOHN HENRY's *hammer clangs*.)

Drivin stakes into the rock, or the mountain, and then fill in the holes they made: dynamite.

GRAHAM. The extreme manual labor explains why versions of the folksong have been adapted by construction crews. By prison crews.

COX. *Not guilty.*

>   (*The music suddenly goes out as* GRAHAM *and* SANDERS *turn to* COX. JOHN HENRY *stops working, not looking at* THEM, *but listening*.)

GRAHAM. Again?

COX. I don't believe he committed any crime. John Henry convicted under the "black codes": Suddenly *vagrancy*'s against the law, black man looking for work and can't find it's a criminal. Suddenly illegal to tout an (*Fingers the quote marks:*) "air of satisfaction" and you know damn well to which race *that* Dixie mandate was directed right after the Civil War, right at the start of Reconstruction.

GRAHAM. (*To audience:*) Reconstruction: a federal effort to level the racial playing field. For a while.

COX. Slavery just declared over, the Cotton Belt knew how to bring back chattel labor. Fill the prisons with black. So here come John Henry, to *them* some Yankee uppity come South, take advantage of post-war Reconstruction.

GRAHAM. This is *not* about the real John Henry.

JOHN HENRY. Reconstruction put a few black men in the Congress.

GRAHAM. This is about folklore, we're here to tell the story of John Henry the *legend*.

JOHN HENRY. And Reconstruction put a slew a black men in the penitentiary.

>   (JOHN HENRY *starts swinging* HIS *hammer again, cueing the return of the carnival music and festive atmosphere*.)

SANDERS. Big John Henry grows up to marry a sweet little lady named Polly Ann.

GRAHAM. Or Lucy, or Julie Ann, depending on the rendition.

SANDERS. John Henry loved him some Polly Ann and Polly Ann loved her some John Henry. Loyal.

GRAHAM. In *some* versions. In others—

COX. (*As* POLLY ANN. *Sings:*) *John Henry had a little woman*
Just as pretty as she could be
They's just one objection I's got to her
She want every man she see

SANDERS. Now John Henry was a big man, *powerful* man, just what the railroad ordered. Doggin track faster 'n any other trackliner, only one other ever had the nerve to challenge him and ten minutes later that challenger draggin home to his woman, her whuppin him with a broomstick cuz he say his paycheck gone, restin easy in John Henry's hip pocket.

(Sudden loud sound of a steam drill. ALL, including JOHN HENRY, look offstage in the direction of the sound. ALL in awe.)

GRAHAM. Then came along the steam engine.

SANDERS. *(Distaste.)* "Progress," they called it.

GRAHAM. Various mechanized drills came to be developed at this time.

SANDERS. Their primary motivation bein speed, mimickin the labor a many men in minimal minutes. But the clunky machines could never match the precision a two workers on their own, the hammer man swingin the sledgehammer down on the chisel,

(JOHN HENRY's hammer clangs down hard.)

the shaker turnin the drill.

(As GRAHAM starts speaking, JOHN HENRY takes interest, stops work to look up and listen to HER.)

GRAHAM. In one version Captain Tommy, dubbed *(Fingers the quote marks:)* "the whitest man on earth," loved John Henry like a son and told him he'd bet the white man running the steam drill that John Henry could drill faster.

COX. John Henry replied to Captain Tommy with "lightnin in his eye,"

(JOHN HENRY now starts to take on the character in the story.)

JOHN HENRY. *(Playing the part, billowing with pride, sings:)* "Cap'n, bet yo lass red cent on me
Fo I'll beat it to the bottom or I'll die—"

JOHN HENRY, COX, GRAHAM and SANDERS. *(All grinning to the audience and singing:)* Lawd, Lawd

JOHN HENRY. *(Sings:)* I'll beat it to the bottom or I'll die.

SANDERS. They faced each other. John Henry on the ground, the White Man perched high up on his whale of a drill, the only time a man had ever looked down to John Henry.

(JOHN HENRY looking up at the imaginary steam drill.)

Well John Henry kissed his hammer (JOHN HENRY *does.*), and the White Man turned on the steam.

(Sound of machine turning on.)

GRAHAM. *(Sings:)* Then the White Man tole John Henry,

SANDERS. *(To GRAHAM, worried:)* Don't sing that part.

GRAHAM. *(Sings:)* "Niggah, damn yo soul"

SANDERS. I said stop singing!

GRAHAM. (*To* SANDERS:) I'm not changing the words to sanitize it, make it palatable. I'm not appeasing your white guilt.

COX. (*Pumping* HER*self up like the cocksure White Man, sings:*) *"You might beat this steamin drill a mine*
When the rocks in the mountain turn to gold"

COX, GRAHAM and SANDERS. (*Singing:*) *Lawd, Lawd*

> (SANDERS *has moved into* JOHN HENRY's *space and stands on something [a block?] that raises* HIM *above* JOHN HENRY. *Now* HE *takes on the persona of The White Man.*)

SANDERS. (*Sings:*) *"When the rocks in the mountains turn to gold."*

> (*Now all sound goes out, and* JOHN HENRY *and* SANDERS *as the White Man stare at each other.* SANDERS' *face still expresses arrogance.* JOHN HENRY's *countenance is more complex. It should not be only anger: also fear, confusion – the consequences for humiliating a white man could be dire. The silence goes on a long time. Then suddenly* GRAHAM, HER *body language indicating* SHE *is acting in some "official" capacity, whistles through* HER *teeth, signaling the start of the race.* SANDERS *will physicalize driving the steam drill while* JOHN HENRY *hammers faster and harder than* HE *has during the entire play. As soon as the race begins* COX *and* GRAHAM *start hooting and hollering, and sound returns: music [different than before], crowds, chaos. The steam drill pulls ahead, then* JOHN HENRY, *then the steam drill, then* JOHN HENRY, *then* JOHN HENRY, *then* JOHN HENRY *– and at some point the race is suddenly over, signaled by the screaming and cheering of* COX *and* GRAHAM *[and the crowd sound], by* SANDERS' *White Man's shock and fury, and by* JOHN HENRY's *exhausted collapse. It is clear that* JOHN HENRY *is the victor. As* JOHN HENRY's *condition gradually dawns upon the onlookers – crawling, clutching* HIS *chest –* COX, *who has now morphed into Polly Ann, races screaming to* HIM, *holds* HIM. SANDERS *from* HIS *perch, back to being the storyteller, turns to the audience.*)

SANDERS. (*Sings softly:*) *John Henry had a little woman*
Her name was Polly Ann
He hugged and kissed her just before he died
Saying,

JOHN HENRY. (*Very weak, speaks rather than sings:*) "Polly, do the very best you can."

> (JOHN HENRY *dies. It should not be corny/cartoon, but not too real either.*)

SANDERS. Well Polly Ann wept her little heart out. (COX *mimes this [no sound].*) But in another version,

GRAHAM. (*Grins:*) This is my favorite part.

SANDERS. (*Sings, belts it out jauntily:*) She walked out to those tracks (COX *as Polly Ann does.*)
Picked up John Henry's hammer (COX *as Polly Ann does.*)
GRAHAM and SANDERS. (*Singing:*) *Polly drove steel like a man* (COX *as Polly Ann does, powerfully.*)
Lawd, Lawd
Polly drove steel like a man.

> (*During the following verse* COX *will leave the hammer to walk downstage and join* GRAHAM *and* SANDERS. JOHN HENRY's *body is now hidden behind* THEM.)

GRAHAM, SANDERS and COX. (*Singing:*) *Well, every Monday morning*
When a bluebird began to sing
You could hear John Henry from a mile or more
You could hear John Henry's hammer ring
Lawd, Lawd

> (*On the second "Lawd" a thunderous hammer clang, sound-enhanced with reverberations.* GRAHAM, SANDERS *and* COX, *startled, jump out of the way and turn around, seeing that* JOHN HENRY *has stood and brought the hammer down.* JOHN HENRY *turns to the audience. Though* HE *will speak of* HIM*self in third person,* HE *should not be completely emotionally distant.*)

JOHN HENRY. After the war, nineteen-year-old John William Henry traveled down to the Reconstruction South looking for work. Accused of petty theft, the charge trumped up to housebreaking and larceny, he was sentenced to a decade in the Virginia Penitentiary. At twenty-one years of age John Henry was farmed out to the Chesapeake and Ohio Railroad. He was five feet one and one-quarter inches tall.

> (JOHN HENRY *seems to shrink before the audience's eyes. This may take a few seconds. When* HE *is finished:*)

The perfect height for tunnel work.

> (*Small* JOHN HENRY *starts swinging the hammer.* HE *seems much weaker, exhausted.*)

SANDERS. The *legend* of John Henry, the strongman, endured and revised itself into a thousand incarnations.

GRAHAM. American communist posters during the Depression adopted his muscled workingman image.

COX. In the comics the black steel-driving man transformed into the white man of steel: Superman.

GRAHAM. (*Moved by the story:*) But the folklore John Henry, the bigger-than-life man born to drive steel and to die by it, his heart giving out at the end of the greatest race: Man Triumphs Over Machine.

COX. Gave his death a poetic quality.

GRAHAM. (*Sensing light sarcasm from* COX, GRAHAM *turns to* HER, *defensively:*) Yes, it *did*.

COX. When in truth he *did* die on the job but what probably killed him like most all of the other tunnel workers, overwhelmingly black men in their young twenties, were the tiny rock bits thick in the air of the caves they created, taking occupation of their lungs.

GRAHAM. Silicosis.

SANDERS. No. Air.

JOHN HENRY. I WAS BORN AND RAISED FREE! THEN COME SOUTH, THE LAW MAKE ME A SLAVE!

> (*This outburst catapults* JOHN HENRY *into an uncontrollable coughing fit.* COX, SANDERS *and* GRAHAM *turn to* HIM, *and lights slowly fade on* THEM *while brightening on* HIM. *JOHN HENRY's coughing becomes unbearable, morphing into a horrible wheezing. As* HE *seems desperately struggling for oxygen, there is a blackout with the terrible wheezing uninterrupted, going on, and on, and on till suddenly: nothing.*)

MIGRANT MAMIE REMEMBERS JOHN HENRY
by Carl Hancock Rux

Talcott. Milboro. Shiloh. Hot Springs. Warm Springs. Burnsville. Bacova Junction. I remember it. Slavery abolished round 'bout five year then. Never know it. No free room and board. Only music tell the tale. I sing it if I could but I tell it better. Back then, do not know how old I was, but I was young, before breasts or blood. No matter. Girls was women then. There was the slow creak of a wagon cart or some crude handmade thing pulling along by the clop clop of a mule and the vibrant off-pitch holler of the handclap... what music has become now. The negro man. The negro preacher. The negro laborer. The negro crook. We all walk the same. Same roads. I come from one big family. Mama give sixteen babies. The first baby born die of fever. The second baby born die in the womb. The third baby born me. Thirteen come after that. All live, I make sure of it. Well, earth, heaven, sky—one big place. Wasn't nuthin' but big hard scrappin' black hands...poor ruff raggedy cotton scrappin' fingers...plantation to plantation...walk the mile road feet...feet tied up... rag feet...toes bleeding...fingers bleeding...what was them days...tobacco farm and steel mills and always somebody with a axe or a hammer ready and miles of walking foot rags hand bleeding cotton scrappin' field to field...pick this pick that. By twelve I take to killing hogs for people...Hotchkiss. Mountain Grove. Sunrise. Switch Back. Chimney Run. Sometimes they give you the innards...sometimes the feet, sometimes the head...I wasn't but nuthin' then...A shadow on the doorsill...just a girl slaughterin' hogs for folks...they pay you with the scraps...pig guts... pig feet...pig head...blood drippin' behind me walkin' back down the road trying to make it home...but if night come you wait for sun up...rest on the long road. Camp up somewhere. Overcrowded shacks and shanties, no running water. Sanitation is an unuttered idea. Contagion, a fact. Congestion a matter of existence. Insects everywhere, feeding upon the host. He come round...lay near beside me...and get to talkin'...I remember everything he say then...whisper it soft...say his name John Henry...big old man...say to me Death is grace. Say Death is reality and nature of life. Say man—every man—is an end in himself, exists for his own sake, and the achievement of his own happiness is his highest moral purpose. Say neither life nor happiness the pursuit of a free man. Just as man is free man got to be free to survive in a random manner, less he perish, less he mindless. Say some things I do not know all what he talkin' about except I like how it sound. Say the

310

torture of frustration all you finds. The problem is time, time as a horizon. Time for the understanding of being. Life. Death. Struggle. Food. Peace. Shelter. Place to rest. Rest stop. Field house. Somewhere before home. Night fallin'. Someplace 'fore pig guts get bad. This one place, I hear the sound of clunking boots on the grass behind me. He pass me. He sat directly in front of me. He was breathing making noises like a crying dog. He was large, big black man big black hands carrying a bag of somethin' other...grunting and saying somethin' in reaction to something. The sounds, the smells, making me ill. It had become stronger, the smell, the night, the not knowin', the liquor men blending the strange olfactory of death...all camped round about together...but he wasn't like them...naw...wasn't so scary...I know he must be on the run from somethin'...most mens was...but he lay beside me in the high grass...night making his body over, measuring his wounds. There are many besides him. Three thousand neat-ankle sons and daughters dispersed far and wide...but he the one I remember from every place alike who serve earth and deep waters. There are many sons of the sky with wings and feet, children who are glorious but he the only one I remember...must been long before Big Bend Tunnel and all that what people tell...I remember 'cause I remember everything...the insects...many rivers. I walked a whole lotta roads feet covered in rags...listening to waters babbling as they flow...but well, this long before them steel driving steam days...this long before his incarceration...that man what lay next to me...son of the Ocean, that John Henry. Must been. Maker of songs. A place for permanent dreaming. A voices of all kinds. I know this I was safe that night in the high grass I know that. That's the night I met John Henry. Never know'd what was in that bag he carry.

JOHN HENRY, POLLY ANN
by Will Power

Images are projected of African-American men working. Abrasive sounds of metal grinding, machinery turning and dogs barking accompany the collage of images. The pictures intensify as the sounds fade. Enter JOHN HENRY, *carrying a hammer, and weary after another day of work. Behind* JOHN HENRY, *enter* PRISON GUARD/RAILROAD CAPTAIN/FEDERAL JUDGE.

PRISON GUARD/RAILROAD CAPTAIN/FEDERAL JUDGE. Get some rest boys, morning bell rings in three hours, and we're at it again.

JOHN HENRY. Yes sir

(JOHN HENRY *enters a small prison cell. Once inside, the* PRISON GUARD/RAILROAD CAPTAIN/FEDERAL JUDGE *closes the cell door and stands guard.*

Lights up on POLLY ANN.)

POLLY ANN. John called for Polly Ann in the night. Called for her like every night since he first went to prison, in 1877

JOHN HENRY. Polly...Polly Ann. I needs to see ya
This 20 pound hammer feel like 40 pounds today
My head is light and my thoughts are heavy
Won't you come by here Polly Ann. Polly Ann! Polly Ann!

PRISON GUARD/RAILROAD CAPTAIN/FEDERAL JUDGE. Quiet up in there boy, Before I give you somethin' to cry about

JOHN HENRY. Yes sir boss man. (*Whispering.*) Polly Ann...

Polly Ann was with the children, a long ways away

POLLY ANN. John Henry, you gonna get out of there soon, and we gonna resume our life, as hard as it was, it don't compare to you bein' in there and me bein' out here. Now tell me, when ya comin' home John? When they gonn' work you to an inch of your life then send you home,

barely a man but my man, I'll take you and nurse you

Till you strong again, find all the pieces of you that's broken and scattered all over and sew you back together.

John needed to hear her voice, but tonight, he was in no mood to hear all that poetic stuff, cause he'd been hearin' it for the last hundred and thirty-somethin' years. Of course he didn't know what Polly should say. In some ways he wished she would just move on with her life, get another man and move on, get a job at CNN down in Atlanta, or go to Hollywood and make movies.

JOHN HENRY. Polly, why you waitin' on me? You know I ain't gettin' outta here. First they say, when you work our fields, then we'll let you out of here, then they said, when you build the railroads, then, and only then, will we let you out, then they said, when you fight our wars, no no when you buy our drugs, no no no, when you work with us on this drug war thing, you play your part, then we promise you John Henry, you'll be released. Well, I been denied parole two hundred sixty seven times. Done broke mo' rocks, and built mo' parts of this country than anyone would believe 'till I show 'em what I built my damn self. But I can't show nobody nothin', can't do nothin', 'cause I'm in here forever.

Polly Ann knew it was gonna be different this time, she just knew it

POLLY ANN. John, didn't you tell me this new Warden is different? He's what they call a liberal, right? He went to UC Berkeley for God sakes.

JOHN HENRY. I don't care where he went, I'm not gettin' out Polly

POLLY ANN. But this Warden—

JOHN HENRY. I asked the Warden Polly, I asked him to please help me. And you know what he say? He say,

> (*The* PRISON GUARD/RAILROAD CAPTAIN/FEDERAL JUDGE *becomes* THE WARDEN.)

THE WARDEN. Well now John, you know I'm a liberal. And you know that I know that you been workin' too long, and it ain't right John, it ain't right! But, I'm just a man and a man can't do nothin' against history, and history say...John, you know how the song go. John Henry dies with a hammer in his hand

POLLY ANN. No John! No you better not...if you die that's a punk move. Baby just hang on, keep your spirits up just a little while longer. See 'cause if you're alive, well then there's still a chance.

JOHN HENRY. Ain't no chance

POLLY ANN. Then you better do somethin', break outta jail or something. See cause I'm tired of doin' it by myself. Your children, my children they ask me they say, where is my daddy, who is my daddy?

JOHN HENRY. Well you the one didn't want them to see me in here, I told you, you can bring them for a visit if you like

POLLY ANN. The hell with a visit John Henry. What I want them to see you in here like this for? I don't want them thinkin' this is normal, no I want them to see they daddy out in the world doin' things

JOHN HENRY. Well what you want me to do Polly Ann? I can't break these bars, I ain't no superman, just a man.

> (*Pause.*)

POLLY ANN. John, I got the new top 40 hit this week.

JOHN HENRY. Oh yeah, what is it, do it for me?

POLLY ANN. It's by this new singer named_____ (*Name of whoever is #1 on Top 40 list that week.*)

JOHN HENRY. (*Name of whoever is #1 on Top 40 list that week.*)? Never heard of him/her before

POLLY ANN. Well, you wanna hear it?

JOHN HENRY. Yeah go ahead

POLLY ANN. OK, now John, I'm not much of a singer but

JOHN HENRY. Polly Ann stop messin' around and let me hear

PRISON GUARD/RAILROAD CAPTAIN/FEDERAL JUDGE. Shut up in there boy, before I give you solitary confinement. I ain't gonna warn you again

JOHN HENRY. I'm sorry boss sir. OK go head, Polly I don't have much time.

POLLY ANN. Alright… (POLLY ANN *sings a few bars of whoever is #1 on Top 40 list that week.*)

JOHN HENRY. That sucks

POLLY ANN. John Henry! You watch your mouth now.

JOHN HENRY. Well it does. Me and the boys sing better than that everyday

POLLY ANN. So you want me to stop singing to you then?

JOHN HENRY. No I—I like when you sing, I bet you sing 'em better than them singers do. Polly Ann, it's time for us to go our separate ways.

POLLY ANN. No

JOHN HENRY. Listen to me. You know it in your heart that we ain't never gonn' be together. The fact that you waited for me through all this time, well…I love you Polly Ann, and now it's time for me to go and for you to go on.

Maybe for the first time in history, Polly Ann knew John Henry was right. If a liberal Warden couldn't help John's cause, well what chance did he have? Polly Ann, she say

POLLY ANN. OK John…I…I guess you're right

JOHN HENRY. I am right Polly. Will you tell the children about me?

POLLY ANN. Of course, and I won't say nothing about prison, I won't say nothing about that. And I'll make you 6 foot five instead of 5 foot two. And I'll make up something about you beatin' a steam engine

JOHN HENRY. A steam engine?

POLLY ANN. Yeah. And you died a hero. How does that sound?

JOHN HENRY. It sounds…it sounds just fine.

POLLY ANN. Goodbye John

JOHN HENRY. Goodbye

      (POLLY ANN *turns to leave*.)

Polly Ann, wait. Honey I got to know

      (JOHN HENRY *sings*.)

Who's gonna shoe your little feet?
Who's gonna glove your hand?
Tell me, who's going to kiss your sweet little lips?
Tell me, who's gonna be your man, lord lord
Who's gonna' be your man?

POLLY ANN. My papa's gonna shoe my little feet
My mama's gonna glove my hand
My sister's gonna kiss my sweet little lips
And you know I don't need no man, Lord, Lord
You know I don't need no man

JOHN
by Regina Taylor

The dance is tap-time steps—
As a chorus of gandy dancers swing metal—

We are seeing JOHN *on the day he dies.*

1 – John
2 – Lucy
3 – Other woman
4 – Steel driving man/ Another John
5 – Overseer/ Carny barker
6 – Steel driving man/ Another John

    We hear in the darkness—
JOHN'S VOICE/1. HUH!
    (*As we hear hammer ringing—*
    A WOMAN'S VOICE—#2—*Ghosts in the same pitch as ringing—*)
2. John!
    (*The strike brings light up on* JOHN/#1.)
JOHN/1. (*Trying to hold onto self.*) I am
2. One
ALL. of many
3. Not the only
ALL. To die
Like…
2 AND 3. A man
1. Doing what I do
As best I can
ALL. (*Striking of hammer.*) huh
5. Name
ALL. John
    (*Striking of hammer.*)
huh
3. Not the only John

4. Number 3—

6. And uh-4 and uh—

2. What's true—

5. (*Like* CARNY BARKER.) Flesh versus tech-no-lo-gy—
> (*We hear: DING!*
> *Of a boxing bell.*)

6. —The rest of the story

1. Belongs to others

4 AND 6. 1 and uh 2 and uh—

ALL. Brothers
In blood
huh

1. (*Singing blues.*) Had me a woman—

2. (*Demands that he remember her.*) What was her name—

3. (*Speaking to* 1.) I want to be married, baby

6. Like I wanna hole in the head

4. (*Singing.*) Had me some women

3 AND 2. (*Demanding for him to remember*—) Their names—

1. (*Blues.*) Had me this woman
Held her in my arms

2. (*Demanding that he speak her name*—) Her name—

3. (*Jealous.*) Named his hammer *Lucille.*

JOHN/1. (*Echoes.*) *My hammer—Lucille*
> (*As he kisses his hammer.*)

2. Is that it?

1. (*Singing.*) Dream about her
Just the same
> (*Speaks.*)

Been a long while since—

ALL. (*Blues.*) Dream about her
Just the same

1. (*Blues.*) Can feel her
In the dark
> (*Speaks.*)

With these hands

ALL. huh

(Shift tempo and rhythm—)

ALL. Hands

1. (*Realization.*) That's who I am

4 AND 6. (1 *echoes.*) Got these hands from my dad

6 AND 4. Like he got his from his dad

1. And so on—

3. And on it goes

5. (*Auctioneer-like.*) Bought and sold!

6. Like the name

3. Passed down

1. And so on

4. John the first and so on—

1. And so—

ALL. huh

1. Convict

ALL. huh

1. Slave

ALL. Huh

5. Number

1. 314-/0

2. (*Howling.*) 0!

ALL. Steel driving—

MAN

Huh

(Shift.)

1. Swing my hammer

ALL. down

huh

1. driving holes into

ALL. into tomorrow

1. My hammer

thirty pounds

ALL. shatters rock

My hammer

Thirty pounds

Shattering rock

(As the Hammer strikes—we hear Hammer ringing and WOMAN'S VOICE—#2—*howling in the same pitch.)*

3. Hear ole Lucille singing

1. No mountain's gonna swallow me.

ALL. huh

(Shift.)

2. Yer n the belly of this beast

ALL. Tun'lin

1. Can't see
what's in front of or—

ALL. around—

1. Swinging this hammer

ALL. Forty/pounds

1. FORTY-two and a-3

ALL. long years
tun'lin
doing time

5. *(Orders them to pick up speed.)* Step!

ALL. 1 and a two and a—

2. Blind

1. Trying to break through to the other side

ALL. O this mountain

1. When I swing my hammer down—
can feel

3. Sweat

4. blood

5. pus

2. Breathe

1. Lungs fill—

ALL. *(Elongated—)* With—Rocks—floating
in the air—

    (Then picking up speed again.)

5. (CARNY BARKER.) side by side
Flesh versus metal!

    (We hear: DING!)

5. *(Pitying them.)* Sisyphean

4. *(Boxer-like.)* Float like a butterfly—

6. (*Preparing for battle.*) Sting like a bee.

5. There's only two ways to be
Give up or fight

2 AND 3. Heroes know when to give—

1. (*On swinging his hammer up*—) Up
2 and a 3 and uh—

5. Got to have some kind of strategy

ALL. To Reach

5. (*Cynical.*) Poor fools

ALL. From here

5. (*Cynical.*) Broker than broke-dicked dogs

ALL. To eternity

5. Choices?

2. Staying alive

5. (*Cynical.*) Huh

1. I'm no Houdini
But I try

ALL. Huh

                (*Shift.*)

1. All I know is

ALL. From can't see
To can't see

Huh

1. (*Affirming self so he won't be swallowed into the darkness of the tunnel.*) My name
is John

5. Like any other

ALL EXCEPT 5. Like so many Johns

3. Buried in the sand

4. Along pounded tracks

1. Hands—calloused

6. cracked

5. Mouths opened wide

6. Parched

ALL. Gimme a cool glass of water before—

1. (*Ghosting.*) Gimme a cool glass of water before I—
                (*Not wanting to speak the word—die*

Not wanting to admit defeat—)

1. (*Indefatigable.*) I am

But who will know I was ever here
In this spot
Pounding rock

(*Contemplative—*)

huh—

(*Light shifts—*
Breaking through the darkness is #2—
He sees her—Lucille—)

1. Told her never to look at another
After
I'm gone
She said

2. yeah

1. The lying two-faced—

2. (*Wanting him to remember and speak her name—*) Lucy!

1. Her name

ALL. Huh

(*Workers continue to work to the rhythm of "Chain Gang" as—at the same time—*

Just as 1 has been swinging his hammer—now—he swings 2 around—jitterbug-like—)

1. I swing her around
She's hot as fire

My Lucille

(*—he kisses the flesh and blood woman.*)

ALL. Huh

(1 *swings* 2 *over and/over and around and around and then* 2 *swings* 1 *around over her back and again—and then both* 1 *and* 2 *are on the ground looking up at the sky—breathing and dreaming.*)

1. A flying machine
Lord
Have you ever seen

2. O what a sight

1. (*Doubtful.*) If man was born to fly

he'd be born with—

2. (*Hopeful/encouraging.*) Wings

ALL. Huh

1. I dream of sometime of later on—
My children's children's time

       (*Light change*—)

Old school—

       (*Overlap.*)

ALL. Old school
Hammer time
1 and a 2 and a shuffle fullap ball-/change

       (*Singing.*)

—chain gang—

1. (*Feeling that he may never see tomorrow/sadly*—) I dream of what's passed on—
What for to labor—

2. (*Seeing him as the dying breed that he is.*) Don't make men like you no more

1. She said

2. *John*—

1. How many will put their

1 AND 2. mouths

1. on

      (1 *and* 2 *kiss.*)

ALL. resuscitating

2. resurrecting

1. me

ALL EXCEPT 1. or some other

3. who will die today—

2. (*Sadly—pulling away.*) drowning in his own spit—

ALL. No one knows the rest—

2. or the next

      (*As* 2 *backs away from* 1—
      bringing back in the darkness.)

1. and so on

ALL. left here to be
eaten up

no bone marrow-dust
is left of us

5. Consumption

4. Floating rocks

4 AND 6. In our lungs

      (Shift.)

1. My story is true
But someone else's name
Grafted to
it

ALL. Keeps repeating

5. (CARNY BARKER.) Man versus Machine!

      (We hear: DING!

      We hear the sound of the Machine and we see—Increase in tempo—tapping and swinging hammers

      —Gandy Dancing faster and faster—

      Then everything stops.)

1. I won!

4 AND 6. *(Echo.)* I Won!

5. *(Cynical.)* Round 1
9 more rounds to go
at least

ALL. *(Tired/spent.)* huh

5. And so we begin—

Again!

      (All resume work.)

1. I gotta hammer
That's fifty pounds
I gotta hammer that's fifty damn
pounds

baby

ALL. Them others
Working so hard
insides fallin'
To the ground

baby

JOHN/1. That / won't / be / me.

HUH!

(*As* JOHN *swings his hammer—for the final time—We hear the last ringing of his hammer—Simultaneously we hear—*

*—*LUCY's *voice and others—continuing his name—beyond the descending darkness—*)

LUCY/2. (*Keening.*) *John—*

ALL. (*Ghosting/speaking/singing—*) John—

End of Play

REMIX 38
by Jackie Sibblies Drury, Idris Goodwin,
Basil Kreimendahl, Justin Kuritzkes
and Amelia Roper

ABOUT *REMIX 38*

This article first ran in the January/February 2014 issue of Inside Actors, *Actors Theatre of Louisville's subscriber newsletter, before rehearsals for the Humana Festival production began.*

Five young writers, ready to add their fresh voices to the Humana Festival's nearly four decades of history. Eight iconic plays of the Festival's storied past. Mix the two together and what do you get? Every year, Actors Theatre commissions a group of playwrights to pen a show for our Acting Apprentice Company, to be performed during the Humana Festival. This year, that show was *Remix 38*: a varied array of short pieces in which five dynamic theatrical minds combined, reimagined, and transformed elements of groundbreaking earlier plays from throughout the Humana Festival's 38 years. It was an imaginative way for Actors (in partnership with some new collaborators) to celebrate our legacy this 50th Anniversary Season.

Those who have attended (or read) previous incarnations of this project written for the Apprentices may recall that in recent Festivals, these experiments have explored a specific theme. This season, however, we tried something different. We gathered a diverse group of playwrights whose singular styles excite us: Jackie Sibblies Drury, Idris Goodwin, Basil Kreimendahl, Justin Kuritzkes, and Amelia Roper. In a nod to the many world premieres that have made the Humana Festival what it is today, we compiled a list of arresting dramatic elements, structural conceits, and vivid images from a representative sampling of particularly influential plays. We then invited our intrepid playwrights to create several short scenes which incorporate items on the list.

The goal wasn't to end up with sequels to the iconic plays, or even pieces that are recognizably linked to the works that influenced them. Rather, the selected details served as points of inspiration. For example, a man looking for his lost skin in José Rivera's *Marisol* (1992) was reimagined into a piece about the search for a friend's missing finger. Audiences needn't have seen any of the earlier Humana shows to fully engage with the scenes in *Remix 38*. (Though for those who *have* been longtime Festival-goers, there is the added fun of occasionally spotting something familiar.) In the music world, to "remix" is defined as mixing and re-recording elements in a different way. That's exactly what we did with this project: we recast the elements of past Humana Festival plays into new stagecraft and new language with its own distinct rhythms.

What hadn't changed about the process is that *Remix 38,* like the projects designed for the Apprentice Company in previous years, was written with its specific cast of performers already in mind. In the fall of 2013, the five playwrights traveled to Louisville to meet the Apprentices and began to generate material with them, over the course of two workshops suffused with fun and spontaneity. For the Apprentices, *Remix 38* was the culmination of a season spent devising, developing, and performing new work—from ensemble creations to solo pieces to new ten-minute plays. Continuing that laboratory for innovation, they moved on to engage with these professional writers' new work throughout every stage of its development, from participating in discussions of ideas and early drafts to bringing the final text to life onstage.

Each year, this Humana Festival venture—commissioned and created from scratch over the course of a season—is marked by the keen curiosity and openness of its creative team, and by a willingness to embrace playful experimentation. *Remix 38* was no exception. Playwrights, Acting Apprentices, and Actors Theatre artistic staff came together to build something lively and new upon the foundation that the creative visionaries of the '70s, '80s, '90s, and 2000s laid down for newer theatre-makers arriving on the scene. A show like *Remix 38* was the perfect gesture to wrap up a year of toasting Actors' 50th Anniversary: it honored the artists who shaped our past, while simultaneously recognizing those who will forge our future.

—Hannah Rae Montgomery

THE PLAYS THAT INSPIRED *REMIX 38*

As a nod to the many world premieres that have made the Humana Festival what it is today, we compiled a list of arresting dramatic elements, structural conceits, and vivid images from particularly influential plays, sampling from throughout the Festival's rich 38-year history. With the authors' blessings, *Remix 38* draws from the following works:

Crimes of the Heart by Beth Henley (1979)

Talking With by Jane Martin (1982)

Marisol by José Rivera (1992)

Polaroid Stories by Naomi Iizuka (1997)

The Trestle at Pope Lick Creek by Naomi Wallace (1998)

Big Love by Charles Mee (2000)

Ameriville by UNIVERSES (Gamal Abdel Chasten, William Ruiz a.k.a. Ninja, Mildred Ruiz, and Steven Sapp, 2009)

The Method Gun created by Rude Mechs, written by Kirk Lynn (2010)

BIOGRAPHIES

Jackie Sibblies Drury's play *We Are Proud to Present a Presentation...* received its world premiere at Victory Gardens Theater, and had its New York premiere at Soho Rep. Other productions of the play include The Matrix Theatre Company, InterAct Theatre Company, Undermain Theatre, Woolly Mammoth Theatre Company, Company One and ArtsEmerson, Available Light, and the Bush Theatre. Drury's play *Social Creatures* was commissioned by Trinity Repertory Company, premiering in March 2013. Her work has been developed at the Sundance Institute Theatre Lab, Berkeley Repertory Theatre's Ground Floor, New York Theatre Workshop, the Lark Play Development Center, Prelude.11, the Bay Area Playwrights Festival, the IGNITION Festival, Soho Rep.'s Writer/Director Lab, and The Civilians' R&D Group. Drury is a New York Theatre Workshop Usual Suspect. She was a Van Lier Fellow at New Dramatists, and is the inaugural recipient of the 2012-2014 Jerome New York Fellowship at the Lark.

Idris Goodwin is an award-winning playwright, essayist, and spoken word artist. His play *How We Got On*, developed at The Eugene O'Neill Theater Center, premiered at Actors Theatre of Louisville's 2012 Humana Festival and was nominated for a Steinberg/ATCA New Play Award. Critically acclaimed and published by Playscripts, Inc., *How We Got On* is being widely remounted across the country. Recent plays include: *This Is Modern Art* (co-written with Kevin Coval), *And In This Corner: Cassius Clay*, and *Bars and Measures*. His play *The Realness* was featured in The Araca Group's New Play Reading Series with American Theater Company. He is the recipient of InterAct Theatre Company's 20/20 New Play Commission. Goodwin has been a writer in residence at The Ground Floor at Berkeley Repertory Theatre, The Kennedy Center, and The New Harmony Project. He is a Core Writer with The Playwrights' Center. Goodwin is an accomplished poet and essayist, and his book *These Are The Breaks* was nominated for a Pushcart Prize. He's performed on HBO, Discovery Channel, and *Sesame Street*.

Basil Kreimendahl is a resident playwright at New Dramatists and a McKnight Fellow. Kreimendahl's play *Sidewinders* won the Rella Lossy Playwright Award from the San Francisco Foundation and had its world premiere at The Cutting Ball Theater in San Francisco as part of their 2013-2014 season, and *Orange Julius* was developed at the 2012 O'Neill National Playwrights Conference and included in La Jolla Playhouse's DNA New Work Series. Kreimendahl was commissioned by Actors Theatre of Louisville for *Remix 38* in the 2014 Humana Festival of New American Plays. Kreimendahl's plays have also been developed by New York Theatre Workshop, About Face Theatre, The Inkwell, Rattlestick Playwrights Theater, WordBRIDGE, The

Lark, and Oregon Shakespeare Festival. Kreimendahl received a Jerome Fellowship from The Playwrights' Center, and an Art Meets Activism grant from the Kentucky Foundation for Women for theatre work with the trans community in Louisville. Kreimendahl has taught playwriting to elementary, high school and college students, founded and ran a playwrights group for queer youth in Louisville called Out On The Edge, and was the 2013-2014 Provost's Visiting Writer at the University of Iowa. Kreimendahl's work has been published by Dramatic Publishing and included in Xlibris' *Becoming: Young Ideas on Gender, Identity, and Sexuality*. *The Cost of a Goat* won a National Science Award at KCACTF in 2012. Kreimendahl received an M.F.A. from the University of Iowa in 2013.

Justin Kuritzkes is a Brooklyn-based writer whose plays have been produced and developed at venues including: The New Group, New York Theatre Workshop, Colt Coeur, Steep Theatre Co., The Brick, Dixon Place, Actors Theatre of Louisville, The Brecht Forum, The 24-Hour Company, The New York International Fringe Festival, Farm Theater Projects, The Tennessee Williams/New Orleans Literary Festival, The Collectin, and the University of New Orleans. He is a member of Ars Nova's 2014 Play Group, and he has been awarded residencies from Yaddo, The MacDowell Colony, the Edward F. Albee Foundation, and SPACE on Ryder Farm, where he was a member of the inaugural writers group: The Working Farm. Kuritzkes has been shortlisted for the 2014 Nick Darke Award, and he is the winner of the 2011 Tennessee Williams/New Orleans Literary Festival One-Act Play Contest. His short play *An Autobiography About My Brother* was published in the University of New Orleans' *Bayou Magazine*. Kuritzkes is a graduate of Brown University, where he earned his B.A. in both Philosophy and Literary Arts and studied playwriting with Gregory Moss, Lisa D'Amour, and Erik Ehn. He is a native of Los Angeles.

Amelia Roper is currently writing for Berkeley Repertory, Yale Repertory, Marin Theatre Company, and Colt Coeur in New York City. New plays and productions include *Everything Is Nice* for Soho Rep.'s 2013-2014 Writer/Director Lab, *Limelight + Rose* for The Rose, Omaha and Prelude NYC 2014, *She Rode Horses Like The Stock Exchange* for Crowded Fire Theatre, San Francisco (2014), and *Lottie in the Late Afternoon*, developed by The Playwrights Realm in New York City. Her work has been developed at the Old Vic in London, the Театр Центр драматургии и режиссуры (Moscow Playwright and Director Center, Russia) in translation, Berkeley Repertory's Ground Floor, and The MacDowell Colony. Publications include *Camberwell House* by Dramatists Play Service, produced nine times in Australia, New

York, Boston and London; and *Big Sky Town*, produced in Australia in 2008 and 2009. Roper originally trained as a designer and worked with Australian and European theatre companies and contemporary arts festivals. She is the 2014 recipient of the National Theatre Conference's Paul Green Award and has an M.F.A. in playwriting from the Yale School of Drama.

ACKNOWLEDGMENTS

Remix 38 premiered at the Humana Festival of New American Plays in March 2014. It was directed by Ian Frank and featured the 2013-2014 Acting Apprentice Company as the Ensemble:

> Jamal Abdunnasir, Rachael Balcanoff, Julia Bynum, Derek Grabner, Peregrine Heard, Jason Huff, David Jackson, Cyndii Johnson, Lindsey Kite, Lauren LaRocca, Madison Niederhauser, Devon Nimerfroh, Daniel Rodriguez, Conrad Schott, Alex Seeley, Mirirai Sithole, Emily Stout, Casey Worthington, and Zach Wymore

with casting for specific pieces as follows:

Every Show You've Ever Seen by Amelia Roper
The Ensemble

Like We Do by Basil Kreimendahl
DANNY .... Jason Huff
FRANK .... Derek Grabner
GUS .... Devon Nimerfroh
LINDA .... Cyndii Johnson

If...Then... by Justin Kuritzkes
EVELYN .... Julia Bynum
ROGER .... Casey Worthington
CHARLOTTE .... Lauren LaRocca
WAITER .... Conrad Schott

a love song // a remix / by Amelia Roper
The Ensemble

Is that what I look like? by Idris Goodwin
LILLIAN .... Cyndii Johnson
BEA .... Mirirai Sithole
CHLOE .... Rachael Balcanoff
TANYA .... Emily Stout
BRAD .... Madison Niederhauser
JIM .... Devon Nimerfroh
HEATHER .... Peregrine Heard
PAUL .... Derek Grabner
JACKIE .... Lindsey Kite
GREG .... Jamal Abdunnasir

FELICIA	Julia Bynum
PARKER	Jason Huff
REED	Alex Seeley
TAYLOR	Daniel Rodriguez
ISAAC	Zach Wymore

War of Attrition by Justin Kuritzkes
The Ensemble

The Sharpening Man by Idris Goodwin

THE SPEAKER	David Jackson
THE ACTOR	Derek Grabner

Finger Play (not a real title) by Basil Kreimendahl

MAY	Lindsey Kite
FORD	Conrad Schott
GRANGER	Madison Niederhauser
HOWARD	Zach Wymore
FERN	Peregrine Heard
JUNE	Emily Stout
CELIE	Cyndii Johnson
GAIL	Mirirai Sithole

and now I only dance at weddings by Jackie Sibblies Drury
The Ensemble, featuring Peregrine Heard

and the following production staff:

Scenic Designer	Daniel Zimmerman
Costume Designer	Kristopher Castle
Lighting Designer	Isabella Byrd
Sound Designer	Lindsay Jones
Original Music	Basil Kreimendahl with Rachael Balcanoff, Madison Niederhauser, Devon Nimerfroh, Daniel Rodriguez, and Zach Wymore
Media Designer	Philip Allgeier
Stage Manager	Mary Elizabeth Penrose
Dramaturg	Hannah Rae Montgomery
Properties Master	Joseph Cunningham
Associate Scenic Designer	Meredith Ries
Directing Assistant	Cara Phipps
Assistant Dramaturg	Eric Werner

Remix 38 was commissioned and developed by Actors Theatre of Louisville. Production supported by the 50th Anniversary NCTF/Ford Foundation Fund for New Work.

The Ensemble
in *Remix 38*

38th Humana Festival of New American Plays
Actors Theatre of Louisville, 2014
Photo by Bill Brymer

REMIX 38

EVERY SHOW YOU'VE EVER SEEN
by Amelia Roper

The actors enter from the back of the auditorium, one by one, or in twos perhaps, subtly, not trying to find their seats or arguing over the price of drinks, just arriving quietly and sitting on the steps, or in empty seats.

Taking off jackets.
Checking phones.
Looking around.

Perhaps two people wave!
Someone takes a sneaky photograph of the stage.

Someone runs in late.

The house lights go down.
The stage lights come up.
The stage is empty but brightly lit.
Someone coughs.

Silence.

The stage is still empty.

Silence.

Someone unwraps candy.

Silence.

The stage will always be empty.

Then from the actors,
one by one, keep it simple.

ACTOR. Think of every show you've ever seen.

ACTOR. Think of the first show, the last show, the best show you've ever seen.

ACTOR. Think of a show with a dining table,

ACTOR. a window,

ACTOR. a light bulb,

ACTOR. rain.

ACTOR. Think of a play you saw with someone you love,

ACTOR. a play you saw alone.

ACTOR. Think of something you saw that just, wasn't very good.

ACTOR. Think of something you saw that was very, very good and made you laugh or cry or both or neither but was, well, very, very good.

ACTOR. Have you ever seen a musical?
Did you like it?
Be honest.

ACTOR. Have you ever seen an actor hit another actor accidentally?

ACTOR. Have you ever seen an actor fall off the stage?

ACTOR. Or off a chair?

ACTOR. Or break a chair?

ACTOR. Or break a cup?

ACTOR. Or break another character's heart?

> (*The sound of a cup dropping and breaking*
> *then,*
> *silence.*)

ACTOR. Haben Sie jemals ein Stück in einer ausländischen Sprache gesehen? [*German*]

ACTOR. 你看过外语的戏剧吗? [*Chinese*]

ACTOR. Ĉu vi iam vidis teatraĵon en fremda lingvo? [*Esperanto*]

ACTOR. Avez-vous vu une pièce dans une langue étrangère? [*French*]

ACTOR. Have you ever seen a play in a foreign language?

ACTOR. Haz visto alguna vez una obra en otro idioma? [*Spanish*]

ACTOR. Questo spettacolo èin una lingua straniera? [*Italian*]

ACTOR. Эта пьеса на иностранном языке? [*Russian*]

ACTOR. Is this play in a foreign language?

ACTOR. Plays translated from a foreign language. Go!

> (*The actors call out the names of plays,*
> *a great many plays,*
> *old and new.*)

ACTOR. In 2002 armed Chechens invaded a theatre in Moscow and took eight hundred and fifty audience members hostage for three days.

ACTOR. Do you remember how many died?

ACTOR. Forty rebels,

ACTOR. seventeen actors,

ACTOR. over one hundred audience members,

ACTOR. some say two hundred audience members.

ACTOR. It was a musical.

> (*The sound of another cup dropping and breaking*
> *Then more smashing crockery*
> *Smashing furniture*
> *A car crash then,*
> *one gunshot*
>
> *then*
>
> *silence.*)

ACTOR. Do you mind seeing guns on stage?

ACTOR. Knives?

ACTOR. Blood?

ACTOR. Guts?

ACTOR. Puppets?

ACTOR. Do you mind seeing kissing on stage?

ACTOR. Do you see kissing on stage and think about all the times those actors must have kissed in rehearsals and if either of them have herpes?

ACTOR. Have you ever seen a penis on stage?

ACTOR. Turn to the person next to you and nod, if you've ever seen a penis on stage.

ACTOR. Nod if you've seen a vagina.

ACTOR. A butt?

ACTOR. A breast?

ACTOR. An overhead projector?

ACTOR. A play with audience participation?

ACTOR. A weird experimental play you didn't enjoy?

ACTOR. A play you read and hated and then saw and loved?

ACTOR. A play you read and loved and then saw and hated?

ACTOR. A racist play?

ACTOR. A sexist play?

ACTOR. A play you've seen more than once?

ACTOR. A play you've seen more than twice?

ACTOR. Think of a day you didn't want to go to the theatre because of the train and the long day and the other thing you missed but you went anyway and you were so, so glad you did.

> (*The recorded but very real sound of footsteps.*
> *The footsteps cross the wooden stage, slowly, and exit.*

Perhaps the curtain flutters.
Perhaps a light change of some sort.
But,
no one is there.)

ACTOR. Think of all the characters you love.

(The actors call out names of characters,
characters they have seen, or played,
or hope to play one day.

Then, all sit.
And watch the stage.
And think about actors.
About famous actors, local actors, young actors,
old actors, funny actors, dead actors.
The footsteps do not return, yet.)

ACTOR. Think of every show you've ever seen.

LIKE WE DO
by Basil Kreimendahl

Workers, working on the roads. We hear the sounds of cars speeding by on the highway. DANNY *and* FRANK *are dealing with the oily gravel fill, spreading it around with shovels.* LINDA *and* GUS *are nearby, on break, doing nothing.*

DANNY. This guy takes my picture. Flash goes off and all that noise. You'd think it's like 1920, I'm covered in oil. Like we are.

FRANK. Like we are.

DANNY. You know how it goes.

FRANK. Like we are.

DANNY. That *is* how it goes. I'm lookin at this picture, it's like black and white like 1920 or somethin. It looks like it's 1920.

FRANK. It's not 1920.

DANNY. Right! It ain't. What the hell? That's what I'm thinkin I'm thinkin what the fuckin hell?
That's somethin, right?

FRANK. I guess.

DANNY. You guess what?

FRANK. Nothin. I guess. I'm just listenin, like I do.
What? I mean I pretty much don't know what the hell you're sayin half the time.

DANNY. You don't know what I'm sayin?

FRANK. No. Look, I don't mind though.

DANNY. All this time, we been workin side by side all the while I'm yammerin on and you don't know what I'm sayin? All this time?

FRANK. Maybe you just gotta be more plain to me.

DANNY. Okay look, I'm sayin I could be my fuckin grandfather, that's all I'm sayin. In the picture? The way I'm lookin, all baggy jeans, white t-shirt, a hard hat just covered in oil. It's like a picture out of another time.

FRANK. But it ain't.

DANNY. That's what I'm sayin. It ain't.
Well, that got to botherin me.

(A car speeds by. GUS *pulls* LINDA *away from the lane the cars are in.)*

GUS. Fuck the cones. You know what you need? Speedo.

LINDA. Speedo.

GUS. Look, you ever play Speedo?

LINDA. Nope.

GUS. Alright, this is a classic right here. The object of the game is to guess the speed of the car. There's a lot involved. Wind conditions. Direction of wind. Type of engine. But mostly it's the blowback. A blowback'll tell ya everything ya need to know. It's all physics. Stand right here next to me on the line.

FRANK. (*To* DANNY.) You're real particular, that's all I'm gonna say. You're particular.

DANNY. What's that mean particular. What's that mean?

FRANK. You gotta be real particular to let somethin like that bother you. I mean what's that mean, so what?

DANNY. I'm about to get real plain.

    (*Silence.*)

FRANK. I'm waitin.

DANNY. It means, everything's the same. That's what I'm sayin. That bothers me, don't that bother you? You and I, we might as well be our grandfathers. Don't that bother you?

FRANK. You sayin there's somethin—hey look—hey now wait a second. My fuckin grandfather had a Purple Heart, okay? I mean my fuckin grandfather worked so—hunched over. The man was hunched over. Is that the kinda man I wanna be? Hell yes it is. Hell fuckin yes. I wanna work so hard the blisters on my hands rip off and there's just meat. Then I wanna keep on workin till the grease and oil cake—till it cakes on my meat. So's the skin grows over and my hands—well till all that work is under my skin and it don't ever wash out.

DANNY. Okay. I think you're missin the point. I'm not tryna talk shit about your grandfather.

FRANK. I know you ain't TRYNA, that's the only reason I haven't busted your face.

DANNY. I'm leadin up to somethin here.

FRANK. Go on. Out your mouth with it.

DANNY. I'm just sayin. Nothin's fuckin changed that's all I'm sayin. Now don't you think don't you think that progress ought to be made? That's what I'm sayin.

FRANK. No.

DANNY. Whatta you mean, no?

FRANK. No, I don't get you. What you talkin bout progress. Progress. What're you sayin bout it?

DANNY. So this guy takes my picture, for the paper, right

FRANK. Why's this guy wanna take your picture for anyway?

DANNY. For the paper. The paper. After Rocky got it.

FRANK. May he rest in peace.

(*Car speeds by,* LINDA *and* GUS *are blown back from the line.*)

LINDA. Whoa!

GUS. That's a…65 mile per hour blowback, right there. What's it say? What's the sign say?

LINDA. 63.

GUS. What'd I tell ya? Alright Linda, batter up. Your turn. Now do like I taught ya. Wind check.

(*They lick their finger and put it up into the air.*)

It's a guster.

On the line, the line. Here she comes.

(*Car zips by, they're blown back.*)

Hot damn! What say you to that?

LINDA. Twelve speed, dual exhaust. Serious blowback. 65!

GUS. 67! Fucker was goin 67 miles per hour. God damn.

DANNY. Looked like 60 years ago or somethin. So to me, that's like starin at me in my face that nothin is different from like 60 years ago. You and me.

FRANK. Lotta shit's different. You gotta toilet that ain't outside. Runnin water. Fuel injection in your truck. So how you wanna say that's not change.

(*Silence.*)

DANNY. Yeah, alright.

FRANK. Alright's goddamn right.

(*Silence.*)

GUS. Sure some a these guys they wanna say this is dangerous. Shouldn't be playin Speedo. That's what they say to me and to that Linda, to that I say, fuck you. That's what I say. Life is fuckin dangerous. You go walk outside your door and danger is lurkin all about you. What're you gonna do, stay inside?

LINDA. Hell no.

GUS. Hell no. You got to pay the bills, get groceries, have human contact. People need people. You got to look danger square in the jaw, open your front door and take the blowback.

DANNY. How come we got all that you're sayin and all, and the pictures still the same?

FRANK. I don't know. Joe Blow's still Joe Blow why you askin me for? You know what? You just thinkin too much bout nothin. You makin a whole lotta nothin into a whole lotta somethin, that's all.

DANNY. Just got to botherin me.

FRANK. You gettin to botherin me today.

DANNY. Maybe that's just cause you don't wanna think about it.

FRANK. You're damn right I don't wanna think about it. Bout your bullshit picture shit. You been offendin me all up and down and sideways. First you wanna say you're too good to be the kinda man your granddaddy was, then you wanna say there ain't been progress made in 60 years, then you wanna say that you and I ain't nothin. Ain't good for nothin, cause we might as well be outta the 1920's. No. You offendin me all kinda ways right now. You'd do best to keep those lips pressed together for the rest of the day. That's what you'd do best to do.

> (*Silence.*
>
> *Car speeds by.* GUS *and* LINDA *are blown back. They laugh and hit each other playfully.*)

LINDA. I think my life just got five times better.

GUS. Yup. What'd I tell ya? If you got somethin a good country song can't fix, Speedo will cure what ails ya. You know what I'm sayin?

LINDA. I know what you're sayin.

GUS. Now a good country song'll make ya feel like workin your shitty job, and havin don't nobody know who you are besides your family, like a real solid good life, you know?

LINDA. Yup.

GUS. That's why I always sing Alan Jackson's "Little Bitty" at Karaoke.

> (*He sings a verse or two of the song. Midway through there's a change. The song no longer makes him feel better. Instead, it reminds the both of them that their lives are small, and maybe that really isn't okay.*)

(*Speaking:*) But when that ain't enough.

LINDA. Speedo   **GUS.** Speedo

DANNY. I ain't said those things you say I said I didn't say that. Nothin bout bein good for nothin. That's not what I'm sayin, what I'm tryna say. I guess I'm just sayin your grandfather most likely didn't dream his grandson would be doin what he done. Right? That's all's botherin me. Don't that bother you?

FRANK. I told you.
I already told you.

> (*...to keep your mouth shut.*)

DANNY. Cause then I get to thinkin bout my kid, my daughter. I mean she could be like Linda over there. Is that what she's gonna be like? Like fuckin Linda over there?

FRANK. Aw man. Hell.

(*Throws his shovel down.*)

What's wrong with fuckin Linda over there?

DANNY. Nothin's WRONG with her.

FRANK. Seems so or else why the hell not would you want your kid to be like her. You must think somethin's not right bout what she is. That what you think?

DANNY. She's 24 years old and she looks bout 35 cause she works so damn hard. That face ain't a happy face.

FRANK. Linda's happy. She's the one who brings in the portable karaoke machine for third Thursday lunch break. Not only is she happy but she makes other people happy. Now this is your final warnin. I'll shut your mouth for you. Quit goin down this road. Next thing you know you won't be able to get outta bed in the mornin.

DANNY. Shut my mouth, like we do.

FRANK. Like we do.

GUS. Once the blowback hits, don't nothin in the whole world exist cept your own heart beatin inside your chest.

(*Silence.*)

LINDA. Gus?

GUS. Linda.

LINDA. You ever think about just jumpin in.

GUS. What's that?

LINDA. Insteada standin at the line? Goin. In.

GUS. Well. Sure. It's crossed my mind, ain't gonna lie. I imagine all a its results. Then I remember that I'm not a lucky man. When I look back I see one unlucky turn of event after another. I don't know about you, but fate conspires against me. I wouldn't die is what I'm sayin. I'd just be paralyzed or brain dead. So I take the small things. Like my heart poundin, knowin I got it there and it's workin.

LINDA. Here comes another.

(*They stand at the line. The car approaches. Blackout.*)

IF...THEN...

by Justin Kuritzkes

NOTE

The actor who says the name of each detainee is responsible for knowing whether that detainee is still being held at Guantánamo.

THE TRAIN PLATFORM

ROGER *and* EVELYN *stand on a train platform.* EVELYN *has luggage.*

ROGER. (*To us.*) If this play is being performed, then the Guantánamo Bay detention camp still exists and is still being operated by the U.S. government at Guantánamo Bay Naval Base in Cuba.

EVELYN. (*To us.*) If we start the play laughing, then a concrete timeline for its closure has yet to be announced.

(*They do or do not laugh.*)

EVELYN. (*To* ROGER.) It's good to see you.

ROGER. You too.

EVELYN. You've grown your beard.

ROGER. (*Looks at her chest.*) You got breast implants.

EVELYN. (*To us.*) If I wink at Roger, then the U.S. military is still withholding information from the media and the public about the number of detainees who are currently on hunger strike.

(*She does or does not wink.*)

ROGER. (*About her breasts.*) They look good.

EVELYN. You always used to be such a fan of natural breasts.

ROGER. Isn't everybody?

EVELYN. No, but you especially. You were militant about it. You'd see a woman with implants and you'd say: "Ugh, she looks like a Barbie."

ROGER. Well, I like yours. Maybe the technology's gotten better.

EVELYN. It has. It really has. Feel.

(*She puts his hand on her breast. He holds it there, awkwardly, for a moment.*)

ROGER. (*To us.*) If I offer to take Evelyn's bag, then it is still standard operating procedure at Guantánamo to force-feed some detainees on hunger strike by removing them from their cells, leading them in handcuffs to a medical room, strapping them down in a restraint seat and inserting a rubber tube down through their noses and into their stomachs.

(He does or does not offer to take EVELYN*'s bag.)*

ROGER. *(To* EVELYN.) Well, shall we get going?

EVELYN. Let's.

ROGER AND CHARLOTTE'S HOUSE

CHARLOTTE *is there waiting for them.*

CHARLOTTE. *(To us.)* The 56 detainee names in this play are from the list that was released by the Justice Department on September 21, 2012 of some of the detainees still being held at Guantánamo who were cleared for release by President Obama's Guantánamo Review Task Force in 2009.[1] Although this play contains only 56 names, at the time the list was released, 86 of the 167 people still being held at Guantánamo had been cleared for release.

(ROGER *and* EVELYN *enter through the front door.)*

There you are! I thought you ran off together.

ROGER. Are we later than you expected?

CHARLOTTE. Only by a few minutes, but, you know, given your history, it was enough to make a girl nervous.

ROGER. *(To* EVELYN.) Did I tell you my wife was a comedian?

CHARLOTTE. I'm just kidding. It's so good to meet you.

(CHARLOTTE *and* EVELYN *hug.)*

EVELYN. *(To us.)* If I brought Roger and Charlotte a thank you gift, then Ibrahim Othman Ibrahim Idris is still at Guantánamo, even though he's been cleared for release.

(EVELYN *does or does not present them with a thank you gift.* ROGER *and* CHARLOTTE *thank her accordingly.)*

CHARLOTTE. Here, come, let's get you set up in the guest room.

EVELYN. That'd be great, thanks.

THE GUEST ROOM

CHARLOTTE *is helping* EVELYN *get settled.*

CHARLOTTE. How long are you staying for again?

EVELYN. Four days.

CHARLOTTE. Right.

EVELYN. That's OK?

---

[1]   This list can be found at: http://images.politico.com/global/2012/09/gitmolist55.pdf.

CHARLOTTE. Yes, yes. Roger told me all the details. I just forgot.

EVELYN. OK. Well, I'm really grateful.

CHARLOTTE. Please, it's nothing.

ROGER. (*To us.*) If I poke my head through the door to check up on them, then Shaker Aamer is still at Guantánamo.

>(ROGER *does or does not poke his head through the door.*
>
>*If* ROGER *pokes his head through the door, the following* **BOLD** *dialogue is spoken:*)

ROGER. Everything OK in here?

CHARLOTTE. You don't trust me to be nice?

ROGER. Just checking in.

EVELYN. All good, Roger.

CHARLOTTE. Roger that.

ROGER. OK.

>(**ROGER** *leaves.*)

CHARLOTTE. (*Looks at* EVELYN.) Wow...

EVELYN. What?

CHARLOTTE. You really are his type.

EVELYN. Does he have one?

CHARLOTTE. Oh yeah.

EVELYN. Well, I'm sure you fit the bill too.

CHARLOTTE. No, actually. It took Roger a while to realize he was attracted to me. Really, we've talked about it. I knew from the moment I saw him that I was attracted, but he took some convincing.

EVELYN. (*A little uncomfortable.*) Oh?

CHARLOTTE. It's OK! He's into me now. I don't question that. It's just, you know, before me I think he usually went after girls who looked a little bit more like you.

EVELYN. What do you mean?

CHARLOTTE. Big breasts for one.

EVELYN. These are implants actually.

CHARLOTTE. No kidding! They look so real.

EVELYN. Yeah.

CHARLOTTE. Can I feel?

EVELYN. Um...

CHARLOTTE. Shit, I'm sorry. That's completely inappropriate.

EVELYN. No, no, please. Go for it.

(CHARLOTTE *starts to reach her hand out towards* EVELYN'*s breasts.*)

CHARLOTTE. (*To us.*) If I manage to touch Evelyn's breast before Roger calls us, then Djamel Ameziane is still at Guantánamo.

(*She does or does not touch* EVELYN'*s breast.*)

ROGER. (*Calling from off.*) Ladies, we're going to be late for dinner!

(CHARLOTTE *smiles at* EVELYN.)

CHARLOTTE. Shall we?

THE RESTAURANT

The three of them are eating a nice meal. WAITER *approaches with a little jug to refill their water glasses.*

WAITER. (*To us.*) If I trip on the way out, then Ridah Bin Saleh Al-Yazidi is still at Guantánamo.

(*The* WAITER *refills their glasses. He does or does not trip on the way out.*)

CHARLOTTE. Evelyn, I've got to say, your work sounds so fascinating.

EVELYN. Does it?

CHARLOTTE. To me at least. I mean, my life is so boring in an office all day. But to be on a different film set every week, doing makeup, it's just…it sounds like some kind of strange fantasy.

ROGER. I'm sure it's not so exciting most of the time.

CHARLOTTE. What would *you* know, Roger?

ROGER. I'm just saying—I'm sure it's just like any other job after a while.

EVELYN. (*To us.*) If I sprinkle pepper on my pasta, then Younous Chekkouri is still at Guantánamo.

(*She does or does not sprinkle pepper on her pasta.*)

CHARLOTTE. Well, tell us, Evelyn. Is it just like any other job?

EVELYN. I don't know. There are some particularly fun days. Like two weeks ago, I did the makeup for…well…a pretty major star.

CHARLOTTE. Who?

ROGER. Yeah who?

EVELYN. I really can't say.

CHARLOTTE. Why not?

EVELYN. They're being really secretive about the whole movie. We all had to sign nondisclosure agreements. Shit, I shouldn't have even brought it up.

CHARLOTTE. Oh, but come on, you have to tell us now!

ROGER. If she can't say, she can't say. Let's not get her into trouble.

CHARLOTTE. I swear, Evelyn, we're not connected to the industry in any way. And we don't have any friends. Really! Ask Roger. We're literally the two people in the world least likely to spread a rumor. Just tell us!

EVELYN. Well…

CHARLOTTE. (*To us.*) If I take a sip of wine, then Ahmed Adnan Ahjam is still at Guantánamo.

> (*She does or does not take a sip of wine.*)

ROGER. You really don't have to.

CHARLOTTE. Shush! She's about to do it!

> (EVELYN *hesitates.*)

EVELYN. OK.

> (*She leans in.*
> *She whispers it to them.*
> CHARLOTTE *gasps.*)

ROGER. (*To us.*) If it was Jack Nicholson, then Hisham Sliti is still at Guantánamo.

CHARLOTTE. (*Does or does not say in disbelief.*) Jack Nicholson?

> (*If the above is not true, then she says the name of a different celebrity.*)

EVELYN. Really, you can't say anything.

CHARLOTTE. I LOVE him.

EVELYN. Yeah, me too. I was freaking out.

CHARLOTTE. Oh, that is so cool.

EVELYN. Yeah.

CHARLOTTE. (*To* ROGER.) See? It's not just like any other job.

EVELYN. But most of the time, it's, you know, commercials. Actors you've never heard of.

CHARLOTTE. Still, that's so cool.

EVELYN. Sure. Yeah.

ROGER. (*To us.*) If I pick something out of my teeth, then Hamood Abdullah Hamood is still at Guantánamo.

> (*He does or does not pick something out of his teeth.*)

CHARLOTTE. I just can't believe they can't afford to put you up in a hotel.

EVELYN. What do you mean?

CHARLOTTE. I mean, you know, it seems kind of crazy that these production companies or these studios wouldn't be able to get even a cheap hotel room for their makeup person.

EVELYN. Oh, no, they offered me a hotel. But I…

CHARLOTTE. (*Confused.*) They…?

EVELYN. (*To* ROGER, *who looks uncomfortable.*) I thought you told her...?

CHARLOTTE. (*To* ROGER.) Told me what?

ROGER. Um...

WAITER. (*To us.*) If I enter to take their plates away, then Fayiz Ahmad Yahia Suleiman is still at Guantánamo.

    (*He does or does not enter.*)

CHARLOTTE. Told me what, Roger?

ROGER. Evelyn, uh, told me she was going to be in town for a few days and that they were going to put her up in a hotel, and I said she should come stay with us instead.

CHARLOTTE. Ah. I see.

ROGER. Sorry.

CHARLOTTE. What are you sorry about?

ROGER. I just...

CHARLOTTE. (*To* EVELYN.) You see, he lied to me earlier.

EVELYN. Oh...

CHARLOTTE. He said you didn't have a place to stay and that it was *you* who asked to stay with us.

EVELYN. Oh...Yeah...No.

CHARLOTTE. Why do you think he'd lie like that?

ROGER. I just thought...you know...

CHARLOTTE. I asked Evelyn.

EVELYN. I don't know.

CHARLOTTE. I mean, it's such a small lie, isn't it?

EVELYN. Yeah.

CHARLOTTE. But the fact that he felt *compelled* to lie makes it seem...I don't know...like it's somehow significant.

EVELYN. I suppose so. Yeah.

CHARLOTTE. (*Looking at* EVELYN.) Ah, look at you. You're so cute.

    (*To* ROGER.)

Did you know that her breasts are fake?

BACK HOME

    Everyone is drunk. CHARLOTTE *is standing on a table with a bottle of wine.*

CHARLOTTE. We're getting hammered tonight, people! Nobody goes to bed until we've each had 300 glasses of wine!

EVELYN. (*To us.*) If I put my head on Roger's shoulder, then Asim Thabit Abdullah Al-Khalaqi is still at Guantánamo.

(*She does or does not put her head on* ROGER's *shoulder.*)

ROGER. (*To* EVELYN, *drunk.*) Let me tell you what's going to happen.

EVELYN. What?

ROGER. She's going to try to get us all to sleep together.

(EVELYN *laughs.*)

I'm serious. That's what she's going to try to do.

CHARLOTTE. Oh, I'm a bad, bad woman.

ROGER. There's no use denying it, Charlotte. That's your plan.

EVELYN. But...why would she want that?

(*To* CHARLOTTE.)

Charlotte, why would you want that?

CHARLOTTE. Why not?

ROGER. To prove to me...that she doesn't mind. That she's not threatened. To feel like she's in control of whether it happens or not.

CHARLOTTE. Oh, Roger, you understand me so well. You have such an acute understanding of my inner workings. What a smart man.

EVELYN. Charlotte, that's not a good idea. I don't think you want that.

CHARLOTTE. But it's too late. I've already decided. It's what we're doing.

EVELYN. What if I don't want to?

CHARLOTTE. (*Starts crying.*) You don't want to????

EVELYN. No, no, I'm sorry. Hey. I want to. I'm sorry.

CHARLOTTE. (*Smiles.*) Oh good. I'd be so devastated.

ROGER. I apologize in advance, Evelyn.

CHARLOTTE. Oh, shut up, Roger. Just shut up shut up shut up. So, how should we do it? Should Evelyn and I start going at it a little bit first while you watch? Or should you and Evelyn start and I'll watch and get a little jealous and then rush in and assert myself? You know: "Hey, if you're gonna fuck my husband, then you're gonna fuck me too!" Or maybe Roger and I go at it first for a little bit while you watch, Evelyn. And you'll be thinking: "Oh, what they have is so nice. Oh, I really shouldn't push my way into this. Oh, but I can't help myself. Oh, I'm so turned on. Oh. Oh."

EVELYN. (*To us.*) If I vomit, then Idris Ahmad Abdu Qadir Idris is still at Guantánamo.

(*She does or does not vomit.*)

THE BEDROOM

They stand still and address us.

CHARLOTTE. *(To us.)* If I kiss her neck, then Falen Gherebi is still at Guantánamo.

ROGER. *(To us.)* If I pull her hair, then Said Muhammad Salih Hatim is still at Guantánamo.

EVELYN. *(To us.)* If I bite his arm, then Sabir Osman is still at Guantánamo.

CHARLOTTE. *(To us.)* If I go under the sheets, then Motai Saib is still at Guantánamo.

ROGER. *(To us.)* If I look into her eyes, then Fahmi Salem Al-Assani is still at Guantánamo.

EVELYN. *(To us.)* If I moan out loud, then Sabry Mohammed is still at Guantánamo.

CHARLOTTE. *(To us.)* If I reach up and touch her face, then Adel Al-Hakeemy is still at Guantánamo.

ROGER. *(To us.)* If I fondle her breasts, then Mohammed Abdullah Taha Mattan is still at Guantánamo.

EVELYN. *(To us.)* If I scratch his back, then Ali Al Shaaban is still at Guantánamo.

CHARLOTTE. *(To us.)* If I come up for air, then Jalal Bin Amer Awad is still at Guantánamo.

ROGER. *(To us.)* If I get on top, then Abdulkhaliq Ahmed Al-Baidhani is still at Guantánamo.

EVELYN. *(To us.)* If I play with myself, then Emad Abdallah Hassan is still at Guantánamo.

CHARLOTTE. *(To us.)* If I grab her hand, then Abdul Sabour is still at Guantánamo.

ROGER. *(To us.)* If I lick her face, then Muieen Adeen Al-Sattar is still at Guantánamo.

EVELYN. *(To us.)* If kiss her mouth, then Omar Hamzayavich Abdulayev is still at Guantánamo.

CHARLOTTE. *(To us.)* If I fondle her privates, then Shawali Khan is still at Guantánamo.

ROGER. *(To us.)* If I start to get close, then Jihad Dhiab is still at Guantánamo.

EVELYN. *(To us.)* If I bite my lip, then Mahmoud Al-Shubati is still at Guantánamo.

CHARLOTTE. *(To us.)* If I start to get close, then Belkacem Bensayah is still at Guantánamo.

ROGER. (*To us.*) If I clench my fist, then Khalid Abd Elgabar Mohammed Othman is still at Guantánamo.

EVELYN. (*To us.*) If I start to get close, then Abdul Qader Ahmed Hussein is still at Guantánamo.

CHARLOTTE. (*To us.*) If I pull his hair, then Mohammad Zahir is still at Guantánamo.

ROGER. (*To us.*) If my eyes roll up, then Mohammed Al-Zarnouqi is still at Guantánamo.

EVELYN. (*To us.*) If my body goes loose, then Mansour Mohamed Mutaya Ali is still at Guantánamo.

CHARLOTTE. (*To us.*) If I come, then Saad Al-Qahtani is still at Guantánamo.

ROGER. (*To us.*) If I come, then Abdul Ghani is still at Guantánamo.

EVELYN. (*To us.*) If I come, then Al Khadr Abdallah Muhammad Al-Yafi is still at Guantánamo.

> (*Pause.*
>
> *They perform an elaborate sex scene composed only of the actions described above that correspond to a true "then" clause.*)

THE TRAIN PLATFORM (AGAIN)

> ROGER, CHARLOTTE, *and* EVELYN *stand on the platform.*
> EVELYN *has her bags at her side.*
> *The train is there.*

CHARLOTTE. It was so good having you.

ROGER. Sad to see you go so soon, Evy.

EVELYN. I may be back if they find the funding again…

CHARLOTTE. Oof. What a crazy business.

ROGER. I can't believe they'd just *pull the plug* like that.

EVELYN. It's what I signed up for, right?

ROGER. Well, you're always welcome back at the house.

EVELYN. Thanks.

CHARLOTTE. Don't even think about staying in a hotel room.

EVELYN. I won't.

ROGER. OK then.

CHARLOTTE. OK.

ROGER. (*Gesturing to train.*) You'd better get on board. I don't want you to miss it.

EVELYN. (*To us.*) If I hug Roger first, then Sharif Al-Sanani is still at Guantánamo.

(*She hugs them both. She does or does not hug* ROGER *first.*)

ROGER. Be well.

CHARLOTTE. Keep in touch.

EVELYN. Of course, guys. Thanks again.

(EVELYN *gets on the train.*)

EVELYN. (*To us.*) If I look back at them, then Nabil Said Hadjarab is still at Guantánamo.

(*She does or does not look back.*)

ROGER. (*To us.*) If I grab Charlotte's hand, then Mohammed Abdullah Mohammed Ba Odah is still at Guantánamo.

(*He does or does not grab* CHARLOTTE*'s hand.*)

CHARLOTTE. (*To us.*) If I blow her a kiss, then Muhammed Ali Husayn Khunaina is still at Guantánamo.

(*She does or does not blow her a kiss.*)

EVELYN. (*To us.*) If the conductor blows the whistle, then Fadhel Hussein Saleh Hentif is still at Guantánamo.

(*The conductor does or does not blow the whistle.*)

ROGER. (*To us.*) If I turn to look at Charlotte, then Khalid Ali is still at Guantánamo.

(*He does or does not turn and look at* CHARLOTTE.)

EVELYN. (*To us.*) If the train starts moving in the next two seconds, then Ahmed Bin Saleh Bel Bacha is still at Guantánamo.

(*The train does or does not start moving in the next two seconds.*)

CHARLOTTE. (*To us.*) If I turn and look at Roger, then Abdul Hadi Omar Mahmoud Faraj is still at Guantánamo.

(*She does or does not turn and look at* ROGER.)

EVELYN. (*To us.*) If I look out the window, then Abdul Bin Mohammed Ourgy is still at Guantánamo.

(*She does or does not look out the window.*)

ROGER. (*To us.*) If we turn and start walking back towards the car, then Suleiman Awadh Bin Aqil Al-Nahdi is still at Guantánamo.

(*They do or do not turn and start walking back towards the car.*)

CHARLOTTE. (*To us.*) If I smile, then Saleh Mohammad Seleh Al-Thabbi is still at Guantánamo.

(*She does or does not smile.*)

EVELYN. (*To us.*) If I think about last night, then Saad Nasir Mukbl Al-Azani is still at Guantánamo.

(*She does or does not think about last night.*)

ROGER. (*To us.*) If I kiss the top of Charlotte's head, then Abdel Ghaib Ahmad Haki is still at Guantánamo.

(*He does or does not kiss the top of* CHARLOTTE's *head.*)

CHARLOTTE. (*To us.*) If I check the time on my phone, then Mohammed Ahmed Salam Al-Khateeb is still at Guantánamo.

(*She does or does not check the time on her phone.*)

EVELYN. (*To us.*) If I take out a book, then Ahmed Abdel Aziz is still at Guantánamo.

(*She does or does not take out a book.*)

ROGER. (*To us.*) If I scratch my nose, then Mohammed Abdul Rahman is still at Guantánamo.

(*He does or does not scratch his nose.*)

CHARLOTTE. (*To us.*) If I think about last night, then Khiali Gul is still at Guantánamo.

(*She does or does not think about last night.*)

EVELYN. (*To us.*) If I'm already in a different town, then Hussain Salem Mohammad Almerfedi is still at Guantánamo.

(*She is or is not already in a different town.*)

A LOVE SONG // A REMIX /
by Amelia Roper

wow.

    wow.

        wow.

            this is great! so, so,

        contemporary.

    yeah.
    contemporary.

but with a nod to the,

to the past.

yeah.

contemporary. nod to the past. yeah.
> (*an art gallery, all rushing, looking, looking, looking for each other, for wine, for sandwiches, for a lover, looking for art. a woman stands with a man, he has opinions.*)

it's not just for the beauty. or the pain. it's not just to show the beauty and the pain, all i meant was, all i meant was, listen to me, all i meant was, don't you also think this guy also, also wanted to be the best god damn artist of his generation?

it's a girl.

don't you think this girl wanted to be the best,
girl painter of her generation?

i just asked you if you liked it.

and i'm telling you.

and you shouldn't say girl.
you should say, woman.
or lady.
> (*others rush past.*)

        what about you?

        what?

what kind of art do you like?

oh i'm not very good at,
i don't know.

do you think this is a heart?
i think it's a heart.

        it could be anything

it's a heart

        it reminds me of,

        it reminds me of,

it reminds me of a heart.

      look at this.
      what is this
      sky?
      the sky's not this blue.
      i've never
      seen the sky
      this blue.

it reminds me of,

oh!

something my grandmother told me?

my, yes,

my grandmother

something my grandmother,

oh!

wait, no.

never forget a love story

never forget a love story!

never forget any love story ever, even if it's boring, even if it's just like all the other love stories, even if there's nothing new, nothing funny nothing well yeah, new. never forget old people's love stories or the love stories in films and most of all, never forget your own.

yes.

           what about you?

what?

what kind of art do you like?

good art.

i like, yeah, good art.

(more people rushing, more plastic cups, more sandwiches.)

oh.
i remember!
they don't remind me of anything,
they remind me of now, that i'm here.

here!

over here!

woo hoo,
here!

no that's not it

if it is a heart, if it's,
well then this,
see this blue and this white,
it's like the american flag,
it's like a red,
white,
and blue heart
breaking,
breaking.
america.
heart.
breaking.

i wish i could paint.

i wish i could play music, the

i wish could play the,

or sing.

i can do this!

(he starts to tap.
those around him make room.
he does one move not quite perfect.
he does it again, trying to get it right.
he does it again, trying to get it right.

he does it again, trying to get it right.
he does it again, trying to get it right.
people stop watching.
he keeps trying.)

(wine and sandwiches.)

oh, i love renaissance too, but think of all the gays! gays, gays. generations of gay painters painting angels for a church that would kill them if it knew. and even now, with all we know, even now with my politics, even now, i love the colors. i hate myself but i love them.

what about you?

what?

i don't know much about art but i know what i like.

what do you like?

hmm.

maybe the sky's this blue when i'm at work.
inside at work.
that's sad.

i like films.
i like, yeah, films.

what kind of films?

good films.

(a woman alone, talking to strangers.)

i drunk this and looked at it.
i ate this and looked at it.
i'm still looking at it and I don't,
i just,

blue is sad.
fuck. now i'm sad.
art is sad.

I can't remember any love stories.

my grandmother said,

my,

she said,

it was an art gallery

    (*on a first date.*)

                so, i really like,
                this is going to
                sound crazy, don't
                laugh, i really like
                those nazi films. i
                don't like the nazis
                but the arty nazi
                films, they're
                good. they're really
                good! but this is so
                much better!
                because i have no
                idea what it is! so i
                don't feel
                complicit. you
                know?

    ah,
                what?
    you like nazi films?
                i like the,
                the arty
                nazi
                films.

she liked art galleries

she went alone sometimes.

                        i go to galleries alone sometimes.

and sometimes she looked
at the colors.

                    sometimes they looked at the colors
                            and thought, god is great,

and sometimes they looked
at the shapes.

                    they looked at the shapes and thought,
                        god is a bastard, man is great!

and sometimes they just liked
the sandwiches

and sometimes they just liked
the ride home,

because they went somewhere
and did something

and the one with the heart, that was nice.

(two strangers are alone. together.
and the tap dancer. still trying to get it right.)

are you going to eat that?

oh, hi.

hi.

do you like the, the

(they notice the tap dancer, watching them.
the tap dancer says,

oh.

(and slowly subtly not so subtly taps slowly away.
backwards.)

are you going to eat that sandwich?

hi.

hi.

here, it's yours.

(she gives someone her sandwich.)

thanks.

(they take the sandwich and leave.
she is alone.)

IS THAT WHAT I LOOK LIKE?

by Idris Goodwin

> LILLIAN *and* BEA—*young African-American women, actresses, take the stage.*

LILLIAN. And then his little funky assistant says to me—

BEA. What'd she say?

LILLIAN. Gon say to me "We're looking for someone with more texture"

BEA. Oooooh.

LILLIAN. Yeah. Texture

BEA. Translation

LILLIAN. some ole hip poppin and neck rollin

BEA. I was absent *that* day at conservatory

LILLIAN. Thing about it—I used to *be that* in real life. When I was younger I was
hip popping and neck rolling, hand clapping, finger snappin
Then I got to conservatory and they shut that shit down.

BEA. Way down.

LILLIAN. Down.

BEA. Dooooooown.

LILLIAN. They beat *round-the-way-girl* up outta me.

BEA. "An actor must be a neutral slate"

LILLIAN. So then I go to audition for round-the-way-girl and I ain't round-the-way enough!
And you know the worst part?

BEA. How could it get worse?

LILLIAN. The director is BLACK!!

BEA. Yeah.

LILLIAN. And English.

BEA. Welsh actually.

LILLIAN. I'm sorry.

BEA. Damon Mfume is from Wales—by way of Ghana

LILLIAN. How do you know?

BEA. He told me.

LILLIAN. You know him like that? His lineage and shit?

BEA. *I* got the part

LILLIAN. Oh.

BEA. Yeah

LILLIAN. Oh.

They think you got the texture huh??

BEA. It's not like that—you know how this whole game is—

LILLIAN. I'm not salty

BEA. Really?

LILLIAN. Of course. I'm happy for you.

BEA. Aw thank you

LILLIAN. Yeah.

BEA. Cuz I was—you know—trippin thinking you'd be—

LILLIAN. I mean why would I?

I'm not naïve

Light skinned girls just get cast more than chocolate girls

BEA. What?

LILLIAN. Am I making this up or something?

BEA. Hello?!!!

LILLIAN. It's true.

BEA. We're the same complexion!! Light skin?

LILLIAN. Nah, not if you look close.

BEA. Oh—stop playin

LILLIAN. Just look. Underneath the chestnut brown you got that red undertone

BEA. We part Cherokee

LILLIAN. Nah you part master Jim or whoever

BEA. We are the *same*—

LILLIAN. Nah, you got that red undertone, see me, I got more of a steady caramel base underneath a dark mahogany

> (*Two women—TANYA, a blonde, and CHLOE, a brunette—enter the park, in the midst of conversation.*)

BEA. I did NOT just get the part because of my so-called red undertone

LILLIAN. I just have a little something called history on my side.

> (*TANYA and CHLOE's conversation increases in volume and BEA and LILLIAN can't help but overhear.*)

CHLOE. And then his assistant says to me—

"We love your look but we're looking for someone a bit more..."

You ready for this?

Airy!!!

TANYA. Oooooh.

CHLOE. Yeah.

TANYA. Noooooo

CHLOE. Yeah. Airy
Come on.
What is that?
Airy
Is that like flighty?

TANYA. You can *do* flighty

CHLOE. I know
I have flighty quirky neurotic hipster girl
DOWN

TANYA. Dooooowwwn. Like when you played that—

CHLOE. Yup

TANYA. And also that—

CHLOE. Right
I mean come on

TANYA. You know, I think I know what they mean by *airy*

CHLOE. It's a bunch of bullshit

TANYA. flighty quirky neurotic hipster girl
but they don't want her to be a downer
you know
they want her to remain—endearing

CHLOE. What're you talking about?

TANYA. You have to learn how to think like a producer.
We don't want to worry about you
Airy means we don't worry
It means we find you charming

CHLOE. So airy means what?

TANYA. Didn't I just kind of explain it?
Lightness.

CHLOE. Ooooooooohhh I know what it means.

TANYA. Right. Gotta think like a director sometimes.

CHLOE. It means blonde!
I guarantee you they gave the part to a fucking blonde
No offense

        (TANYA *is offended.*)

TANYA. Flighty quirky neurotic hipster girl never gets to be a blonde

CHLOE. This one has to be. Come on. They want airy—as in ARY-AN

TANYA. We're not *airy.*
Just because of our hair color

CHLOE. Of course you don't see it.

You're operating from a place of blonde privilege.

TANYA. What!?

CHLOE. Which means you don't know how to scrap and hustle.

TANYA. I know how to scrap and hustle

CHLOE. You've never done a bad thing in your entire life have you?

TANYA. Of course I have.

CHLOE. Yeah right.

TANYA. I have.

CHLOE. Like what?

TANYA. (*A significant change in tone.*) Plenty. You don't need to know what I've done.

I have done things.

There is nothing airy about the things I've done.

Or the things I might do.

Or the things I could do

The thing I could do to you.

   (CHLOE *steps to* TANYA, *unafraid.*)

CHLOE. And what's that Tanya?

   (*Stare down.*)

Do something.

Come on.

I took five years of stage combat.

   (BRAD *and* JIM *enter in mid-conversation, diffusing the tension.*)

BRAD. and his assistant says we're looking for someone with a more structured jaw

JIM. Wow

   (*As they continue,* BRAD *complaining*
   and JIM *being a good friend.*
   HEATHER *and* PAUL *enter.*)

HEATHER. And then he said, "Someone with more overseas appeal"

PAUL. Wha?

   (*Same thing as* JACKIE, *who is on crutches—she demands the attention of all the others.*)

JACKIE. Hey!

Think that's bad.

They told me they wanted someone *not* injured

   (GREG *enters.*)

GREG. Someone more olive toned

(FELICIA *enters.*)

FELICIA. They said they were looking for someone less me.

(PARKER *enters.*)

PARKER. Someone not hooked on chewable children's tablets.
Because I am.

(PARKER *opens a bottle and dumps a bunch in his mouth as* REED *and* TAYLOR *and* ISSAC *enter.* REED *very animated.*)

REED. So I marched up there to the table where the director, the assistant director, the casting agent and the producer were sitting. I slapped both my hands on the table.

TAYLOR. Fucking A.

REED. And I said, "I can be anything
I can be all and anything
any and all parts big and small"

(*The others overhear. Sounds good to them.*
Maybe they nod or say "uh huh" as REED *preaches the real.*)

REED. Villains come in all different sizes and shades

TANYA. So do flighty quirky neurotic hipster girls

LILLIAN. and black people

REED. I told them all, each of them, right to their damn faces
"I am a trained actor. I know how to morph and hide to illuminate. Don't tell me you're looking for someone with bonier elbows. I am trained. I can make my bones look anyway I want them to. Any way YOU need them to."

ISSAC. What else did you say?

REED. That was it. That's all I said.

TAYLOR. What'd they say?

REED. "Okay fantastic. Thank you. We'll get back to you."

(*Everyone claps.*)

Right? Encouraging right? Now who wants to help me rehearse for my callback?

(*Hands shoot up.*)

Well, come on!

(*Everyone follows* REED *off*
except for GREG.)

GREG. Pssssshhh
He didnt get that shit.

WAR OF ATTRITION
by Justin Kuritzkes

Lights up on an empty stage.

Then:

From opposite sides of the stage, two armies march in. They are both dressed in 18th century European army garb, but in different colors. They both carry muskets. Both armies are composed of one general and many soldiers.

They halt at opposite sides of the stage with some distance between them.

Hold.

The two armies face each other for a moment. They eye each other over. Both look very polished. The uniforms are beautiful.

The two generals look across the field at one another. They wave.

They walk forward and meet in the center of the field to see if they can come to an agreement before a battle takes place.

They shake hands, gentlemanly. They open their mouths to speak.

Lights shift: in the middle of the stage, the generals mime-talk in darkness. On the sides, the soldiers are illuminated. They stare across the field at each other. They can't hear what the generals are saying.

Lights shift back. The generals have not been able to come to an agreement.

They turn around in distaste and walk back toward their troops.

The generals raise their swords in the air as a signal to their troops to load their muskets.

The soldiers do.

The generals point their swords toward the other side as a signal to their troops to aim.

The soldiers do.

The generals drop their arms to their sides as a signal to their troops to fire.

The soldiers fire.

On each side, about a third of each army falls to the ground, dead.

The generals briefly look over their losses.

They look out across the field at one another. They wave.

They walk forward and meet each other in the center of the field.

The generals shake hands, gentlemanly. They open their mouths to speak.

Lights shift: in the middle of the stage, the generals mime-talk in darkness. On the sides, the remaining soldiers are illuminated. They stare across the field at each other. They can't hear what the generals are saying.

Lights shift back. The generals have once more not been able to come to an agreement.

They turn around in distaste and walk back toward their troops.

They raise their swords in the air as a signal to their troops to load their muskets.

The soldiers do.

They point their swords toward the other side as a signal to their troops to aim.

The soldiers do.

They drop their arms to their sides as a signal to their troops to fire.

The soldiers fire.

On each side, another third of each army drops to the ground, dead.

The generals briefly look over their losses.

They look out across the field at one another. They wave.

They walk forward and meet each other in the center of the field.

They shake hands, gentlemanly. They open their mouths to speak.

Lights shift: in the middle of the stage, the generals mime-talk in darkness. On the sides, the few remaining soldiers are illuminated. They stare across the field at each other. They can't hear what the generals are saying.

Lights shift back. The generals have once again not been able to come to an agreement.

They turn around in distaste and walk back toward their troops.

They raise their swords in the air as signal to their troops to load their muskets.

The soldiers do.

They point their swords toward the other side as a signal to their troops to aim.

The soldiers do.

They drop their arms to their sides as a signal to their troops to fire.

The soldiers fire.

On each side, all of the remaining soldiers drop to the ground, dead.

Only the two generals remain standing.

They briefly look over their losses.

They look out across the field at one another. They wave.

They walk forward and meet each other in the center of the field.

They shake hands, gentlemanly. They open their mouths to speak.

Lights shift: in the middle of the stage, the generals mime-talk in darkness. On the sides, the soldiers are illuminated. They are all dead.

Lights shift back. The generals have once more not been able to come to an agreement.

They turn around in distaste and walk back toward their sides.

The generals load their own muskets.

The generals aim their own muskets at each other.

The generals fire.

Neither of them is hit.

They briefly pat their bodies for bullet holes.

They look across the field at one another and see that the other general is still standing.

Annoyed, the generals load their own muskets again.

They aim their own muskets at each other again.

They fire.

Again, neither of them is hit.

They pat their bodies for bullet holes.

They look across the field at one another and see that the other general is still standing.

More annoyed, the generals load their own muskets again.

They aim their own muskets at each other again.

They fire.

Again, neither of them is hit.

Repeat again and again and again—with the generals getting more and more annoyed—as the lights very slowly fade.

THE SHARPENING MAN
A MONOLOGUE FOR TWO
by Idris Goodwin

NOTE

So, this is what I call a "page play." The idea is that we are seeing a body on a stage describing stage action. We may or may not see it enacted in front of us. This is up to director discretion, though I lean toward the latter.

SPEAKER. You're sitting in your seat.
We begin to hear the pulsing of a locomotive closer and closer
The lights come up, of course
For about a five count.

There's an actor onstage

We're watching this actor sharpen a blade

We hear the *shink shuck shink shuck* of the blade as he works

The train gets closer

This actor is portraying a man who has murder on his mind. The man being played by this actor, he was the last fella you'd expect to be sharpening a blade.

You would've expected him to be mowing the lawn or serving soup to the homeless and insane—whistling the whole time

He was that sort of man. But now the actor is portraying the man he became.

The sharpening man we'll call him was driven to this…

You see, much has been said about life's challenges and rocky terrains.

Life has been called a jungle sometimes, a box of sweets, a stage upon which we're all players or something to that effect, but life, if I may contribute to the stew pot of analogy,

Life, at least for the sharpening man, is couscous.
Underwhelming.
Hearty? Yes.
Sustaining.
Sometimes spice helps…but only a little

The sharpening man doesn't like couscous on his plate

He appreciates life, more or less.
Or he did until he found the world around him ungrateful
ugly
spoiled
self-centered
greedy
consuming
sloths

The systems that fail him
The education, it fails him daily—can't take it back
The health insurance ain't free and yet when he uses it—still has to pay
ACTOR. "It's as if heaven ain't free."
SPEAKER. He thinks
And not that he was a saint but it's hard to shimmer in a shower of shit
The train gets closer
ACTOR. "The sharpening man is gonna make them pay"
SPEAKER. This is what the actor is thinking
This is what motivates his choices as the actor chosen to play…this man
SPEAKER. The actor is thinking,
ACTOR. "I will make everybody understand that
they can't stick their fingers in my couscous anymore"
SPEAKER. The train is real close. We can feel it rumble under our seats

the actor wipes his brow

shick shuck shick shuck shick shuck

The actor leaps up with the knife
And the spotlight reflects off the blade

he breathes

The actor is very convincing

He doesn't look a thing like me

Does he really understand?
How method his approach?

I wonder how much he understands.

I'm not allowed to be in the audience for this show but I know what comes
next.

A sea of people, walking across the stage and he swings wildly cutting and
carving
swish swoosh swish swoosh
screams, of course screams, because there were

and the sharpening man stands there.

As the train rumbles by

Spotlight on the blade with the blood. The lights spread into the house
And the audience looks a bit puzzled

The actor lunges into the aisles
after each and every patron

swish swoosh

Each and every person

the train distant now

every person

will pay

swish

will pay

swoosh

the train
all of you
will pay
all of you
every single
last
one

even the actor playing me
will pay

FINGER PLAY (NOT A REAL TITLE)
by Basil Kreimendahl

> MAY *and* FORD *are sitting together. She pushes her toes to him, seductively. He's barely paying attention to her. Lost.*

MAY. You like it?

FORD. What's that?

MAY. The toes. My toes. You like it?

FORD. Your toes are fine.

MAY. Did you look at 'em? Look.

FORD. Yeah. They're fine, what's wrong with 'em?

MAY. I did 'em up. Jesus. Forget it.

FORD. They look good.

MAY. You're fuckin out of it or somethin.

FORD. I got shit on my mind.

MAY. You're bein weird.

FORD. No I'm not. I'm not being weird.

MAY. Yeah you are, what the hell?

FORD. Listen, just somethin happened is all.

MAY. What?

FORD. I just found somethin that happened. That happened to me.

MAY. And?

FORD. I mean it doesn't just happen, it like never happens, okay it happens to people, sure, but only probably once every five years. Maybe. Some lady chomps into a taco and BAM. Bam there it is. Pointin right at her.

MAY. What are you talkin bout?

FORD. Nothin important ever happens to people like us.

MAY. That ain't true.

FORD. Yeah, it is. We just keep goin till— People like us aren't ever in the paper or on TV unless we're goin to jail.

MAY. What're you talkin bout, Ford?

FORD. In my cooler, out there, in the hall closet.

MAY. In your cooler?

FORD. Go on. Just look.

> *(She steps out of his sight [In Shadow?] to look inside the cooler. He speaks sort of to her, sort of aside.)*

I just found it. There it was. Out there in that field I walk through from work? You know? Gleamin at me. Wantin me to have it. Wantin somethin important to happen to me. To me, May.

MAY. (*From the hall.*) Ford?

FORD. You can't fuckin tell anyone, seriously. / Somethin fuckin happened to me.

> (GRANGER*'s hand is bandaged. He's missing his finger. He looks out from his own window. It overlooks the field where* HOWARD *and* FERN *are searching for the finger so it can be reattached.*)

GRANGER. (*Aside.*) Somethin fuckin happened to me.

> (FORD *and* MAY *disappear, in lights? They are replaced by* HOWARD *and* FERN, *off in the distance searching the field.* GRANGER *watches them.*)

The kinda thing that makes one reevaluate their life. Take stock in the things you have. Appreciate them. That's what they say. I mean that's how you gotta look at it. When you lose somethin. But you didn't lose everything. You gotta be like "It was a god damn miracle. Coulda lost everything." It's just one finger. I mean I got nine other ones.

Of course it's my right hand and I'm freakin right handed, and it's my index finger so I can't…point at anything.

Which you want to do more than you think.

Out the window I can see the field, and Fern and Howard, out there, lookin for my finger. I wanted to point at 'em and say "There's Fern and Howard lookin for my finger"

> (FERN *and* HOWARD *wave at him.*)

but then I realized I wasn't pointin at anything because it was a / ghost finger.

> (*At some point* GRANGER *fades into shadow.*)

HOWARD. Ghost finger.

FERN. It ain't a ghost finger you fuckin lost it. You had it. We were done. How could you lose his fuckin finger?

HOWARD. It just—in all the excitement I / just

FERN. That's like somethin you hold onto. *Precious cargo,* you don't drop that.

HOWARD. How far could it have gone?

FERN. Who knows! We've been lookin for an hour. Jesus.

HOWARD. I don't think I could face 'em. You know if we can't—

FERN. Well, you're gonna have to, cause it ain't my fuckin fault/

HOWARD. Shouldn't a let me carry it. Can't hold on to nothin. You know that. Why'd you let me carry it?

Everything I touch turns to shit. Somethin's gotta change. Somethin's gotta give.

FERN. Look. We're gonna find it.

HOWARD. If we do / I'm gonna kiss it.

> (MAY *is sitting in a cramped space inspecting the finger. We see her as* MAY *and* HOWARD *say "I'm gonna kiss it."* FERN *and* HOWARD *in a sharp blackout? We later discover* MAY *is in a toilet stall in a bar.*)

MAY. (*Aside.*) I'm gonna kiss it.

I put it up to my finger, like right next to it. So I could really see it. How it's not the same. It's somethin— I mean it's—I don't know—it's like I'm gonna know—No, understand some—

When I saw it in the cooler—somethin happened. It was like—like the sky opens and the sun streaks through like the fuckin praise picture in my grandma's place. All God's grace and shit. Like that—that happened. So I took it. Ford. He doesn't—I'm gonna give it back.

After I figure it out. After I kiss it. You touch somethin. With your hands— they can't really feel—lips, lips are all just nerve endings.

I've been starin at it for fifteen minutes, and I'm definitely gonna kiss—

> (*Someone bangs on the bathroom door.*)

Hey! I'm in here. Chill out. Fuck. Give me a minute!

> (*She puts the finger up to her lips, runs the skin over her skin, kisses it and shoves it into her purse. She opens the nonexistent door and loud club music blares. She's on the dance floor where* JUNE *is waiting for her.*)

MAY. I swear these fuckin people.

JUNE. Somethin's different about you.

MAY. Really?

JUNE. Yeah. What'd you do?

MAY. Nothin. I didn't do nothin—what?

JUNE. You are really different.

MAY. Stop starin at me. You're freakin me out. Seriously. Stop. Can we just dance?

JUNE. Alright, don't tell me.

MAY. There's nothin to tell.

JUNE. Fine.

> (*They start to dance with the crowd, everything seems pretty normal.*)

MAY. (*Aside.*) Somethin is different though. It's like the entire club is just in motion around me, for me. I'm on some kinda fire.

> (*The crowd starts all dancing at* MAY, *and they sing the words of whatever song directly to her.*)

And it freaks me out.

(We hear her breathing over the music.

To JUNE.)

I gotta go. Bathroom emergency.

JUNE. Wait! / May?!

*(*FORD, *briefly passing through light. He's somewhere else searching for* MAY.)

FORD. May?!

MAY. I gotta go.

(She closes the door, sits, quiet.

Aside.)

That was a bad idea. This finger is fucked up. I shoulda left it in the cooler. It's bad mojo. I shoulda left it in the fuckin cooler. Aw shit, aw shit, / aw man.

(She places it on the floor after "fuckin cooler" and leaves the bathroom as CELIE *enters. They pass each other.)*

CELIE. Aw man. What the hell? What the—

Hey ya'll, someone fuckin left a— a— a

(She decides maybe not to tell anyone. And hell, when are you ever gonna find a severed finger in your whole entire life? Maybe she should keep it.)

Shit. Alright Lord. You put the thing in my path. I say alright, I'll / take it.

(Fast lights down on CELIE *up on* HOWARD *and* FERN. *They're losing hope of ever finding the finger. It's starting to get dark.)*

HOWARD. *(Pointing his finger out.)* Take it, go on just take it. Don't even count or nothin, surprise me.

FERN. What're you talkin bout?

HOWARD. Just take my finger / it's all my

FERN. Oh shut up. Jesus, Howard.

HOWARD. Like I said, somethin's gotta change.

FERN. Quit it will ya. We're losin light.

HOWARD. It's hopeless. Just take my finger, Fern. A needle in a haystack, it is. I'm willin to do somethin different, stop tryna hold on to nothin. Do somethin important. So take it.

FERN. Forget that shit.

HOWARD. I ain't even wasted right now. I'm dead fuckin serious.

FERN. Howard—man—

HOWARD. Been / out here forever

JUNE. *(In the bathroom of the club.)* Out here forever. / May? You here?

*(*FORD, *briefly passing through light. He's somewhere else searching for* MAY.)

FORD. May? You here?

(CELIE *comes out of the bathroom stall.*)

JUNE. Celie?

(*She shows* JUNE *the finger.*)

/ Shit.

(GRANGER, *still looking out the window at the field.*)

GRANGER. Shit. When one is missin something essential, like an index finger. You gotta start thinkin different. Turn your mind so's it all makes sense. For instance, I mean, really, that fuckin finger got in the way. My middle finger's longer. If somethin fell down the sink drain, I could better get it out with my long middle finger now that it ain't obstructed by my index finger. That's just one thing. Probably other things too.

Maybe— Maybe I oughta thank the stars that aligned to make that saw jam, and my dumb ass for tryna push through it. Maybe I oughta thank that. I ask "What have I got?" What's a guy like me got? And the world and the people who run it, they say, "You got your body, Granger." And the world and the people take everything you've got. One piece at a time. Mostly you don't get to notice that. You just look in the mirror one day and it hits ya, that your body's all used up.

So am I a lucky son of a bitch? One piece at a time. Seen my finger spin in the saw, shoot straight up and fly out into the field. And the world and the people who run it don't give you your pieces back. Shit. Howard and Fern been out there forever, seems like. They say you gotta look at the bright side / I'm dead fuckin serious.

(CELIE *and* JUNE *are showing* GAIL *the finger.*)

CELIE. I'm dead fuckin serious, man. On the bathroom floor.

JUNE. On the bathroom floor.

CELIE. Layin there. Now I know. You're thinkin, that shits disgustin I'd fuckin puke if I saw a bloodless severed finger in the ladies bathroom. Ladies bathroom, but I get the strong sense this a man's finger. Okay?

JUNE. There's a story here. This a man's finger.

CELIE. I wrapped it up in some TP like a used up tampon. Stuffed it down in my purse and we was out.

GAIL. Ahm.

Okay.

Watchu want me to do?

CELIE. I don't know. Shit.

You're all fuckin spiritual and stuff. You got that Buddhist flag thing on your porch.

GAIL. That's not / mine.

CELIE. I mean the universe put the finger in my path. So what can I get for it?

JUNE. We. What can we get for it? What? There's enough to go around.

GAIL. Watchu mean what can you get for it? What?

CELIE. It's got some kinda spiritual currency, am I right?

JUNE. This like a magical object.

GAIL. What kinda magic does it make?

CELIE. I don't know.

JUNE. Let's just / put it up here.

FERN. Put it up here.

> (*Blackout except for* HOWARD *and* FERN.)

HOWARD. (HOWARD *puts his pointy finger on the block.*) Do it.

FERN. (*Raises a small axe.*) Don't look at me, man. Fuck. I can't do it if you look at me.

HOWARD. Alright, Alright.

FERN. (*Raises the axe.*) Look. Why you gotta be so quiet for?

HOWARD. This ain't easy for me either.

FERN. I'm not gonna do it. This is /

HOWARD. Don't.

FERN. I'm not /

HOWARD. No, do it /

FERN. Which one is it?

HOWARD. Don't NOT do it. Do it.

Don't take— Look, I fuckin lost the finger okay, you didn't lose it. Like I lose everything. And I got a chance here, got chance right here, right now, to make it right, but I need you not to puss out. Help me out. Don't make me— You know I ain't good at nothin, you know it's true. You seen me all this time. And I can't take one more thing I done wrong weighin on me. This is it. Help me out. I'm askin for it.

FERN. Alright. Alright, man, but really this—

> (HOWARD *sings the first three lines of "Proud To Be An American" by Lee Greenwood.*)

FERN. What're you doin?

HOWARD. Not bein Quiet. Just do it!

FERN. I hate that fuckin song.

> (HOWARD *starts singing from the 5th line of "Proud To Be An American."*)

(*As* HOWARD *sings* FERN *prepares herself with the axe. Swinging but stopping. She swings the axe to the beat and starts to sing with him on the 11th line of the song. On the beat at the end of the 13th line she makes one final swing and BAM! cuts off* HOWARD*'s finger.*)

HOWARD. /Agghhh!!

(*Blackout on* HOWARD *and* FERN.

MAY *and* FORD. *He's upset. She's consoling him.*)

MAY. Agghhh. Right like that. Agh. Right?

FORD. Are you serious?

MAY. Yes, I'm serious. You should fuckin thank me.

FORD. Are you fuckin with me May?

MAY. Ford, I'm tellin you. This dude was all fuckin Sleepy Hollow and shit only without his finger. He had his head. All grotesque head, like Walking Dead rotted flesh. But this big space where his finger shoulda been. I just fuckin threw it at him and ran like hell.

FORD. Man.

MAY. I'm sorry, baby. I know it was kinda special to you. I mean I was totally gonna give it back to you.

FORD. Somethin like this will never happen to us again.

To me, anyway. You know? There ain't nothin special ever gonna happen to me. That's my life May, nothin special.

MAY. Come on, Baby.

FORD. You know I don't believe you, right?

MAY. /Yeah.

(GRANGER, HOWARD *and* FERN. HOWARD *hands him a Ziploc full of ice and* HOWARD*'s finger. He keeps his mutilated hand in his pocket.*)

GRANGER. Yeah?

HOWARD. Fuck yeah, man. We got it.

GRANGER. Ohh, hell!

FERN. It was all Howard.

(*Silence.* GRANGER *inspects* HOWARD*'s finger.* HOWARD *and* FERN *look at each other a little concerned.*)

Everything alright?

GRANGER. No. It's just weird, right? When it's not attached. / It looks weird.

(CELIE *and* GAIL *sit transfixed by the finger.*)

GAIL. It looks weird.

JUNE. You gotta relax your mind.

CELIE. Whoa.   **JUNE.** Fuck.   **GAIL.** Shit.

(*Blackout. End of* Finger Play.)

AND NOW I ONLY DANCE AT WEDDINGS
by Jackie Sibblies Drury

Hey. It's THE BRIDE.
THE BRIDE *isn't dressed as a bride, fyi.*
She's dressed however.
She talks to us.

THE BRIDE. Hey you guys.
Can I tell you something?
Every once in a while it's like
I hate something
So Much
that I can't believe that anyone else actually likes it.
Do you know what I mean?
It's like I feel so solid and settled in my hatred—

> (THE GOOFY YET LOVEABLE VIRGIN *jumps spastically into the space and really sticks the landing—gymnastics style. It punctuates* THE BRIDE's *speech as indicated:*
>
> THE GOOFY YET LOVEABLE VIRGIN *lands, knees bent [maybe wobbles].*)

Like I'm totally sure I like haaaaaaaate it—

> (THE GOOFY YET LOVEABLE VIRGIN *straightens, arms straight at sides.*)

It might be when I feel the most certain of anything at all, actually.

> (THE GOOFY YET LOVEABLE VIRGIN *raises his/her arms as a salute, salutes each side of the audience [or salutes judges, audience, and teammates, if you like] as* THE PITY BRIDESMAID *laughs at him/her, a little too loud, a little desperately, turning for the benefit of a crowd of people we don't see:*)

THE PITY BRIDESMAID. (*Laughing.*) That's so funny! Isn't that funny?
Omigod you're so so funny.

THE BRIDE. Anyway, but then—

> (THE GOOFY YET LOVEABLE VIRGIN *lowers arms and makes an "ain't I a goof!" gesture/noise/face;*
> THE BRIDE *continues as* THE GOOFY YET LOVEABLE VIRGIN *walks away making "get outta here!" gestures/noises/faces.*
>
> THE PITY BRIDESMAID *stands alone, waiting for* THE BRIDE *to notice her.*)

THE BRIDE. I remember that other people like Love it and then I feel bad.

Like I look at my sister.

You know?

And I'm like.

You probably love this.

> (THE PITY BRIDESMAID *pretends to say hello to someone on the other side of the room, and leaves, trying to bear some semblance of self-respect.*)

THE BRIDE. I mean she'd have to love this—it would be weird if she didn't love it.

It's her wedding and she's not a total asshole.

And my Mom loves it.

And my Dad too I guess.

But he might kinda hate it

but he'd never say

or like it sort of doesn't matter when my Dad hates things

because he sort of doesn't *like* things

so my Mom and my sister are just like (*She waves her hand, dismissing.*)

And it sucks because it's like the only time I'm happy in the whole thing is when I allow myself to hate every part of it.

THE LIFE OF THE PARTY. Because now I only dance at weddings.

> (*Hey it's* THE LIFE OF THE PARTY.
> *S/he isn't drunk yet.*
> THE BRIDE *might notice him/her,*
> *but doesn't pay him/her much mind.*
> *Obviously* THE LIFE OF THE PARTY *doesn't notice*
> THE BRIDE *at all, s/he talks to us.*)

THE LIFE OF THE PARTY. I used to dance all the time.

All the fucking time.

I feel like, I don't know, last fucking year I danced like every five minutes and now it's like

I'm only dancing when like my fucking put-together friends are getting married

and it's like I don't know if I even believe in marriage

and you're really too young to be getting married

but I'm glad your parents got me drunk, like it's awesome to be dancing

even if it's to like motherfucking Earth Wind and Fire.

But also thank God it's Earth Wind and Fire because I don't want to be like Dancing

like to like Partition or something with like your fucking uncle looking at me or something.

(THE BRIDE *looks at* THE LIFE OF THE PARTY.)

THE LIFE OF THE PARTY. (*Bitchface.*) What.

THE BRIDE. (*To* THE LIFE OF THE PARTY, *and then to us.*)
My family is like all girls.

	THE LIFE OF THE PARTY.
My mother had four sisters:	(*Blink blink.*)
Lee, my mother, E-E Lee, and her sisters	Ooooo—
Lisa, Leigh—E-I-G-H Leigh, Lee-Anne,	—oooo—
and Leighton.	—ookay.
Lee, my mother had two girls:	
Me and my sister Lori.	(*Fake.*)
	Woooow.
Lisa had three girls:	
Larkin, Laura, and Laren.	Yeah. Um.
Leigh—E-I-G-H Leigh had two girls,	Mmm-hmm. Mmm-hmmm.
Lauda and Louise	Yeah, I'll be right—I'm just
Lee-Anne had one girl, Lois	going to get a
And Leighton, the youngest, had five like	(*Motion of drinking a drink.*)
her mother	(*Exits.*)
Liss, Lithe, Laurent, Loon, and Listen.	

All of the girls in my family have gotten married.
All of them.
This means that I have been in one dozen weddings.
I have sung in four of them
I've read five poems
I've caught one bouquet
I've made out with two groomsmen
I've danced to the "YMCA" ten times
I've danced to "Little Red Corvette" four times
I've danced to "Hava Nagila" twice.
Twelve pictures of fourteen brides and ten grooms are displayed on the mantle of my parents' fireplace. Twelve.
I don't think I hated all of the weddings.
I don't think I hate all weddings.
But I do hate, like, *weddings.*

THE PHOTOGRAPHER. Can you squeeze in a little?

> (THE BRIDE *takes a step to her left or right.*
> *She doesn't need to actually be in any real relationship*
> *to* THE PHOTOGRAPHER.)

A little bit more?
Yeah, a little bit more?

Can you squeeze in a little bit more?
You on the end, can you squeeze in a little bit more?
Yeah, a little bit more?
You're family right? Ha ha. Get close.
Yeah, a little bit more—THERE we GO.
BIG smiles people!
One two three.
And again, big smiles, one two three.
Great.
And a fun one. Let's say Lori's special daaaaay. One two three:

>   (*Mouths "Lori's special daaaaay."*)

Greeeaaaat.

>   (THE PHOTOGRAPHER *exits.*)

THE BRIDE. I am the last of my generation to be married.
I don't know if I ever want to be married.
I think that some of you want to be married.
I'm pretty sure that some of you are married.
I'm pretty sure that some of you thought you would be married by now.
I'm pretty sure that some of you think that you will never get married.
I'm pretty sure that some of you don't think very much about marriage.
I'm pretty sure that some of you don't think very highly of marriage.
But none of that really matters.
Not to my mother.
As I sang "Ave Maria," and I looked and my Mother and I thought I was twenty-three
And then Lori said I do and I thought I was twenty-three
And Lori kissed her bride and I thought I was twenty-three
And Lori cut her cake and I thought I was twenty-three
And Lori danced to Earth Wind and Fire and I thought I was twenty-three
And Lori danced to UB40 and I thought I was twenty-three
And Lori danced to Journey and I thought I was twenty-three
And I was dancing and a little drunk and everyone was dancing and a little drunk
and I caught my Mother's eye and my Mother looked at me
with this Look
and realized that I was Thirty.

>   (*Beat.*

>   BRIDESMAIDS *run on giggling.*)

THE SECOND BRIDESMAID. Why aren't you dancing?
THE BRIDE. I don't feel like it.

(*Giggles.*)

THE PITY BRIDESMAID. You're so funny!

THE FIRST BRIDESMAID. Come on.

> (*She pulls at* THE BRIDE *and tries to make her dance.*
> *She pulls at her arms like a puppet as:*)

THE PITY BRIDESMAID. Omigod it's so so funny! Look how much she doesn't like it, it's so funny!

THE BRIDE. I just don't—

THE SECOND BRIDESMAID. It's like you don't even want to be here.

THE BRIDE. Well, I—

THE FIRST BRIDESMAID. It's like, live a little you know? Like live your life just a little. This is what life Is. Cheers!

> (*Music fades in and UP.*
> *People fade in and UP.*)

THE BRIDE. What?

THE THIRD BRIDESMAID. Cheers!

THE BRIDE. What?

THE SECOND BRIDEMAID. Cheers!

THE BRIDE. WHAT?

> (*By this last "WHAT?" the music should be loud and the wedding reception should be at its drunken height. All the guests are sloshed, shoes are off, people are making out, someone is pissed and wants to go home, someone is telling someone how much they are loved, someone is still trying to get everyone to take shots, people are singing along in howling screams, errebody is drrrtay dancing.*
>
> *We stay in this last dance long enough for it to establish itself.*)

THE BRIDE. (*To us.*) What IS this?

> (*NEW SOUND CUE: fun height of dancing at the height of the reception. People are less sober, but not sober, no one is crying, shoes are put on, people are flirting,* THE GOOFY YET LOVEABLE VIRGIN *is doing a silly dance.*
>
> *Once it's established,* THE LIFE OF THE PARTY *enters the dance floor, and everybody cheers! Because YAY! DANCE CIRCLE!*
> *A few people get into the middle of the dance circle,* THE LIFE OF THE PARTY *dances at least three times,* THE GOOFY YET LOVEABLE VIRGIN *does a funny mime dance like "shopping cart" or "sprinkler" or something more baroque that people might like a little bit less.*
>
> THE BRIDE *doesn't dance.*

THE BRIDE *is a bit outside it all. Walking through it, like Scrooge with the Ghost of Christmas Past.*

Maybe we dance in slow motion, we see things slowly, silently so that we can hear the bride say:)

THE BRIDE. Yeah. All of this. Is completely, one hundred percent, unfuckingbelievably awful.

Unless it's yours.
I guess.

If it's yours it's unique and special
If it's yours its precious.
Artisinal.
Indefinable. Cherished.
Loved
If it's yours then,

       (Eyeroll—I can't believe I'm saying this:)

then I guess it's really yours.

       (We see other moments from a wedding reception, specific glimpses: the electric slide. The bouquet toss.)

I mean, when these stupid things are yours, or like—
from inside this hateful person that's everything you're not
Things seem—but also things don't seem so—

DJ. And now!
It's time!
For! The! Caaaake!

THE PITY BRIDESMAID. *(Too excited.)* Yaaaaaaaaaaay!

      (Cake for everyone! Everyone gets a piece!
      All of us get a little piece! It's difficult and great!
      And during:
      Music.
      Some couples dancing a bit—the early ones, the bold ones, the awkward ones,
      THE LIFE OF THE PARTY.

      Clicking of a glass.
      If we were able to give everyone champagne, this is when that would happen, and it would be awesome.

      THE BEST (WO)MAN *gives a toast. It's the end of a personal anecdote or story, and then a line about how they're happy to be here, or whatever. It's a toast. A lovely toast. It could change for every performance. A version of one of the toasts that Madison Niederhauser, Acting Apprentice extraordinaire, came up with is below, for reference.)*

THE BEST (WO)MAN. And she says, "I'll pass on the quinoa, because quinoa is a cash crop that ruins local farmers' lives. So me? I'll just stick to the bulgur wheat." And that's when I realized how lucky I've been to get to stand by your side all this time, and how fortunate we all are to be here with you on your special day.

> *(We continue on our trajectory, touching on moments of a wedding reception, of a wedding ceremony, in reverse order. Hopefully, the progression has a dreamy aspect.*
> *We rest lightly, specifically—glimpses of moments—recognizable specific moments, like:*
> *A hug leaving the ceremony,*
> *church bells, throwing rice,*
> *sitting or standing in rows like a congregation,*
> *a friend performing a song, a sibling reading a poem—*
> *glimpses, arrangements, looks.*
> *The atmosphere should become slightly more lovely.*
> *Slightly more earnest. Slightly more heartfelt.*
> *Slightly more in love.*
> *In the midst we have a moment for THE PERSON OF THE CLOTH.)*

THE PERSON OF THE CLOTH. *(Beneficently, with gravitas.)* Love.

Is Patient.

Love is Kind.

> *(And on we go.*
> *We don't settle too long in any of these moments—it's an impressionistic wash, until we get to:*
>
> *The Processional.*
>
> THE BRIDE *looks towards someone in the "congregation."*
> THE SOLOIST *walks up to the front,*
> *beaming at the* BRIDE.
> THE BRIDE *beams back.*
>
> THE SOLOIST *stands in front of the "congregation"*
> *takes a breath*
> *and begins to sing "Ave Maria."*
> *S/he sings the first few lines, as* THE BRIDE *begins to "process" down an aisle in the middle of the congregation.*
>
> *As* THE BRIDE *gets to the middle, perhaps the whole congregation joins the*

song. In beautiful harmony.
Perhaps the entire company sings "Ave Maria"!
A capella. To us in the audience.
They sing Softly. Sweetly. It's just lovely.

Or perhaps they don't—
perhaps there is beautiful music instead.

As they sing, or if they don't sing, as their hearts sing, they all look at us, the audience, with looks of love.
The kind of love a groom might bestow on his bride or his groom as they see each other at the altar.
The kind of love a bride might bestow on her bride or her groom as she walks up an aisle.
The kind of love a friend might bestow on a couple saying "I do."

It should be a human, stupefyingly earnest moment.
And maybe, in spite of ourselves, we might smile.)

End of Play